AMERICAN WOMEN

of the Nineteenth Century

AMERICAN WOMEN WRITERS SERIES
Joanne Dobson, Judith Fetterley, and Elaine Showalter, series editors

AMERICAN WOMEN POETS

of the Nineteenth Century

An Anthology

Edited by Cheryl Walker

RUTGERS UNIVERSITY PRESS

New Brunswick, New Jersey

Second paperback printing, 1995

Library of Congress Cataloging-in-Publication Data

American women poets of the nineteenth century : an anthology / edited by Cheryl
Walker.
      p.   cm. — (American women writers series)
   Includes bibliographical references.
   ISBN 0-8135-1790-7 (cloth) — ISBN 0-8135-1791-5 (pbk.)
      1. American poetry—Women authors.   2. American poetry—19th
century.   3. Women—United States—Poetry.   I. Walker, Cheryl,
1947–   .   II. Series.
811'.30809287—DC20   91-33080
                                                                  CIP

British Cataloging-in-Publication information available

CONTENTS

Contents

Contents

Contents

Contents

Contents

Contents

Contents

Contents

Contents

INTRODUCTION

In the nineteenth century the world of publication opened up to women poets to a startling, some even felt alarming, degree. Though modern readers are generally unaware of the many women who made a career of writing poetry in the nineteenth century, readers of an earlier period, both male and female, were familiar with such names as Lydia Sigourney, Alice and Phoebe Cary, Frances Harper, and Ella Wheeler Wilcox. This anthology is designed to introduce the contemporary reader to the range and substance of nineteenth-century women's poetry, acknowledging that much of this poetry was written for the popular press. The poems here are a representative sampling of the conventional and the less usual, however, and are included in the hope that reintroducing these voices will lead to a broader understanding of nineteenth-century literary history and a recognition that some of these poets, long considered of merely antiquarian interest, deserve to be better known.

In order to provide a context for evaluation today, this introduction will address five major issues relevant to modern interests. First, what were the cultural and material conditions that encouraged the surprising increase in numbers of women writing poetry in America? These conditions include social, economic, political, and technological changes in American life, many of them familiar to students of American history but until recently often overlooked in the study of poetry.

Second, what were the specifically literary conditions that fostered increased publication by women poets? Who encouraged women to write, for instance? To feminist critics belongs the credit for emphasizing the importance of female friendships and support networks to women in the nineteenth century. It is true that Maria Brooks, Sarah Helen Whitman, Edith Thomas, and Celia Thaxter (to say nothing of Emily Dickinson) were encouraged at important points in their careers by women. It is also true, however, that few of these poets could have entered the world of publication without male assistance. Supportive men played key roles as friends, editors, patrons, and literary mentors.

Nevertheless, the realm in which women's poetry flourished was for most of the century considered a distinctly separate sphere. There were

Introduction

poets and there were *women* poets, as one can see from the two enormously
influential anthologies compiled by Rufus Griswold: *The Poets and Poetry of
America* of 1842 (which included only a few women) and *The Female Poets of
America* (1849). One feature of the literary conditions to be considered here
will be the conventions of female poetics, conventions that exerted a
strong influence over both style and content in women's poems.

A discussion of these literary conditions will provide some under-
standing of the broad historical and literary contexts needed by the mod-
ern reader to put nineteenth-century women's poems into perspective. In
addition, however, the curious reader wants to know something more
specific about these women's lives. After the discussion of literary condi-
tions, therefore, I will present several lives and personalities, to suggest
representative patterns and to highlight obstacles and opportunities gener-
ally shared by women poets at this time.

Fourth, consideration will be given to the reception these women
poets received both in their own time and in later periods. Though the
typical pattern of reception remains broad recognition followed by total
neglect, some figures were resurrected—if only briefly—in twentieth-
century commentaries. Louise Bogan, for instance, wrote a 1936 essay for
the *New Yorker* entitled "Poetesses in the Parlor," bringing such women as
Frances Osgood and Maria Brooks to the attention of readers who had
never before heard their names.

No such introduction would be complete without some assessment
of the strengths and weaknesses of the poetry offered here. Lastly, then, I
shall open a modern perspective on what now seems appealing and unap-
pealing about the female poetry considered effective in the nineteenth
century. At that point I shall also identify those writers whose poetry
stands out from the rest as deserving of greater attention. Though the
attempt to single out a few individuals at the expense of others may strike
some readers as dangerous in a climate as hostile to canon-formation as our
own, such a practice can be defended on the grounds that this group of
women is hardly in danger of preempting the cultural center. That almost
all these women are equally unfamiliar to a modern reader is, in fact, a sign
of how thoroughly marginal they have become. Furthermore, the argu-
ment that all nineteenth-century women poets were equally talented is not
really necessary for us to feel that a much larger selection of poets and
poems should be available for study.

Introduction

Leaving aside the issue of female contributions to oral traditions, we can fairly say that women have *written* poetry in North America at least since the early years of major European settlement. Anne Bradstreet stands out as a poet whose work impressed not only the early Puritans but also English readers back home where she was dubbed "the tenth muse." Her work went through several editions in the seventeenth century, the first made up principally of long scientific meditations, on such subjects as the four humors and the four ages of man, modeled on the poems of the French Puritan, Guillaume du Bartas. The second edition is the one most favored today, however, since it includes more of Bradstreet's personal and religious lyrics.

Bradstreet was admired by her fellow Puritans, it seems, and her work was prefaced by encomia of all sorts, including one teasing bit of praise from crusty Nathaniel Ward, drafter of the first code of laws for the Massachusetts Bay Colony and a man who had little favorable to say about women. In the next generation Bradstreet drew praise as a model gentlewoman and heroine of early colonial settlement from one of the severest Puritans of all, Cotton Mather.

Yet, despite her generally respectable position in the New World, abetted no doubt by her status as the daughter of one governor of Massachusetts Bay and the wife of a man who would become governor after her death, Anne Bradstreet was apparently not exempt from criticism. She has furnished twentieth-century readers a tantalizing hint that, even with powerful supporters, a woman writer was vulnerable to attack. In her "Prologue" to *The Tenth Muse,* Bradstreet writes:

> I am obnoxious to each carping tongue
> Who says my hand a needle better fits,
> A poet's pen all scorn I should thus wrong,
> For such despite they cast on female wits:
> If what I do prove well, it won't advance,
> They'll say it's stol'n, or else it was by chance.

We know from the journal of John Winthrop that another literary female, Ann Hopkins, drew criticism from the colonial fathers, who felt it was unseemly for a woman to put too much energy into writing. Winthrop explains Hopkins's loss of her wits by remarking that she had written many books instead of attending to the domestic work for which God had intended women. Similarly, a now forgotten woman writer of the period was scorned by her brother for publishing a book, a defection from her assigned role which he felt "doth rankly smell." Such stories make clear that, as far back as the seventeenth century, American culture offered a confusing array of opportunities and dangers to female writers. Not infrequently they elicited both praise and blame just because they were stepping out of the typical female role.

Still, as European settlements expanded, English-speaking women poets became less of an oddity, and the eighteenth century witnessed the proliferation of women writers of all sorts. Some of these, such as Jane Turrell, were publishing verse in the early years of the century but without a doubt female publishing intensified in the second half when such poets as Mercy Warren came to the fore. European Enlightenment ideas, beginning to infiltrate the cosmopolitan centers of the New World, surely had a positive influence on the opportunities afforded women. Furthermore, the Revolutionary War opened up avenues for the expression of various popular sentiments. Newspapers and pamphlets were passed from hand to hand, and popular literature had a currency never before known in America.

In her anthology *Women Poets in Pre-Revolutionary America 1650–1775,* Pattie Cowell divides her poets into two categories: those who were prolific and those who published infrequently. In the first category she includes eleven eighteenth-century women, among them Mercy Warren, Judith Sargent Murray, and Phillis Wheatley. The "infrequent poets" number twenty-seven. Phillis Wheatley, brought to America as an African slave, has generated the most twentieth-century interest. She was a careful poet, a "literary daughter of Milton"; her work so impressed her elders that she was forced to submit to an oral examination in order to "prove" that she could have composed such elevated lyrics. Anne Bradstreet's prediction—"They'll say it's stol'n"—turned out also to be true for Phillis Wheatley.

Though we now know that a surprising number of women both wrote and published poetry in the eighteenth century, the beginning of what we can reasonably call a female literary establishment comes in the nineteenth. Until that time women writers were still the exception. In a rapidly expanding republic, however, conditions began to create clusters of female voices and, therefore, feminine norms.

To understand how this came about, we should keep in mind that

Introduction

before the Revolution the colonies were in no sense unified. Transporta-
tion from one place to another was time consuming and difficult, as Frank-
lin's *Autobiography* makes abundantly clear in its chronicling of the young
Ben's journey from Boston to Philadelphia. Though printing presses were
common enough in the bigger cities, there was no system for extensive
distribution of either books or newspapers. Nor was there telephone, tele-
graph, a national mail system, or even a common currency: no wonder that
in the eighteenth century only a privileged lady or a "phenomenon" like
Phillis Wheatley could hope to reach more than a few readers. Newspapers
and pamphlets did publish women writers but these were ephemeral me-
dia by and large. Books remained in the hands of the fortunate few.

It took some years before these limitations could be overcome in the
new republic, but the Revolutionary War and the War of 1812 hastened
the process by necessitating the building of numerous roads for troop
transportation. In due time the problems of a national currency, of inter-
urban transportation, and of mail distribution diminished. European tech-
nology making possible the use of continuous-action roller presses, fed by
cheap wood pulp paper, revolutionized the printing industry. The tele-
graph became commonplace, lyceum lectures grew popular, and condi-
tions were ripe for the development of greatest importance to fledgling
women poets: the establishment of a market for their productions.

Political and technological changes brought the market for women's
poetry into being as did social, cultural, and, of course, economic ones. As
America became industrialized, fewer people lived on farms and more
moved to urban centers. Rural subsistence and barter economies were
replaced by production for city dwellers who no longer grew and pro-
cessed their own food. Cash-crop farmers, industrialists, merchants, and
bankers made money. As in Europe, the expansion of the middle class and
the decline of illiteracy contributed to the creation of a reading audience,
and those who did the most reading, of popular literature at least, were
women.

In 1792 Mary Wollstonecraft's *A Vindication of the Rights of Women* was
published amid considerable controversy. Generally, the book was severely
attacked in the American press, and yet here and there voices were raised
in its defense. Judith Sargent Murray in her *Gleaner* essays echoed many
of Wollstonecraft's points about women's education. This discussion ush-
ered in a century of debate over women's roles in which both rationalist
Enlightenment views and liberal Romantic sentiments were marshaled
against conservative arguments for the strict subjugation of women.

Introduction

Catharine Beecher's elevation of the mother's domestic role as a powerful determinant in the health of the republic opened the door for broader female education. Beecher's argument for educating mothers, however, was only one strand of many that made up the discursive rope tugging women away from the positions fixed within home and family, positions that conservatives wished them to maintain. Secondary schools and even colleges were founded, ready to train young women's minds. More women worked outside the home; though, for the middle class, such work was understood chiefly as interim employment until the more respectable work of making a home for a man became available.

From his vantage point as an outsider, Alexis de Tocqueville was keen enough to spot the tensions democratic women were experiencing: young girls, he felt, were given extraordinary freedoms and encouraged to think and question, but married women were expected to restrict their ambitions and interactions with the opposite sex to a far greater degree than European women of a similar class. Nevertheless, Tocqueville felt that the success of democracy in America would to a significant extent depend upon American women whose potential he found to be unusually great.

Among the middle and upper-middle classes, female voices were heard more and more often throughout the century. At the Seneca Falls Convention of 1848 women met for the first time to develop a national platform for change and female advancement. Women took an active part in a host of projects and organizations outside the home: abolition; charity and child welfare work; world peace efforts; Polish, Greek, Jewish, and Irish relief; women's suffrage leagues; temperance campaigns; aid to fallen women; the Underground Railroad; cultural uplift; church administration. By the end of the century, women were doctors, lawyers, preachers, actresses, educators, lyceum lecturers, and—certainly—writers. In light of all this, Edmund Stedman half-seriously referred to this era as the "woman's age."

In many ways, of course, this blithe picture of gradual and ever-increasing opportunity is untrue. For women of color and working-class women, life was probably no easier at the end of the century than it had been at the beginning, though the abolition of slavery must be recognized as a major step forward for black women who no longer ran the risk of being set up on the auction block. For Native American women the enormous disruptions of traditional life effected by the Reservation Movement—in full swing in the last third of the century—probably meant that life was to a great extent *more* difficult in 1900 than it had been in 1800. And

Introduction

immigrant women struggling to make a living in the teeming cities were hardly in a position to benefit from the expansion of opportunities enjoyed by some of their more fortunate sisters.

Nevertheless, it cannot be denied that literary life in America was an arena distinctly more favorable to women in the late nineteenth century than it had been in its earliest decades. In an 1887 memoir of Lydia Sigourney, John Greenleaf Whittier reflected: "She sang alone, ere womanhood had known / The gift of song that fills the air today" (*AWW* 4:80). By the 1870s the many minor poets who found their way into the popular magazines were about equally male and female.

THIS PICTURE OF CHANGE offers one dimension of the historical context necessary for an understanding of women's literary production in the nineteenth century. Just as important, however, is a recognition of several features of the literary scene which affected women writers throughout the century. Chief of these was the magazine market for women's poems. As early as 1830 Lydia Sigourney was earning an income by selling her productions to over twenty periodicals. In his 1843 preface to *The Sinless Child* by Elizabeth Oakes-Smith, H. T. Tuckerman wrote effusively of the potential influence of the magazines, saying: "We doubt not, that many of her sweet fancies and holy aspirations, *winged by the periodical press over our broad land,* have carried comfort to the desponding and bright glimpses to the perverted" (xxxii; emphasis added). For many of these women, material compensation was an even greater inducement than influence, however. Even late in the century Celia Thaxter and Rose Terry Cooke were able to supplement their inadequate family incomes through magazine publication, though by this time popular taste had begun to turn away from poetry.

In the first half of the century, women's poetry was a staple of the women's magazines such as *Godey's Lady's Book, Graham's Magazine,* and the *Lady's Wreath,* which also published such male writers as Poe, Hawthrone, and Longfellow. Lydia Sigourney was adept at pleasing the editors of these widely read periodicals. At one point she was paid as much as $100 for four poems, but as the century progressed, the women's magazines (though they increased in number) changed their formats, giving less space to literature and more to domestic science. Now more prestigious publications such as the *Atlantic Monthly, North American Review,* and *Century*

Magazine were preferred by contributors. They paid less than the fledgling juvenile magazines, however, a fact that may explain why so many women poets chose to publish so much poetry for children.

The ability to earn significant amounts of money by publishing poetry in the popular media certainly provided an impetus for women to write verse. Until relatively recently, however, it was assumed that women were composing their poems in isolated cottages or garrets, cut off from the mainstream of literary life. In *Literary Women,* for instance, Ellen Moers asserted: "Women through most of the nineteenth century were barred from the universities, isolated in their own homes, chaperoned in travel, painfully restricted in friendship. The give-and-take of the literary life was closed to them" (43). The Brontë sisters and Emily Dickinson were taken to be typical of woman's lot. Today, in contrast, we know that Emily Dickinson was very much the exception among American women poets. By and large, literary women on this side of the Atlantic were not isolated from one another, secretly composing in an upstairs bedroom, but were actively involved with a world simultaneously social and intellectual. One feature of this world was the literary salon.

Women participated in literary salons from the eighteenth century onward, and in several notable cases they supervised these social occasions themselves, holding salons for the great and the near great in their homes. One of the most famous was the New York salon run by Anne Lynch (later Botta) which entertained writers such as Poe, Emerson, Frances Osgood, Rufus Griswold, Margaret Fuller, the Cary sisters, and Elizabeth Oakes-Smith. Edith Thomas's career was launched at one of Botta's evening entertainments. Such salons were often inbred and typically thrived on gossip, but they also played a significant role in establishing networks of literary inter-relationships. In her autobiography Elizabeth Oakes-Smith gives a fascinating account of one evening at Emma Embury's during which Frances Osgood sat adoringly at the feet of Poe and the guests engaged in witty repartee. She remarks: "I remember Fannie Osgood and Phoebe Cary rather excelled at this small game, but Margaret Fuller looked like an owl at the perpetration of a pun, and I honoured her for it" (91).

Though the most elaborate salons probably belonged to the big cities such as New York and Boston, smaller communities were not necessarily without literary life. Celia Thaxter, for instance, conducted a famous salon on Appledore Island, one of the Isles of Shoals off the New England coast. For thirty summers Thaxter entertained artists, musicians, and such writers as Hawthorne, Lowell, Whittier, Twain, Harriet Beecher Stowe, Thomas Bailey Aldrich, and Sarah Orne Jewett.

In the Far West Ina Coolbrith held salons in Oakland and San Francisco, which added interest to an otherwise frustrated life and brought her into close contact with other writers. Bret Harte, John Rollin Ridge (known as Yellow Bird), Jack London, Joaquin Miller, Ambrose Bierce, Charlotte Perkins Gilman, Mark Twain, George Stoddard, Mary Austin, John Muir, and Isadora Duncan all visited her home. In her day Coolbrith's was the most famous artistic salon in northern California.

As the example of Coolbrith suggests, not all nineteenth-century women poets lived in New England. Some such as the Cary sisters and Ina Coolbrith were westerners by birth. Others such as Lizette Woodworth Reese identified more strongly with the South. Nevertheless, New York as the funnel of New England culture continued to dominate the publishing world throughout the nineteenth century. Women's poetry demonstrates the ongoing influence of New England Puritanism in American letters, and even the thoroughly western Ina Coolbrith adapted much of her poetry to the tastes of an eastern readership.

Indeed, the powerful male figures who shepherded the reputations of so many of these women were all New Yorkers or New Englanders: Poe (during the time of his influence), Whittier, Lowell, Emerson, the publisher James C. Fields, Oliver Wendell Holmes, and Thomas Wentworth Higginson. The influence these men had on the women poets included here will be shown in the headnotes preceding individual selections, but two of the most influential deserve separate mention here: Rufus Griswold and Edmund Clarence Stedman.

Like Louis Untermeyer in the twentieth century, Rufus Griswold was a New Yorker, a man-about-town, who knew a great many writers and had enormous influence on popular literary taste. Sarah Helen Whitman, for instance, held Griswold mainly responsible for the negative reception Poe's work received after his early death. According to John Evangelist Walsh, Griswold was bitter about Poe's treatment of Frances Osgood and fostered the view that the poet was a drug addict. Griswold could be a powerful ally as well as a bitter antagonist, however, and he deserves recognition for bringing many women poets—Maria Brooks, Frances Osgood, and the Cary sisters, for example—to the attention of the general reading public.

Though there were competing anthologies of women poets

published by Caroline May and others, Griswold's was the model anthologists inevitably followed and, in large part, slavishly copied. His *Female Poets of America* went through many editions and was still an influential text in the 1870s, though its 1873 updating was accomplished by R. H. Stoddard; Griswold had died in 1857. Louise Bogan used Griswold as a principal source for her *New Yorker* essay.

At the end of the century Rufus Griswold was supplanted by Edmund Clarence Stedman, a poet and successful Wall Street broker, who, like Griswold, knew the literati personally as well as professionally. His *American Anthology 1787–1900* (1900) brought together earlier women poets with the most important later figures: Louise Imogen Guiney, Lizette Woodworth Reese, Celia Thaxter, Edith Thomas, and the discovery of the 1890s, Emily Dickinson. Stedman's anthology is much more comprehensive than Griswold's. It brings together male and female poets, adding many southern, midwestern, and western women writers to the predominantly eastern list that Griswold had assembled.

Both Griswold and Stedman had strong opinions about women's poetry. Neither man acknowledged the existence of black women poets (though Stedman includes a selection of Negro spirituals) and both catered to a largely sentimental view of the female imagination. Griswold compared women's poems to "dews and flowers" gratefully encountered after the "glaciers and rocks" of male productions. He had no fondness for women who indulged in "rude or ignoble passion," praising Frances Osgood in *The Memorial* because "she had no need to travel beyond the *legitimate* sphere of woman's observation" (29; emphasis added).

In comparison, Stedman seems far less limited in his views, but his assessment that much women's poetry "has been exquisite, some of it strong as sweet," gives an indication of the nature of his late Victorian literary ideology. "The tuneful sisterhood," as he calls the women poets in *An American Anthology,* appear typically preoccupied with love, nature, children, death, and religion. The twenty Dickinson poems he includes strike a modern reader as peculiarly unchallenging and tame compared to her best work. Rose Terry Cooke's strong political poem about John Brown is absent from his selection, as is Ina Coolbrith's critique of the Columbian Exposition. Apparently, neither Griswold nor Stedman thought politics part of woman's poetic province.

In a world of publication dominated by such presences, the poems by women most typically praised were those that dealt with themes deemed appropriate to feminine life: the events that favor religious consolation, noble deeds and sentiments, a woman's secret sorrow. Nature also furnished topics to many women poets. At mid-century the seasons were especially popular with Indian Summer a particular favorite, perhaps because its juxtaposition of different seasonal moods helped a poet to illustrate her mixed feelings about so much in her life and culture.

In similar fashion, "the language of gems" and "the language of flowers" provided opportunities for women poets to write about "feminine" moods, objects of affection, and situations while exploring the metaphorical possibilities of such natural phenomena as beryl, fern, monotropa, and Indian pipes. Some of these poems are included here, even when they are not particularly striking in themselves, because they both illustrate conventional subject matter and offer the astute comparatist the chance to reflect on Emily Dickinson's usage of similar themes and images.

Though women poets frequently used their own domestic lives as material for their poems, the number of "exotic" poems dealing with foreign figures (Zinzendorff, Napoleon, Guido, for example) or faraway places (Asia, Africa, Alaska, Cuba, Hawaii, or the Middle East) is striking. Maria Brooks's *Zóphiël, or, The Bride of Seven* is but one example among many of a work whose action occurs in a time and place far from the American scene. Nativist poems, however, such as those commemorating American wars, praising features of American geography, or saluting American heroes or ideals, are not far behind the exotics in numbers and popularity.

Faced with these women poets' unabashed boosterism and their ornate fantasies of exotic life, the modern reader must confront the fact that nineteenth-century conventions were strikingly different from those of our own time. In addition to variations from contemporary practices in topics, attitudes, and settings, nineteenth-century women poets had recourse to particular poetic paradigms now no longer popular. *The Nightingale's Burden* (1982), my study of early women's poetry, analyzes some of these so-called archetypes. The free-bird poem, for instance, begins with a salute to the beauty and freedom represented by a bird winging its way across the sky. In the course of a poem like Elizabeth Oakes-Smith's "An Incident," however, the speaker rejects the model of rebellion and flight she has invoked, usually concluding with a renunciation similar to Smith's "I would not soar like thee, in loneliness to pine."

Other poems that seem to have had a wide currency include the sanctuary poem, which expresses longing for a private realm protected from incursions from the outside world; the forbidden lover poem, in which the speaker voices her frustration at not being able to be joined to her spirit's mate; the power fantasy, in which the poet briefly explores forbidden territory within a dream frame or under another neutralizing cover; and the poem of secret sorrow, in which she reveals that her life has been blighted by experiences she hides from public scrutiny.

Much of this poetry shows the influence of Felicia Hemans (1793–1835) who was probably the single most important model for American women poets. Hemans's early poem "The Wings of the Dove," for instance, probably furnished the paradigm for the free-bird poem. A British poet of considerable renown, Hemans authored the famous shipwreck ballad "Casabianca," used for a century of school memorizations, which begins "The boy stood on the burning deck." Many poets, both black and white, followed in Hemans's footsteps. Her work was praised by such male contemporaries as Shelley and Wordsworth, and both Emma Embury and Lydia Sigourney were saddled with the title "the American Hemans."

Moralistic and pious, Hemans's poetry combined Romantic interest in nature and intense feeling with Victorian insistence on duty and responsibility for others. Thus, it agreed perfectly with the type of sensibility women poets in the nineteenth century were expected to possess. On the one hand, the poetess was stereotypically represented as a dreamy soul standing apart from the harsh realities of everyday life and cherishing a special sensitivity to things of the spirit. On the other, she was expected to confirm prevailing social values, accommodating herself to the very world with which other aspects of her nature were supposed to be so much at odds. In no way was a woman poet (any more than a man) expected to provide serious political, social, or religious challenges to the status quo. Though she might criticize certain social practices as lacking in compassion or disproportionately burdensome to women, her critique was at all times understood to advocate reform not revolution.

In this respect most nineteenth-century women poets could hardly be called Romantic if we think of the Romantics in terms of such men as Blake, Byron, and Shelley, all of whom shared a radicalism different from what one finds among these women. Their Romanticism was more akin to Wordsworth's mystical nature poetry, though German literature (and Goethe) was for many of them a far stronger influence than either English or French culture. Wordsworth was remembered best by the nature poets, Lucy Larcom, Lydia Sigourney, Alice Cary, and Sarah Helen Whitman, for example.

For the most part, these women saw their task as providing memorable expression for the prevailing sentiments of liberal Christianity, domestic piety, American nature romanticism, and nationalist fervor. To this must be added the fact that many turned to poetry to provide relief from personal crises such as the deaths of loved ones or disillusionment with their lives. Modernist aesthetic principles—privileging linguistic disruption, extreme perceptions, epistemological doubt, and trenchant political critique—were alien to the minds of most of them. Unlike the moderns, nineteenth-century women poets typically saw the role of art as an intensification of familiar aspects of life rather than as a separate realm with its own, sometimes antisocial, values and resonances.

Yet the so-called feminization of American culture analyzed by Ann Douglas deserves a second look. From this distance it is hard to know to what extent women writers engineered the rather bland version of culture they often seemed to advocate. Writing on "Modern Women" in the *Nation* (22 Nov. 1868), Henry James was of the opinion that his female contemporaries were "remarkably well-disposed to model themselves on the judgment and wishes of men" rather than vice versa. We do have evidence that women poets were strongly critical of their own productions. Lydia Sigourney was frustrated that her economic situation required her to reproduce "slight themes" in order to please editorial appetites. She saw herself as serving rather than defining popular taste, commenting memorably: "If there is any kitchen in Parnassus, my Muse has surely officiated there as a woman of all work and an aproned waiter" (see *NB* 57).

Indeed, many women poets reported that they felt themselves restricted to certain subjects and forms. Sarah Josepha Hale, the influential editor of *Godey's Lady's Book,* made it clear that women could not range freely over literary subjects like the "lords of creation." Frances Osgood was even more emphatic:

> Ah! woman still
> Must veil the shrine,
> Where feeling feeds the fire divine,
> Nor sing at will,
> Untaught by art,
> The music prison'd in her heart!

In spite of inhibitions, however, women did write a great deal. Books of poetry often ran to three or four hundred pages, though the length of such books diminished considerably toward the end of the century. Expansiveness was a feature not only of books but also of individual poems in which the aim often seems to be discursiveness rather than condensation. Regular in meter and rhyme scheme, consistent in tone, comprehensive in treatment of its subject, operating within the fixed boundaries of a shared discourse rather than aiming at surprise, the typical nineteenth-century work by a popular woman writer is nothing like what twentieth-century critics, strongly influenced by modernist aesthetics, construe as a "good poem." And yet, for one who is willing to evaluate this work outside of the confines of modernist thinking or even sometimes within them, there are numerous good poems among these examples.

THE MORE ONE READS Emily Dickinson the less like her contemporaries she seems. Nevertheless, there are features of the poetesses' world that agree in detail with Dickinson's life and experience. It is helpful to consider some trends in women poets' lives in the nineteenth century. Generalizations should not be overemphasized, of course, but identifying some patterns is useful for seeing how nineteenth-century careers typically took shape and where a particular poet's experience represents the norm or diverges from it.

In the biographies of these women, one frequently reads that a particular poet was precocious. Catharine Sedgwick gives a full account of the way Lucretia Davidson covered pages with poems even as a young child. Both Frances Harper and Emma Lazarus wrote poetry in their teens and published volumes of their juvenilia. Rose Terry Cooke was writing poems and plays from childhood onward.

To get a sense of the emphasis given to precocity in nineteenth-century accounts of these women's lives, it is worth looking at a passage in the memorial prefacing the 1869 edition of Emma Embury's poems where the writer claims: "As a child [Embury] was most precocious, and learned to read almost intuitively. She early developed a talent for compositions, and her juvenile productions are remarkable for their graceful and flowing rhythm." This statement is repeated in a slightly varying form in many early biographies, and it suggests that the norms for feminine poetry (here described in terms of "graceful and flowing rhythm") put no necessary boundary between juvenile and adult productions. One also suspects that by seeming precocious, a girl could establish an identity as an exception, worthy to be further educated and encouraged. Girls who were not precocious were less likely to be able to nurture a literary talent at a more advanced age. Precocious young women however were comparatively blessed in the nineteenth century by opportunities to read and study. Though public education could not be counted upon until late in the century, private seminaries, such as the Emma Willard School in Troy, New York (which Lucretia Davidson attended), Mount Holyoke Female Seminary, and the Hartford Female Seminary in Connecticut, provided good schooling much earlier. Most of the women poets in this collection received some form of advanced education, generally including study in classical literatures, German, French, geography, and basic mathematics. Handwork skills, such as needlework, and home economics were also part of many of these young women's educations, but lessons in dancing and decorum usually did not outweigh more scholarly studies, as they often did in England.

Interestingly enough, the minority women represented in this anthology did not necessarily suffer in terms of education. Lucy Larcom, for instance, whose working-class life in the Lowell Mills placed unusual strains on her time, attended lectures and night classes and was tutored in her off hours by her sister. She later attended Monticello Female Seminary. Though Jewish at a time of violent anti-Semitism, Emma Lazarus grew up in a wealthy and fashionable New York City home. She was privately tutored in French, German, and Italian and traveled extensively in Europe.

Even black women poets, suffering from both racism and sexism, were not always disadvantaged in terms of their education. Henrietta Cordelia Ray, for instance, the daughter of a Congregational minister in New York City who edited the influential black journal *Colored American,* was one of three sisters all achieving advanced degrees: Charlotte graduated from Howard University Law School in 1872 and became Washington's first black woman lawyer. Henrietta and Florence both earned masters degrees in pedagogy from the University of the City of New York. Henrietta taught mathematics, music, languages, and English literature.

Of course, the possession of an inquiring mind and advanced education did not protect any woman from a white patriarchal hegemony that imposed restrictions on all women and on minority women in particular. One of the patterns most frequently repeated in these poets' biographies is precocity, adolescent distinction, marriage, followed by disillusionment and years of difficult adjustment to an unpalatable wifely role. Elizabeth Oakes-Smith, who became a lyceum lecturer in support of women's rights, expressed the frustration of many women when she wrote: "I felt painfully that had I been a boy, time and space would have been allowed me to fill up this arrested beautiful development, while marriage, which a girl must not refuse, was the annihilation of her" (46).

Stressful marriages blighted the lives of Sigourney, Osgood, Howe, Oakes-Smith, Brooks, Thaxter, Menken, and Coolbrith. Others, like Larcom, who wanted to be free to pursue their literary lives, remained single. The Cary sisters, Guiney, Ray, Thomas, and Reese also did not marry. Financial difficulties often hounded them however. The life of a single woman was frequently marked by some sort of dependency. Through most of the century it was difficult for women to travel alone and there were few occupations open to them that provided more than minimal wages. Several of these women—Larcom, Ray, and Reese—were schoolteachers. Louise Guiney worked briefly, under great stress, as a postmistress. Ina Coolbrith spent many years as a librarian in Oakland, California, but was eventually removed by a male board of supervisors who found her independent spirit unsettling. All of these women led precarious lives financially and sought ways of supplementing their incomes through writing.

Though a single life frequently made women vulnerable to financial strains, marriage provided no guarantee of security. In fact, one notable feature of several poets' biographies is the conjunction of marriage and a precipitous descent into poverty brought on by a husband's reverses in business. Elizabeth Oakes-Smith is a prominent example of this pattern. Her husband lost all their money through land speculation. In her autobiography she reflects on the false position of the wife in such circumstances: "I saw the shipwreck before us, but made the best of it, and it was nothing I could in any way prevent. Internally, I vented my spleen upon the false position held by women, who seemingly could do nothing better than suppress all screaming and go down with the wreck" (73). Like Oakes-Smith, Lydia Sigourney, Rose Terry Cooke, Julia Ward Howe, and Celia Thaxter were forced to turn to writing to offset the dire consequences of their husbands' debts.

In addition to financial worries and dissatisfaction with marriage, a host of griefs afflicted the women poets represented here. Some were tormented by severe illnesses such as tuberculosis, which killed Lucretia

Davidson, Frances Osgood, the Cary sisters, and Maria Lowell, or cancer, which cut short the career of Emma Lazarus. Davidson, Osgood, Lowell, and Embury have left behind chilling poems recording the distresses of the sickroom.

Several women poets were devastated by the deaths of their children. Sigourney, Jackson, Osgood, Lowell, Coolbrith, and (probably) Fordham fall into this category. Jackson's poem "The Prince Is Dead" is a very powerful example of this genre, undoubtedly written out of her own experience with grief, but even Lizette Woodworth Reese, who was childless, wrote a moving lyric on this subject entitled "Rachel."

We must remember, of course, that death was much more likely to bear down on the life of a young family in the nineteenth century than is typically the case today. It was common to lose at least a parent, a sibling, a husband, or a child before one was thirty. Many of the women in this collection, however, seem to have taken these deaths particularly hard. Jackson, who lost both her first husband and her two sons, attributed her vocation as a writer to a decision to "sing off charnel steps."

Though most of the lyrics written about children's deaths are unremarkable in the way they represent parental suffering and religious consolation, a few stand out. Brooks, for instance, ends one poem—called "On Hearing of the Death of a Beautiful Child" from *Judith, Esther, and Other Poems*—with this stark portrait of grief:

> And, sufferer, though to the regions of bliss,
>> And light, love, and music, and beauty, she's gone,
> Oh! the heart just bereft of an earth-hope like this,
>> Though thousands console, must be bleeding and torn.

In Lowell's poem the "slave-mother" of the title hopes that her child will die rather than face a lifetime of debasement as a female slave. Equally unconventional is Osgood''s "A Mother's Prayer in Illness," which begs God to take her children *first* and then let her die and repose at their feet.

Religion played an enormously important role in the lives of many of these women. Though they adhered to a variety of faiths—Catholic, Episcopal, Congregationalist, Methodist, Unitarian, and Jewish,—most of them drew intense spiritual satisfaction from their connection to a higher power. Howe became a preacher in her later years. Oakes-Smith finally gave institutional form to her mystical leanings by taking on the ministry of an independent congregation in Canastota, New York. Many religious poems written by these women seem repetitious, uncreative, *merely* pious, and therefore forgettable. But some, such as Cooke's "Iconoclast," Oakes-Smith's "Strength from the Hills," Alice Cary's "To Solitude," Phoebe Cary's "Drawing Water," and Guiney's "Borderlands," demonstrate intensity of spirit, originality, and lyrical power.

In summary, the typical nineteenth-century American woman poet was well educated and spiritually keen, showed unusual intellectual promise before she was out of her teens, either remained single or found married life frustrating, suffered intensely and relatively early from the deaths of loved ones, turned to writing to ease financial burdens or a troubled heart, and sought the support of an influential male. Whittier proved to be an unusually energetic supporter of nineteenth-century women poets, championing Sarah Helen Whitman, Lucy Larcom (with whom he collaborated), Alice Cary, Ina Coolbrith, and Celia Thaxter. Like Whittier, women poets tended to favor reform (most were abolitionists) and to find religion spiritually present in nature.

Popular women poets often wrote in a variety of genres—poetry, fiction, essay—and published many works in large-distribution magazines before issuing them in book form. Though no one was able to support herself entirely from the publication of poetry, some women—Sigourney, the Cary sisters, Howe, Harper, Larcom, and Wilcox—added significantly to their incomes by publishing verse.

Still, Louise Imogen Guiney's essay, "The Point of View: On Being Well-Known" (published in *Scribner's Magazine* in January 1911) provides an ironic commentary on the way so-called popularity could coexist with poverty. Guiney began to publish after the decline of emphasis on poetry in women's magazines, in an era in which more and more people preferred to read prose. In her essay she humorously recounts the references made to her supposed popularity while letting us know that she has earned almost nothing from the publication of her works. Guiney's tart revelations help to confirm a sense that, by the end of the century, the market for women's poetry seemed to be shrinking. Few of these poets lived long enough to see it expand again in the 1910s and 1920s when some women poets (Amy Lowell, Sara Teasdale, and Edna St. Vincent Millay) found thousands of readers for their verse.

Despite indications that women poets generally were not reaching as many readers as they had earlier, Emily Dickinson's poems, first published in book form in the 1890s, found a large audience. *Poems of Emily Dickinson,* edited by Mabel Loomis Todd and Thomas Wentworth Higginson, went through three editions: a First Series in 1890, a Second Series in 1891, and a Third Series in 1896. Responses to the poems were mixed but the poetry met with far more approval than Todd and Higginson had dared to expect. In part, this had to do with changing taste, which was much more tolerant of idiosyncrasy than it had been forty years earlier.

Another woman poet popular in the last decades of the nineteenth century was Ella Wheeler Wilcox, whose *Poems of Passion,* first published in 1883, gave rise to "the Erotic School" of writers, which insisted on the artistic right to explore sexual feelings in defiance of Victorian morality. Wilcox became the target of searing attacks as well as the heroine of a more liberated younger generation. Her champion was William Randolph Hearst.

Both Dickinson and Wilcox were received enthusiastically in the 1890s. To clarify the range of responses women poets in the nineteenth century received, I shall also explore more negative elements in the reception given "popular" women poets, limiting the term "popular" to women who had a reasonably large readership during their lifetimes. It was these women, rather than Dickinson, whose poems populated the century's literary landscape and who gave wide currency to the figure of the "poetess."

Many male writers who dominate the literary canon today expressed themselves at some point on the subject of the popular woman poet. By and large, they disapproved of her, Poe and Whittier notwithstanding. Mark Twain's portrait of Emmeline Grangerford in *The Adventures of Huckleberry Finn* is probably the most familiar caricature. Emmeline's poems, written without much thought or polish, are uniformly morbid. To Huck, his new friend Buck's sister seems a prodigy:

> She didn't ever have to stop and think. [Buck] said she would slap down a line, and if she couldn't find anything to rhyme it with she would just scratch it out and slap down another one, and go ahead. She warn't particular, she could write about anything you choose to give her to write about, just so it was sadful. (ch. xvii)

Twain probably had both Lydia Sigourney and Sara Lippincott in mind when he created this satirical portrait, but many of its barbs were aimed at a broad range of female writers.

Walt Whitman also took a dim view of the current increase in literary women. In 1857, just after he quarreled with James Parton over a loan, he wrote in the Brooklyn *Daily Times* an indictment of women writers that mentioned by name Parton's wife Sara, the popular writer Fanny Fern. According to Justin Kaplan, Whitman insisted that the "majority of people do not want their daughters trained to become authoresses and poets. We want a race of women turned out from our schools, not of pedants and bluestockings. One genuine woman is worth a dozen Fanny Ferns" (225).

In *The Portrait of a Lady* (1881) Henry James provides his own satire of female poetic pretensions through the characters of Lady Pensil and Mrs. Osmond. Lady Pensil is given to artistic affectations, including the writing of verse. Similarly, Gilbert Osmond's mother, "the American Corinne," is described by Mme. Merle as a woman "who had bristled with pretensions to elegant learning and published descriptive poems and corresponded on Italian subjects with the English weekly journals" (ch. XXVI). There is some implication that her literary distractions prevented her from taking adequate care of her children who have turned out as adults to be morally stunted.

If some like Hawthorne resented the strength of this new "mob of scribbling women," others simply felt that it was indecent for a woman to expose herself by publishing at all. According to Ann Douglas, "in a long letter of 1827, [Lydia Sigourney's husband] mercilessly described her career in terms of sexual desire: she evinced a '*lust* of praise, which like the *appetite* of the cormorant is not to be satisfied,' and was guilty of an 'apparently unconquerable *passion* of displaying herself" ("Mrs. Sigourney" 166). Julia Ward Howe's husband felt the same way about his wife's frequent appearances upon the public stage. Caroline Howard Gilman was covered with shame when she realized that one of her poems had been secretly passed to a Boston paper. Her alarm when she saw it in print was as great "as if I had been detected in man's apparel" (*NB* 34). To Gilman and others there was an indication of something not only unseemly but even licentious in a woman willing to come before the public in print. Charles Sigourney's outrage at his wife's urge to publish makes this connection even clearer. In asking "Who wants or would value a wife who is to be the public property of the whole community?" he probably spoke for many who were unsettled by these women's assertion of an identity independent of that of wife and mother.

Nevertheless, the history of American criticism abounds with examples of men willing to make an exception for a particular woman of their acquaintance whose publicity somehow thrills rather than disgusts them. James Russell Lowell was eager to see his wife Maria receive the public acclaim he felt was her due. "I will not compare her with any of our 'poetesses' because she is not comparable with them," he wrote to a friend, "but I should like to have [her poems] go into G[riswold]'s volume. He ought to have a poem or two in it by way of salt" (Vernon 30). Similarly, George Stoddard expressed his enthusiastic appreciation of his friend Ina Coolbrith, pronouncing her an exception to the general pattern: "She has no superior among the female poets of her own land, and scarcely an equal" (AWW1; 401). The woman who is thus praised achieves her status at the expense of her sisters. Furthermore, the exaggeration of some of these women's talents suggests that such men were generally unfamiliar with women's poetry. Maria White Lowell's poems are interesting but not in a class by themselves.

No doubt, these women poets' popularity was due more to their female than to their male readers, but a few men were willing to take women's poetry seriously. One was Edgar Allan Poe. Poe paid court to more than one woman poet in New York and became embroiled in some complicated and nasty intrigues because of this, but he knew women's poetry in the 1840s in detail. Because he was so often involved in editorial magazine work (including a stint at *Graham's*), he read what women were writing. His essays on popular women poets (now in volume eight of the collected works edited by Stedman and Woodberry) provide interesting insights into nineteenth-century aesthetic standards. Poe evaluates Emma Embury, Frances Osgood, Anne Lynch, Mary Hewitt, Amelia Welby, the Davidson sisters, and Elizabeth Oakes-Smith among others. He makes fun of the grand praise for Lucretia Davidson's *Amir Kahn* as "twaddle" and calls Elizabeth Ellet a "plagiarist." His highest praise goes to Frances Osgood for the warmth of her style. The poets he found the most effective simply in terms of skill were Osgood, Lynch, and Sigourney.

Other attempts to survey the field of women's poetry include Griswold's introduction to *The Female Poets of America* and Stedman's introduction to his *American Anthology*. Griswold begins his mid-century appraisal by saying: "It is less easy to be assured of the genuineness of literary ability in women than in men." Since women are "naturally" given to emotional sensitivity and moral delicacy, one should not confuse the presence of such sentiments with good poetry in their case, whereas with men, who are naturally given to abstract thought, good poetry often does depend upon the possession of these "feminine" traits. Griswold praises particularly Brooks, Oakes-Smith, Osgood, and Whitman, finding in their work "as high and sustained a range of poetic art, as the female genius of any age or country can display" (4). Yet Griswold remains patronizing in his judgments of women poets, gallantly leaving to others the task of serious discrimination among female talents.

Stedman's anthology contains both male and female poets, so his introduction is not primarily concerned with women. He does say, however, that he finds in America "a succession of rarely endowed women-singers, that began—not to go back to the time of Maria Brooks—near the middle of the century, [and] still continues unbroken." While energetically defending his decision to include women poets, he warns against overenthusiasm, remininding his readers: "Not that by force of numbers and excellence women bear off the chief trophies of poetry, prose fiction, and the other arts; thus far the sex's achievements, in a time half seriously styled 'the woman's age,' are still more evident elsewhere" (xiv). It is not clear to a modern reader what he means by "elsewhere."

If both Griswold and Stedman convey a certain fastidiousness about being either too appreciative or too critical of women's writing (and indeed both back away from the task of making serious distinctions), nineteenth-century women readers were far more frankly enthusiastic. Poems by members of their own sex had a special appeal. Lucy Larcom talks about her love of several poems by Felicia Hemans. Emily Dickinson cherished the works of Elizabeth Barrett Browning, especially *Aurora Leigh*. Edith Thomas fell deeply under the spell of Helen Hunt Jackson. Willa Cather insisted that Louise Imogen Guiney's poems were passed from hand to hand when Cather worked at *McClure's Magazine,* and Guiney herself expressed delight that so many women poets were coming to the fore in America. To an English male friend, she wrote, with a good deal of satisfaction: "The women over here are regular Atlantas in the poetic race" (*NB* 125).

Yet Emily Dickinson's letters tell us that she paid little attention to the American women poets popular in her lifetime. She treasured Helen Hunt Jackson as a friend (and once spoke admiringly of her poems, calling them "stronger than any written by Women since Mrs.—Browning, with the exception of Mrs. Lewes" # 368), but Jackson does not seem to have influenced her much. When Higginson recommended that she read Maria White Lowell, she wrote back (26 Sept. 1870): "You told me of Mrs. Lowell's Poems. Would you tell me where I could find them or are they not for sight?" (# 352). One wonders how genuine this question was, since her brother and sister-in-law (who lived next door) owned a copy of *The Household Book of Poetry* which contained one of Maria Lowell's most popular poems. Though the Dickinson library apparently did not include a copy of Griswold's anthology of women poets, Emily was still exposed to women through the magazines such as the *Atlantic Monthly,* which printed many poems by Rose Terry and Julia Ward Howe. Even Longfellow's *Kavanaugh* (a favorite among the younger generation of Dickinsons) contains an extract from Maria Brooks's *Zóphiël.* But Emily's extant letters, with the exception of the above two references, never mention the American women poets of her day.

These contradictions suggest that the politics of reading were more complicated in the nineteenth century than one might at first assume. That a woman poet was "popular" did not mean that every aspiring woman writer necessarily knew her work, though in Dickinson's case one suspects that she knew more than she admitted. On the other hand, poetry in general was read by a much larger segment of the literate population than is the case today. Melville includes part of a poem by Oakes-Smith in his Extracts, prefatory to *Moby Dick.*

In the last years of the century, women's poetry finally seems to have moved out of its ghetto, becoming a dominant force. According to Amy Lowell in *Poetry and Poets,* the poets of the 1890s, no matter what sex they belonged to, were more "feminine" than "masculine." Lowell contrasts her own generation, which she sees as primarily masculine, with that of the earlier era, concluding:

> This little handful of disconnected souls, all unobtrusively born into that America [of the late nineteenth century] which sighed with Richard Watson Gilder, wept with Ella Wheeler Wilcox, permitted itself to dance delicately with Celia Thaxter, and occasionally to blow on the beribboned trumpet of Louise Imogen Guiney, was destined to startle its progenitors. (111)

In many ways the chorus of 1890s female voices simply signaled the beginning of a rout; almost all nineteenth-century women poets, with the exception of Dickinson, drifted into obscurity within a few decades. Lizette Woodworth Reese continued to write well into the 1930s, but her moment had passed with the passing of the late nineteenth-century generation to which she primarily belonged. Like Reese, Louise Imogen Guiney was remembered by a few writers, Louise Bogan notable among them, but she too faded. Helen Hunt Jackson preserved a reputation based on her Indian novel, *Ramona*. Her poetry went out of print.

There are already signs of erasure in Jessie Rittenhouse's 1915 anthology, *The Little Book of American Poets*. Though Rittenhouse goes back as far as eighteenth-century Philip Freneau, she includes no poems by Brooks, Osgood, Oakes-Smith, Embury, Cooke, or any black women. The white women who came to the fore in the late nineteenth century— Lazarus, Dickinson, Coolbrith, Thaxter, Thomas, Guiney, and Reese—do make an appearance. But of the poets who were particularly popular in the middle years, only the Cary sisters, Larcom, Whitman, and Howe are represented. Rittenhouse acknowledges in her notes that the Cary sisters, though popular in their day, are no longer read. Larcom is remembered mainly for having worked in the Lowell Mills, Whitman for having been engaged to Poe (the only poem used to illustrate her work is a tribute to Poe), and Howe is given credit for writing only one poem of enduring interest, "The Battle-Hymn of the Republic."

Here and there in the twentieth century, a poet or critic has noted the earlier contributions made by some nineteenth-century women poet. Amy Lowell, for instance, "discovered" her distant relative, Maria White Lowell, and her enthusiasm eventually led to the first major edition of Maria's poems, published by Brown University Press and edited by Amy's friend, S. Foster Damon. Emma Lazarus has enjoyed considerable appreciation within the Jewish community and Frances Harper has been similarly revered by African-Americans.

Yet Louise Bogan is one of the few early twentieth-century critics to attempt a survey of nineteenth-century women poets. In her "Poetesses in the Parlor," Bogan adopts a tone mostly patronizing toward these women, making errors of both fact and attribution, but accurately judging Maria Brooks and Frances Osgood to be of more than passing interest. Though she doesn't name Rose Terry Cooke, she mentions several of Cooke's poems. In the years following 1936, Bogan began to feel more generous toward nineteenth-century women's verse. When she came to write her book *Achievement in American Poetry* (1951), she was ready to say: "the line of poetic intensity which wavers and fades out and often completely fails in poetry written by men [in the later years of the nineteenth century] on the feminine side moves on unbroken" (19). The "poetess" had moved out of the parlor and into the main arena.

THE LATE TWENTIETH CENTURY has seen several attempts to reassess the contributions of nineteenth-century women poets. Generally, the strategy has been to play Emily Dickinson off against the lesser-known women in order to highlight Dickinson's greatness at their expense. But in works by Paula Bennett, Joanne Dobson, Alicia Ostriker, Emily Stipes Watts, and myself, popular nineteenth-century poets have been treated more even handedly as deserving attention of their own. The selected Bibliography lists some of these texts.

In addition *Legacy: A Journal of American Women Writers* has become an important source of material concerning both poets and prose writers. The essays and profiles in *Legacy* (which began as a newsletter in 1984) have considerably enriched the field of scholarship on nineteenth-century women poets. Finally, several books on individual women (Larcom, Harper, Menken, and Howe) have been published in recent years, with more due out in the near future.

The greatest strength of nineteenth-century American women's po-etry—and the reason for continued interest in it—is that it represents the liberation of primitive literary energies, that is, it comes from a group of women who have only recently begun to feel themselves empowered to speak and who thus write with an urgency and dedication that separates them from most of their male counterparts. This explains Bogan's idea that the line of feeling is stronger in women's than in men's poems during the nineteenth century.

The weaknesses one discovers often have similar origins unfortu-nately; as Adrienne Rich writes about Marie Curie, their "wounds came from the same source as [their] power." Virginia Woolf in *A Room of One's Own* also identifies some of the circumstances affecting women trying to write well with little in the way of tradition or education behind them. Their lack of authority, finally, may make them imitative, on the one hand, or merely provocative on the other. One can readily see in women's poetry the truth that freedom needs (some) power to express itself effectively.

It is difficult from this distance to evaluate adequately the works of so many women, and impossible to do so without imposing some standards that derive more from twentieth-century critical perspectives than from nineteenth. We must remember that most of the poets selling their productions in the nineteenth-century literary marketplace were working with a conscious aesthetic that differed significantly from the norms of today's poetry. Above I have sketched out the lineaments of this aesthetic and suggested the way it differed from what we now tend to value. Nevertheless, even when writing a poem about a child's death (as Jackson did in "The Prince Is Dead") or when celebrating the inspirational value of nature (as Oakes-Smith did in "Strength from the Hills"), these poets were sometimes able to develop effective responses to conventional *topoi*.

In my view the most interesting poet of the first generation is Maria Brooks, whose work remains stirring and provocative even in the late twentieth century. Not only was Brooks a passionate and effective stylist, she also investigated bizarre psychological phenomena that many today would find fascinating. Indeed, as the headnote to her selection indicates, Brooks has attracted several admirers in our time.

Of mid-century writers Frances Osgood, Lucy Larcom, and Julia Ward Howe represent three quite distinct modes of talent, all of which deserve further study. Osgood achieves something rare: a recognizable voice, a sensibility announcing itself as female in tones of simultaneous seduction and challenge. In poems such as "He Bade Me Be Happy" and "Forgive and Forget," Osgood teases and mocks her lovers in lines that have no counterpart until Edna St. Vincent Millay. "Caprice" represents a triumph of female narcissism unequaled in its time. Though her work is uneven, as is the case with all of these highly prolific poets, Frances Osgood illustrates one powerful mode of literary subversion: she is adept at what Alicia Ostriker calls "stealing the language," seizing the male perogative for her own use.

Lucy Larcom is almost her opposite: down to earth where Osgood is flighty, intellectual where Osgood is emotional, modest where Osgood is vain. Yet both women represent in their poems memorable forms of resistance to the dominant attempt to contain female force. Larcom stands her ground as a worker, a thinker, a woman who respects herself first of all. "The Rose Enthroned" is an extraordinary composition, drawing upon contemporary theories of evolution to imagine cosmic time bringing to birth a new understanding of love and life.

Though born before Larcom, Julia Ward Howe belongs to a slightly later generation of poets, less influenced, for instance, by nature. Howe's best work—"The Soul-Hunter," "The Telegrams," and "A New Sculptor" are good examples—has a dark and thrilling mystery about it which refuses to unveil itself. Howe, like Melville's Ishmael, is "quick to perceive a horror, and could still be social with it," should it seem rewarding. Her feminism is not without an edge, as "The Tea-Party" demonstrates. Howe was a tireless reformer who looked to women to bring about the new order, discovered in them a "royal will," and gave them her most serious charge: don't sit by and watch the world become corrupt. "Redeem the church, reform the state!"

My personal favorite, however, is Rose Terry Cooke. In Cooke's work we certainly feel the liberation of primitive energies, the celebration of an excess that seeks to rupture the bonds of womanhood. Though Cooke's work became less interesting as she grew older, her first book of poetry, published in 1861, is studded with gems. "Blue-Beard's Closet"—with its haunting refrain "The chamber is there!"—seems to make male violence against women the obscenity that corrupts civilization. Yet, Cooke herself plays with the sensuality of violence in such poems as "Fantasia," "After the Camanches," and "The Squire's Boar Hunt." On almost every score, Cooke refuses to play by women's rules. She is appetitive rather than renunciatory, openly sexual in "Semele" and "In the Hammock," and politically radical in her tribute to John Brown. Though her life was full of constraints, her imagination was wild and even cruel, the mind of a sorceress rather than a nun.

At the end of the century, four talented women poets came to the fore: Helen Hunt Jackson, Louise Imogen Guiney, Lizette Woodworth Reese, and Edith M. Thomas. Jackson, the earliest, was the favorite of both Emerson and Higginson, and for good reason. She was adept at the use of literary forms. "The Prince Is Dead," for instance, is a stark and powerful poem that uses simple, declarative statements reminiscent of Thomas Hardy, along with an intricate rhyme scheme of her own devising. Jackson's control of prosody was striking indeed, and both Guiney and Thomas learned from her example.

Guiney's poems have that peculiar combination of brazen trumpets and quiet flutes that appealed to both Amy Lowell and Louise Bogan, whose works also vacillated between abstinence and passion. One of Guiney's most interesting poems is "Tarpeia," a ballad typical of the poet's archaic and militaristic imagination but here inflected with feminist insight. Guiney left this work out of her selected poems, *Happy Ending,* and it has been overlooked in other anthologies for this reason. Even in the late twentieth century, however, Tarpeia's fate and "the deed they had loved her for, doing, and loathed her for, done," remain resonant. On the more delicate side, Guiney's "Open, Time" is as lovely and poignant an elegy as any I know.

Thomas and Reese, though more limited, also achieved moments of lyric beauty and vitality. Reese's work began the drift toward narrow, compact lyrics with pungent endings which came to be associated with Sara Teasdale and other similar women poets of the 1910s and 1920s. Thomas's transformation of Greek motifs gives her work a strength and purity that looks forward to the imagistic poetry of H. D.

In all nineteenth-century anthologies the political content of women's poetry was either downplayed or actively suppressed. Women's poetry was political however, from the beginning to the end of the century—from Lydia Sigourney's poems about slaves, Africans, and Indians to Ina Coolbrith's "The Captive of the White City" in 1893. This collection contains stirring political poems by the Cary sisters, Harper, Lowell, Lazarus, and many others. What Griswold disdained, as a violation of female norms, many modern readers will recognize as an important expression of nineteenth-century thought and feeling.

To counter the assumption that all nineteenth-century women poets (except for Dickinson) were morbid or melancholy, I have included some humorous poems in my selections. One of the wittiest is Embury's "Lament" (of One of the Old Régime)," but there is humor in the work of Lynch Botta, Osgood, Larcom, the Cary sisters, and Wilcox as well. "The Coming Woman" by Mary Weston Fordham is wryly satirical about the reversal of male and female roles, as is Lucretia Davidson's earlier poem "Auction Extraordinary."

Given the almost total neglect accorded nineteenth-century popular women poets, it is a pleasure to be able to show through an anthology that these writers were neither all alike nor without merit. If I have left many poets out, I did so because it seemed preferable to present fewer poets and thereby offer a greater number of representative poems. Women such as Margaret Fuller who were mainly prose writers have been excluded. And the selections do not reflect all of what nineteenth-century women wrote. I have not included poems written for children, for instance, and my choices tend to favor secular over sacred poetry.

Another feature of this anthology is that some poems have been chosen for the purposes of comparison; topics such as the washerwoman, opium addiction, and the practice of suttee were addressed by several women. I could, however, have chosen other poems and found similar patterns of repetition; my choices should not suggest that these were the *only* themes women poets shared.

The exclusion of Emily Dickinson from this anthology was a decision made for the sake of space and coherence. Dickinson's work is easy to obtain, the facts of her life are well known, and an enormous amount of criticism is available about her. Though this anthology aims to inspire new comparative work that would connect Dickinson to other nineteenth-century women poets, its purpose is mainly to bring to the attention of modern readers the long-forgotten texts of nineteenth-century women poets who are not already widely known and recognized. In this sense the anthology is designed to be revisionist. I hope it will be received as a point of departure for a very lively conversation about history, literature, the canon in general, and women in particular. I have learned much from the study of these poets. In the years to come, others also involved in such research might very well want to revise and expand the selections I have made. I look forward to the widening of the circle.

Works listed in the Selected Bibliography are given only partial reference in the Selected Criticism sections at the end of the individual poets' biographies.

The following abbreviations have been used in the Introduction and Notes to this volume.

AWW	*American Women Writers*
NAW	*Notable American Women 1607–1950*
NB	Walker, Cheryl. *The Nightingale's Burden*

American Women Writers. Ed. Lisa Maniero. 4 vols. New York: Frederick Ungar, 1979, 1980, 1981. (*AWW*)

Bennett, Paula. *Emily Dickinson, Woman Poet.* Iowa City: U of Iowa P, 1990.

Bogan, Louise. *Achievement in American Poetry.* Chicago: Henry Regnery, 1951.

————. "Poetesses in the Parlour." *New Yorker,* 5 Dec. 1936. 42 ff.

Coultrap-McQuin, Susan. *Doing Literary Business: American Women Writers in the Nineteenth Century.* Chapel Hill: U of North Carolina P, 1990.

Cowell, Pattie, ed. *Women Poets in Pre-Revolutionary America 1650–1775.* Troy, NY: Whitston, 1980.

Dickinson, Emily. *The Letters of Emily Dickinson.* 3 vols. Ed. Thomas H. Johnson and Theodora Ward. Cambridge: Harvard UP, 1958.

Dobson, Joanne. *Dickinson and the Strategies of Reticence: The Woman Writer in Nineteenth-Century America.* Bloomington: Indiana UP, 1989.

Douglas, Ann. *The Feminization of American Culture.* New York: Knopf, 1977.

————. "Mrs. Sigourney and the Sensibility of the Inner Space." *New England Quarterly* 45 (June 1972): 163–81.

Duyckinck, Evert A. and George L. *Cyclopaedia of American Literature.* 2 vols. New York: Scribner's, 1855.

Finch, Annie. "The Sentimental Poetess in the World: Metaphor and Subjectivity in Lydia Sigourney's Nature Poetry." *Legacy* 5 (Fall 1988): 3–18.

Griswold, Rufus, ed. *The Female Poets of America*. 1848. Rev. ed. R. H. Stoddard. New York: James Miller, 1874.

————, ed. *The Poets and Poetry of America*. Philadelphia: Perry & McMillan, 1856.

Kaplan, Justin. *Walt Whitman: A Life*. New York: Simon, 1980.

Keller, Karl. *The Only Kangaroo among the Beauty: Emily Dickinson and America*. Baltimore: Johns Hopkins UP, 1979.

Kelley, Mary. *Private Woman, Public Stage: Literary Domesticity in Nineteenth-Century America*. New York: Oxford UP, 1984.

Lowell, Amy. *Poetry and Poets*. Boston: Houghton, 1930.

Marchalonis, Shirley, ed. *Patrons and Protégées: Gender, Friendship, and Writing in Nineteenth-Century America*. New Brunswick: Rutgers UP, 1988.

May, Caroline. *American Female Poets*. Philadelphia: Lindsay & Blakiston, 1856.

Memorial, The: Written by Friends of the Late Mrs. Osgood. Ed. Mary E. Hewitt. New York: George Putnam, 1851.

Moers, Ellen. *Literary Women*. New York: Doubleday, 1976.

Notable American Women 1607–1950. Ed. Edward T. James et al. 3 vols. Cambridge: Harvard UP, 1971. (*NAW*)

Oakes-Smith, Elizabeth. *The Autobiography of Elizabeth Oakes-Smith*. Ed. Mary Alice Wyman. Lewiston, MD: Lewiston Journal, 1924.

Ostriker, Alicia Suskin. *Stealing the Language: The Emergence of Women's Poetry in America*. Boston: Beacon, 1986.

Pattee, Fred Lewis. *The Feminine Fifties*. New York: Appleton, 1940.

Poe, Edgar Allan. *The Literati—Minor Contemporaries, Etc.*, in *The Works of Edgar Allan Poe*, vol. 8. Ed. Edmund Clarence Stedman and Clarence Woodberry. New York: Scribner's, 1895.

Reynolds, David. *Beneath the American Renaissance: The Subversive Imagination in the Age of Emerson and Melville*. New York: Knopf, 1988.

Rittenhouse, Jessie B. *The Little Book of American Poets*. Boston: Houghton, 1917.

St. Armand, Barton Levi. *Emily Dickinson and Her Culture: The Soul's Society*. Cambridge: Cambridge UP, 1984.

Sherman, Joan R., ed. *Collected Black Women's Poetry*. 4 vols. The Schomburg Library of Nineteenth-Century Black Women Writers. Gen. ed. Henry Louis Gates, Jr. New York: Oxford UP, 1988.

————. *Invisible Poets: Afro-Americans of the Nineteenth Century*. Urbana: U of Illinois P, 1974.

Stedman, Edmund Clarence, ed. *American Anthology 1787–1900.* Boston: Houghton, 1900.

Stern, Madeleine. *Publishers for Mass Entertainment in Nineteenth-Century America.* Boston: G. K. Hall, 1980.

Vernon, Hope Jillian. Biographical Preface to *The Poems of Maria Lowell.* Providence: Brown UP, 1936.

Walker, Cheryl. *The Nightingale's Burden: Women Poets and American Culture before 1900.* Bloomington: Indiana UP, 1982. (*NB*)

Walsh, John Evangelist. *Plumes in the Dust: The Love Affair of Edgar Allan Poe and Fanny Osgood.* Chicago: Nelson-Hall, 1980.

Watts, Emily Stipes. *The Poetry of American Women from 1632 to 1945.* Au' tin: U of Texas P, 1977.

A NOTE ON THE TEXTS

For all selections I have used the versions printed in the poet's volumes published during the nineteenth century. I have generally retained the original spelling and punctuation as given. The only exception to this practice is Maria Brooks's *Zóphiël* which required changes due to inconsistent spellings (of Medea and Sardius, for example), occasionally confusing punctuation, and obvious typographical errors. I also omitted Brooks's footnotes, which seemed neither necessary nor very helpful. In other cases, I have occasionally included author's footnotes, adding my own when a word or reference might be obscure to the reader.

ACKNOWLEDGMENTS

For advice and help in preparing this manuscript, I wish to thank Ellen Finkelpearl, Margaret Mueller, Nancy Burson, Michael Roth, Bradford Blaine, Michael Harper, Paula Bennett, Roswitha Burwick, Sara Adler, Melvin Sands, and especially Joanne Dobson.

AMERICAN WOMEN POETS
of the Nineteenth Century

LYDIA SIGOURNEY

(1791 – 1865)

LYDIA HOWARD HUNTLEY was the most famous woman poet in America during the first half of the nineteenth century. She adored her father, a gardener, and her literary tastes were nurtured by the family who employed him. It was through this family (in particular, Daniel Wadsworth of Hartford) that her first book of poetry, *Moral Pieces,* was published in 1815. She taught school in Hartford and relinquished her job with some regrets when in 1819 she married Charles Sigourney, a widower with three children. The marriage was not happy. She had two children of her own, but the younger one, Andrew, whom she deeply loved, died of tuberculosis at the age of nineteen. Her husband's hardware business failed. Having been a great reader since childhood, she turned again to writing, a pursuit her husband greatly resented because of its publicity.

An energetic and indomitable writer, Sigourney published 46 distinct volumes and 2000 articles in 300 journals. Since she was one of the earliest popular nineteenth-century women poets, her name alone was worth money. *Godey's Lady's Book* offered $500 for the right to list her as an editor. Though she clearly exploited her reputation to earn support for her family, she was often dissatisfied with the quality of what she had to produce.

Sigourney became known for her moralistic sentiments and her poems about death. "The Mother of Washington" and "Death of an Infant" were perennial favorites. She has since been much maligned as a sentimentalist. In her defense, however, we should note that she was actively involved in political and social issues and much more interested in the world than in her own emotions. Like many women poets she was an abolitionist and supporter of American Indian causes, though insistent on the benefits of conversion to Christianity. Sigourney was confident that her religion would confer the blessings of civilization upon the heathen, but in "Christian Settlements in Africa" her usual optimism about the positive effect of Christianity is absent.

Mother Sigourney, as she was sometimes called, was a stalwart, generous woman who supported women's education, worked hard as a professional writer, and occasionally—as one can see in "To a Shred of Linen"—was able to laugh as well as sermonize. "The Stars" and "The Suttee" show her talents to advantage. She was an early progressive, moralistic to be sure, but not without her share of warmth. Her memoirs, *Letters of Life* (1866), provide a lively sense of this woman's mind and heart.

Selected Works: Letters to Young Ladies. 1833; *Report of the Hartford Female Beneficent Society.* 1833; *Zinzendorff, and Other Poems.* 1835; *Pocahontas, and Other Poems.* 1841; *Select Poems.* 1842; *Sayings of the Little Ones, and Poems for Their Mothers.* 1855; *The Man of Uz, and Other Poems.* 1862.

Selected Criticism: De Jong, Mary G. "Profile of Lydia Sigourney. *Legacy* 5 (Spring 1988): 35–43; Dobson; Douglas; Finch; Haight, Gordon S. *Mrs. Sigourney: Sweet Singer of Hartford.* New Haven: Yale UP, 1930; Kramer, Aaron. *The Prophetic Tradition in American Poetry, 1835–1900.* Rutherford: Farleigh Dickinson UP, 1968.

THE STARS

Make friendship with the stars.
                    Go forth at night,
And talk with Aldebaran, where he flames
In the cold forehead of the wintry sky.
Turn to the sister Pleiades, and ask

Lydia Sigourney

If there be death in Heaven? A blight to fall
Upon the brightness of unfrosted hair?
A severing of fond hearts? A place of graves?
Our sympathies are with you, stricken stars,
Clustering so closely round the lost one's place.
Too well we know the hopeless toil to hide
The chasm in love's fond circle. The lone seat
Where the meek grandsire, with his silver locks,
Reclined so happily; the fireside chair
Whence the fond mother fled; the cradle turn'd
Against the wall, and empty; well we know
The untold anguish, when some dear one falls.
How oft the life-blood trickling from our hearts,
Reveals a kindred spirit torn away!
Tears are our birth-right, gentle sister train,
And more we love you, if like us ye mourn.
—Ho! bold Orion, with thy lion-shield;
What tidings from the chase? what monster slain?
Runn'st thou a tilt with Taurus? or dost rear
Thy weapon for more stately tournament?
'Twere better, sure, to be a son of peace
Among those quiet stars, than raise the rout
Of rebel tumult, and of wild affray,
Or feel ambition with its scorpion sting
Transfix thy heel, and like Napoleon fall.
Fair queen, Cassiopeia! is thy court
Well peopled with chivalric hearts, that pay
Due homage to thy beauty? Thy levee,
Is it still throng'd as in thy palmy youth?
Is there no change of dynasty? No dread
Of revolution 'mid the titled peers
That age on age have served thee? Teach us how
To make our sway perennial, in the hearts
Of those who love us, so that when our bloom
And spring-tide wither, they in phalanx firm
May gird us round, and make life's evening bright.

—But thou, O Sentinel, with sleepless eye,
Guarding the northern battlement of heaven,
For whom the seven pure spirits nightly burn
Their torches, marking out, with glittering spire,
Both hours and seasons on thy dial-plate,
How turns the storm-tost mariner to thee!
The poor lost Indian, having nothing left
In his own ancient realm, not even the bones
Of his dead fathers, lifts his brow to thee,
And glads his broken spirit with thy beam.
The weary caravan, with chiming bells,
Making strange music 'mid the desert sands,
Guides, by thy pillar'd fires, its nightly march.
Reprov'st thou not our faith so oft untrue
To its Great Pole Star, when some surging wave
Foams o'er our feet, or thorns beset our way?
—Speak out the wisdom of thy hoary years,
Arcturus! Patriarch! Mentor of the train,
That gather radiance from thy golden urn.
We are of yesterday, short-sighted sons
Of this dim orb, and all our proudest lore
Is but the alphabet of ignorance:
Yet ere we trace its little round, we die.
Give us thy counsel, ere we pass away.
—Lyra, sweet Lyra, sweeping on with song,
While glorious Summer decks the listening flowers,
Teach us thy melodies; for sinful cares
Make discord in our hearts. Hast thou the ear
Of the fair planets that encircle thee,
As children round the hearth-stone? Canst thou quell
Their woes with music? or their infant eyes
Lull to soft sleep? Do thy young daughters join
Thy evening song? Or does thine Orphean art
Touch the warm pulses of the neighbor stars
And constellations, till they higher lift
The pilgrim-staff to run their glorious way?

—Hail, mighty Sirius! monarch of the suns,
Whose golden sceptre subject worlds obey;
May we, in this poor planet speak to thee?
Thou highest dweller, 'mid the highest heaven,
Say, art thou nearer to His Throne, whose nod
Doth govern all things?
                              Hearest thou the strong wing
Of the Archangel, as it broadly sweeps
The empyrean, to the farthest orb,
Bearing Heaven's watch-word? Knowest thou what report
The red-hair'd Comet, on his car of flame,
Brings the recording seraph? Hast thou heard
One whisper through the open gate of Heaven
When the pale stars shall fall, and yon blue vault
Be as a shrivell'd scroll?
                              Thou answer'st not!
Why question we with thee, Eternal Fire?
We, frail, and blind, to whom our own dark moon,
With its few phases, is a mystery!
Back to the dust, most arrogant! Be still!
Deep silence is thy wisdom! Ask no more!
But let thy life be one long sigh of prayer,
One hymn of praise, till from the broken clay,
At its last gasp, the unquench'd spirit rise,
And, unforgotten, 'mid unnumber'd worlds,
Ascend to Him, from whom its essence came.

THE MOTHER OF WASHINGTON

On the laying of the Corner-stone of her Monument at Fredericksburg, Virginia

Long hast thou slept unnoted. Nature stole
In her soft ministry around thy bed,

Spreading her vernal tissue, violet-gemmed,
And pearled with dews.

                She bade bright Summer bring
Gifts of frankincense, with sweet song of birds,
And Autumn cast his reaper's coronet
Down at thy feet, and stormy Winter speak
Sternly of man's neglect.

                But now we come
To do thee homage—mother of our chief!
Fit homage—such as honoreth him who pays.
   Methinks we see thee—as in olden time—
Simple in garb—majestic and serene,
Unmoved by pomp or circumstance—in truth
Inflexible, and with a Spartan zeal
Repressing vice and making folly grave.
Thou didst not deem it woman's part to waste
Life in inglorious sloth—to sport awhile
Amid the flowers, or on the summer wave,
Then fleet, like the ephemeron,[1] away,
Building no temple in her children's hearts,
Save to the vanity and pride of life
Which she had worshipped.

                For the might that clothed
The "Pater Patriæ," for the glorious deeds
That make Mount Vernon's tomb a Mecca shrine
To all the earth, what thanks to thee are due,
Who, 'mid his elements of being, wrought,
We know not—Heaven can tell.

                Rise, sculptured pile!
And show a race unborn who rests below;
And say to mothers what a holy charge
Is theirs—with what a kingly power their love
Might rule the fountains of the new-born mind.
Warn them to wake at early dawn—and sow

1. This insect in its winged state lives only one day.

Good seed before the world hath sown her tares;
Nor in their toil decline—that angel bands
May put the sickle in, and reap for God,
And gather to his garner.
                       Ye, who stand,
With thrilling breast, to view her trophied praise,
Who nobly reared Virginia's godlike chief—
Ye, whose last thought upon your nightly couch,
Whose first at waking, is your cradled son,
What though no high ambition prompts to rear
A second Washington; or leave your name
Wrought out in marble with a nation's tears
Of deathless gratitude;—yet may you raise
A monument above the stars—a soul
Led by your teachings, and your prayers to God.

TO THE FIRST SLAVE SHIP

First of that train which cursed the wave,
    And from the rifled cabin bore,
Inheritor of wo,—*the slave*
    To bless his palm-tree's shade no more.

Dire engine!—o'er the troubled main
    Borne on in unresisted state,—
Know'st thou within thy dark domain
    The secrets of thy prison'd freight?—

Hear'st thou *their* moans whom hope hath fled?—
    Wild cries, in agonizing starts?—
Know'st thou thy humid sails are spread
    With ceaseless sighs from broken hearts?—

Lydia Sigourney

The fetter'd chieftain's burning tear.—
　　The parted lover's mute despair,—
The childless mother's pang severe,—
　　The orphan's misery, are there.

Ah!—could'st thou from the scroll of fate
　　The annal read of future years,
Stripes,—tortures,—unrelenting hate.
　　And death-gasps drown'd in slavery's tears.

Down,—down,—beneath the cleaving main
　　Thou fain would'st plunge where monsters lie,
Rather than ope the gates of pain
　　For time and for Eternity.—

Oh Afric!—what has been thy crime?—
　　That thus like Eden's fratricide,
A mark is set upon thy clime,
　　And every brother shuns thy side.—

Yet are thy wrongs, thou long-distrest!—
　　Thy burdens, by the world unweigh'd,
Safe in that *Unforgetful Breast*
　　Where all the sins of earth are laid.—

Poor outcast slave!—Our guilty land
　　Should tremble while she drinks thy tears,
Or sees in vengeful silence stand,
　　The beacon of thy shorten'd years;—

Should shrink to hear her sons proclaim
　　The sacred truth that heaven is just,—
Shrink even at her Judge's name,—
　　"Jehovah,—Saviour of the opprest."

The Sun upon thy forehead frown'd,
   But Man more cruel far than he,
Dark fetters on thy spirit bound:—
   Look to the mansions of the free!

Look to that realm where chains unbind,—
   Where the pale tyrant drops his rod,
And where the patient sufferers find
   A friend,—a father in their God.

FEMALE EDUCATION

Addressed to a South American Poet[1]

Thou, of the living lyre,
   Thou, of the lavish clime,
Whose mountains mix their lightning-fire
   With the storm-cloud sublime,
We, of thy sister-land,
   The empire of the free,
Joy as those patriot-breasts expand
   With genial Liberty.

Thy flowers their fragrant breast
   Unfold to catch its ray,
And Nature's velvet-tissued vest
   With brighter tint is gay,
More blest thy rivers roll
   Full tribute to the Sea,

---

1. The South American poet may well be Sor Juana Inés de la Cruz (1652–95) who wrote in favor of female education.

And even Woman's cloister'd soul
　Walks forth among the free.

Aid with thy tuneful strain
　Her bold, adventurous way,
Bid the long-prisoned mind attain
　A sphere of dazzling day,
Bid her unpinion'd foot
　The cliffs of knowledge climb,
And search for Wisdom's sacred root
　That mocks the blight of time.

MEETING OF THE SUSQUEHANNA WITH THE LACKAWANNA

Rush on glad stream, in thy power and pride,
To claim the hand of thy promis'd bride;
She doth haste from the realm of the darken'd mine,
To mingle her murmur'd vows with thine;
Ye have met—ye have met, and the shores prolong
The liquid notes of your nuptial song.

Methinks ye wed, as the white man's son,
And the child of the Indian king have done;
I saw thy bride, as she strove in vain,
To cleanse her brow from the carbon stain,
But she brings thee a dowry so rich and true
That thy love must not shrink from the tawny hue.

Her birth was rude, in a mountain cell,
And her infant freaks there are none to tell;
The path of her beauty was wild and free,
And in dell and forest, she hid from thee;
But the day of her fond caprice is o'er,
And she seeks to part from thy breast no more.

Pass on in the joy of thy blended tide,
Through the land where the blessed Miquon[1] died;
No red man's blood with its guilty stain,
Hath cried unto God from that broad domain—
With the seeds of peace they have sown the soil,
Bring a harvest of wealth, for their hour of toil.

On, on, through the vale where the brave ones sleep,
Where the waving foliage is rich and deep;
I have stood on the mountain and roam'd through the glen
To the beautiful homes of the western men;
Yet naught in that realm of enchantment could see,
So fair, as the vale of Wyoming to me.

THE BUBBLE

Out springs the bubble, dazzling bright,
With ever-changing hues of light,
And so amid the flowery grass
Our gilded years of childhood pass.
Yet bears not each with traitor sway,
Beneath its robe, some gem away?
Some bud of hope, at morning born,
Without the memory of the thorn?
Some fruit that ripen'd, free from care?
Where are those vanish'd treasures? *where?*

Then knowledge, with her letter'd lore,
Demands us at the nursery-door,
Reproves our love of vain delights,

---

1. The Indian name given to William Penn.

And on the brow, "sub jugum,"[1] writes.
But the sweet joys of earliest days,
The buoyant spirits, wing'd for praise,
Escape,—exhale. We thought them seal'd
For wintry days, their charm to yield.
Where have they fled? Go, ask the sky,
Where fleet the dews, when suns are high.

Upborne by history's arm, we tread
The crumbling soil, o'er nations dead.
The buried king, the mouldering sage,
The relics of a nameless age,
We summon forth, with vain regret;
And in that toil our heart forget:—
Till, warn'd, perchance, by wayward deeds,
How much that realm a regent needs,
Renew, with pangs of contrite pain,
The study of ourselves again.

While thus we roam, the silver hair
Steals o'er our temples here and there,
And beauty starts, amaz'd to see
The ploughshare of an enemy.
—What is that haunt, where willows wave?
That yawning pit? The grave! the grave!
The turf is set, the violets grow,
The throngs rush on, where we lie low.
Our name is lost, amid their strife,
The bubble bursts,—*and this is life!*

---

1. Lat., under the yoke.

Lydia Sigourney

FUNERAL OF MAZEEN

The Last of the Royal Line of the Mohegan Nation

'Mid the trodden turf is an open grave,
And a funeral train where the wild flowers wave,
And a manly sleeper doth seek his bed
In the narrow house of the sacred dead,
Yet the soil hath scantily drank of the tear,
For the red-brow'd few are the mourners here.

They have lower'd the prince to his resting spot,
The deep prayer hath swell'd, but they heed it not,
Their abject thoughts 'mid his ashes grope,
And quench'd in their souls is the light of hope;
Know ye their pangs, who turn away
The vassal foot from a monarch's clay?

With the dust of kings in this noteless shade,
The last of a royal line is laid,
In whose stormy veins that current roll'd
Which curb'd the chief and the warrior bold;
Yet pride still burns in their humid clay,
Though the pomp of the sceptre hath pass'd away.

They spake, and the war-dance wheel'd its round,
Or the wretch to the torturing stake was bound;
They lifted their hand, and the eagle fell
From his sunward flight, or his cloud-wrapt cell;
They frown'd, and the tempest of battle arose,
And streams were stain'd with the blood of foes.

Be silent, O Grave! o'er thy hoarded trust,
And smother the voice of the royal dust;
The ancient pomp of their council-fires,

Their simple trust in our pilgrim sires,
The whiles that blasted their withering race,
Hide, hide them deep in thy darkest place.

Till the rending caverns shall yield their dead,
Till the skies as a burning scroll are red,
Till the wondering slave from his chain shall spring,
And to falling mountains the tyrant cling,
Bid all their woes with their relics rest
And bury their wrongs in thy secret breast.

But, when aroused at the trump of doom,
Ye shall start, bold kings, from your lowly tomb,
When some bright-wing'd seraph of mercy shall bend
Your stranger eye on the Sinner's Friend,
Kneel, kneel, at His throne whose blood was spilt,
And plead for your pale-brow'd brother's guilt.

THE SUTTEE

She sat upon the pile by her dead lord,
And in her full, dark eye, and shining hair
Youth revell'd.——The glad murmur of the crowd
Applauding her consent to the dread doom,
And the hoarse chanting of infuriate priests
She heeded not, for her quick ear had caught
An infant's wail.——Feeble and low that moan,
Yet it was answer'd in her heaving heart,
For the Mimosa in its shrinking fold

The title refers to the practice associated with Hinduism of burning the widow
on her husband's funeral pyre.

From the rude pressure, is not half so true,
So tremulous, as is a mother's soul
Unto her wailing babe.——There was such wo
In her imploring aspect,——in her tones
Such thrilling agony, that even the hearts
Of the flame-kindlers soften'd, and they laid
The famish'd infant on her yearning breast.
There with his tear-wet cheek he lay and drew
Plentiful nourishment from that full fount
Of infant happiness,——and long he prest
With eager lip the chalice of his joy.——
And then his little hands he stretch'd to grasp
His mother's flower-wove tresses, and with smile
And gay caress embraced his bloated sire,——
As if kind Nature taught that innocent one
With fond delay to cheat the hour which seal'd
His hopeless orphanage.——But those were near
Who mock'd such dalliance, as that Spirit malign
Who twined his serpent length mid Eden's bowers
Frown'd on our parents' bliss.——The victim mark'd
Their harsh intent, and clasp'd the unconscious babe
With such convulsive force, that when they tore
His writhing form away, the very nerves
Whose deep-sown fibres rack the inmost soul
Uprooted seem'd.——

              With voice of high command
Tossing her arms, she bade them bring her son,——
And then in maniac rashness sought to leap
Among the astonish'd throng.——But the rough cord
Compress'd her slender limbs, and bound her fast
Down to her loathsome partner.——Quick the fire
In showers was hurl'd upon the reeking pile;——
But yet amid the wild, demoniac shout
Of priest and people, mid the thundering yell
Of the infernal gong,——was heard to rise
Thrice a dire death-shriek.——And the men who stood

Near the red pile and heard that fearful cry,
Call'd on their idol-gods, and stopp'd their ears,
And oft amid their nightly dream would start
As Frighted Fancy echoed in her cell
That burning mother's scream.

THE SICK CHILD

Thy fever'd arms around me,
    My little, suffering boy—
'Tis better thus with thee to watch,
    Than share in fashion's joy.

The pale nurse-lamp is waning
    Upon the shaded hearth,
And dearer is its light to me
    Than the gay flambeau's mirth.

I've lov'd the merry viol
    That spurs the dancer's heel,
And those soft tremblings of the lute
    O'er summer's eve that steal;

But when hath richest music
    Been to my soul so dear,
As that half-broken sob of thine
    Which tells that sleep is near?

I knew not half how precious
    The cup of life might be,
Till o'er thy cradle bed I knelt,
    And learn'd to dream of thee;

Lydia Sigourney

Till at the midnight hour I found
    Thy head upon my arm,
And saw thy full eye fix'd on mine,
    A strong, mysterious charm;

Till at thy first faint lisping
    That tear of rapture stole,
Which ever as a pearl had slept
    Deep in the secret soul.

A coffin small, and funeral,
    With all their sad array,
Gleam as my broken slumbers fleet
    On sable wing away.

Rouse, rouse me, ere such visions
    My heated brain can sear,
For still my baby's heavy knell
    Comes booming o'er my ear.

Cling closer, round my bosom
    Thy feeble arms entwine,
And while the life-throb stirs thy heart,
    Be as a part of mine.

That start, that cry, that struggle!
    My God—I am but clay,
Have pity on a bruised reed,
    Give thy compassions way;

Send forth thy strength to gird me,
    Impart a power divine,
To wring out sorrow's dregs, and say
    "Oh! not my will but thine."

Lydia Sigourney

DEATH OF A YOUNG LADY

AT THE RETREAT FOR THE INSANE

Youth glows upon her blossom'd cheek,
  Glad beauty in her eye,
And fond affections pure and meek
  Her every want supply:
Why doth her glance so wildly rove
  Some fancied foe to find?
What dark dregs stir her cup of love?
  Go ask the sickening mind!

They bear her where with cheering smile
  The hope of healing reigns
For those whom morbid Fancy's wile
  In torturing bond constrains;
Where Mercy spreads an angel-wing
  To do her Father's will,
And heaven-instructed plucks the sting
  From Earth's severest ill.

Yet o'er that sufferer's drooping head
  No balm of Gilead stole,
Diseas'd Imagination spread
  Dark chaos o'er the soul;
But recollected truths sublime
  Still fed Devotion's stream,
And beings from a sinless clime
  Blent with her broken dream.

Then came a coffin and a shroud,
  And many a bursting sigh,
With shrieks of laughter long and loud,
  From those who knew not why;

For she, whom Reason's fickle ray
    Oft wilder'd and distress'd
Hush'd in unwonted slumber lay,
    A cold and dreamless rest,

Think ye of Heaven! how glorious bright
    Will break its vision clear,
On souls that rose from earthly night
    All desolate and drear;
So ye who laid that stricken form
    Down to its willing sleep,
Snatch'd like a flowret from the storm,
    Weep not as others weep.

DEATH OF AN INFANT

Death found strange beauty on that polished brow,
And dashed it out. There was a tint of rose
On cheek and lip. He touched the veins with ice,
And the rose faded. Forth from those blue eyes
There spake a wishful tenderness, a doubt
Whether to grieve or sleep, which innocence
Alone may wear. With ruthless haste he bound
The silken fringes of those curtaining lids
For ever. There had been a murmuring sound
With which the babe would claim its mother's ear,
Charming her even to tears. The spoiler set
The seal of silence. But there beamed a smile,
So fixed, so holy, from that cherub brow,
Death gazed, and left it there. He dared not steal
The signet ring of Heaven.

Lydia Sigourney

CHRISTIAN SETTLEMENTS IN AFRICA

Winds! what have ye gathered from Afric's strand,
As ye swept the breadth of that fragrant land?
The breath of the spice-bud, the rich perfume
Of balm and of gum and of flowret's bloom?
"We have gather'd nought, save a pagan prayer,
And the stifling sigh of the heart's despair."

Waves! what have ye heard on that ancient coast
Where Egypt the might of her fame did boast,
Where the statue of Memnon[1] saluted the morn,
And the pyramids tower in their giant scorn?
"We have heard the curse of the slave-ship's crew,
And the shriek of the chain'd as the shores withdrew."

Stars! what have ye seen with the glancing eye
From your burning thrones in the sapphire-sky?
"We have mark'd young hope as it brightly glow'd,
On Afric's breast whence the blood-drop flow'd,
And we chanted the hymn which we sang at first,
When the sun from the midnight of Chaos burst."

---

1. An Ethiopian prince, the son of Eos (Dawn), Memnon fought in the Trojan War and was killed by Achilles. Amenophis's statue in Thebes was thought by the Greeks to represent Memnon.

Lydia Sigourney

TO A SHRED OF LINEN

Would they swept cleaner!—
                          Here's a littering shred
Of linen left behind—a vile reproach
To all good housewifery. Right glad am I,
That no neat lady, train'd in ancient times
Of pudding-making, and of sampler-work,
And speckless sanctity of household care,
Hath happened here, to spy thee. She, no doubt,
Keen looking through her spectacles, would say,
"This comes of reading books:"—or some spruce beau,
Essenc'd and lily-handed, had he chanc'd
To scan thy slight superfices, 'twoud be
"This comes of writing poetry."—Well—well—
Come forth—offender!—hast thou aught to say?
Canst thou by merry thought, or quaint conceit,
Repay this risk, that I have run for thee?
———Begin at alpha, and resolve thyself
Into thine elements. I see the stalk
And bright, blue flower of flax, which erst o'erspread
That fertile land, where mighty Moses stretch'd
His rod miraculous. I see thy bloom
Tinging, too scantly, these New England vales.
But, lo! the sturdy farmer lifts his flail,
To crush thy bones unpitying, and his wife
With 'kerchief'd head, and eyes brimful of dust,
Thy fibrous nerves, with hatchel-tooth[1] divides.
———I hear a voice of music—and behold!
The ruddy damsel singeth at her wheel,
While by her side the rustic lover sits.
Perchance, his shrewd eye secretly doth count

---

1. A hatchel or heckle was a tool used for combing flax.

The mass of skeins, which, hanging on the wall,
Increaseth day by day. Perchance his thought,
(For men have deeper minds than women—sure!)
Is calculating what a thrifty wife
The maid will make; and how his dairy shelves
Shall groan beneath the weight of golden cheese,
Made by her dexterous hand, while many a keg
And pot of butter, to the market borne,
May, transmigrated, on his back appear,
In new thanksgiving coats.
                              Fain would I ask,
Mine own New England, for thy once loved wheel,
By sofa and piano quite displac'd.
Why dost thou banish from thy parlor-hearth
That old Hygeian harp, whose magic rul'd
Dyspepsia, as the minstrel-shepherd's skill
Exorcis'd Saul's ennui? There was no need,
In those good times, of callisthenics, sure,
And there was less of gadding, and far more
Of home-born, heart-felt comfort, rooted strong
In industry, and bearing such rare fruit,
As wealth might never purchase.
                              But come back,
Thou shred of linen. I did let thee drop,
In my harangue, as wiser ones have lost
The thread of their discourse. What was thy lot
When the rough battery of the loom had stretch'd
And knit thy sinews, and the chemist sun
Thy brown complexion bleach'd?
                              Methinks I scan
Some idiosyncrasy, that marks thee out
A defunct pillow-case.—Did the trim guest,
To the best chamber usher'd, e'er admire
The snowy whiteness of thy freshen'd youth
Feeding thy vanity? or some sweet babe
Pour its pure dream of innocence on thee?

Say, hast thou listen'd to the sick one's moan,
When there was none to comfort?—or shrunk back
From the dire tossings of the proud man's brow?
Or gather'd from young beauty's restless sigh
A tale of untold love?
               Still, close and mute!—
Wilt tell no secrets, ha?—Well then, go down,
With all thy churl-kept hoard of curious lore,
In majesty and mystery, go down
Into the paper-mill, and from its jaws,
Stainless and smooth, emerge.—Happy shall be
The renovation, if on thy fair page
Wisdom and truth, their hallow'd lineaments
Trace for posterity. So shall thine end
Be better than thy birth, and worthier bard
Thine apotheosis immortalise.

MARIA GOWEN BROOKS

(1794–1845)

❦❦❦❦❦❦

THOUGH SHE PUBLISHED only two books of poetry, Maria Brooks impressed both English and American readers in the nineteenth century and has continued to appeal to such writers as Louise Bogan and Alicia Ostriker, who have examined her work in the twentieth. In "The Doctor" Robert Southey called her "the most empassioned and most imaginative of all poetesses" (*NAW* 1:245).

Orphaned at the age of fifteen, Maria Gowen was able to continue her education thanks to a wealthy friend of the family, John Brooks. The fifty-year-old Boston merchant insisted upon marrying his young ward in 1810, and Maria, who was grateful to Brooks, felt unable to deny him this favor. She was miserable in the marriage, however, and fell in love with a Canadian officer when the family moved to Maine. Unable to acknowledge her love publicly, she "wept and prayed in agony." In 1823, after a number of financial reverses, John Brooks died. His widow moved to a Cuban coffee plantation belonging to relatives. According to her son, she always wore white (with a passion flower in her hair) and devoted herself to her children in the tropical setting she hád come to love, moving back to the United States only to be near them. Though she was once engaged to her lover after her husband's death, the marriage was mysteriously called off. Twice she attempted suicide by means of opium. Eventually, she traveled to Europe. In England she befriended Robert Southey and stayed with his family, but when she returned to Cuba in the 1840s, Brooks contracted a tropical fever and died.

Maria Gowen Brooks

With the assistance of Southey, *Zóphiël; or, The Bride of Seven* was published in London in 1833. Both Rufus Griswold and Charles Lamb were entranced by it, Lamb reportedly commenting: "Southey says it's by some Yankee women. As if there were ever any woman capable of anything so great!" (*NB* 80). Though she had published a slim volume of poems in 1820, *Zóphiël* was unquestionably her masterwork. In this book-length poem, Egla—a virtuous Hebrew maiden living in a hostile kingdom—is pursued by a tormented fallen angel, Zóphiël, who is compared to both Apollo and Lucifer. Zóphiël is sometimes a victim and sometimes a victimizer. In the selection included here, Brooks treats Egla's courage and beauty, Zóphiël's sensitivity and passion, and (in the song from the final canto) Egla's despair. In her last years, Brooks wrote a psychological novel *Idomen*, which (like *Zóphiël*) is highly autobiographical. All of Maria Brooks's work is scholarly as well as personal, however. Trained in the literatures of several languages, she was a student of Milton, but always a passionate Romantic as these extracts show.

Selected Works: Judith, Esther, and Other Poems. 1820; *Idomen: or the Vale of Yumuri.* 1843.

Selected Criticism: Grannis, Ruth S. *An American Friend of Southey.* New York: De Vinne Press, 1913; Griswold; Gustafson, Zadel B. Intro. to *Zóphiël*, 1879; Mabbott, T. O. "Maria del Occidente." *American Collector* 2 (Aug. 1926): 415–24.

ZÓPHIËL; OR, THE BRIDE OF SEVEN

PLOT SUMMARY OF ZÓPHIËL

Egla is the heroine, a young and beautiful Jewish woman, who lives near the city of Ecbatane in the country of Medea. She and her parents, Zoroh and his wife, have survived the slaughter of the captive Jews by hiding in a cave. Now a kinder and younger king rules Medea, Sardius. Egla has been prevailed upon by her mother to agree to marry Meles, a nobleman of Medea, who is the first of the six husbands to fall prey to a mysterious death in the bridal chamber. In Canto 2 Egla defends herself from the charge of his murder. *Attracted by her beauty, five more members of Sardius's court attempt marriage and Egla, warned by the king's minister Idaspes not to resist if she wishes to preserve her father's life, watches each new bridegroom meet the same fate. Alcestes, Ripheus, Philomars, Rosanes, and finally, Altheëtor—the fair flower of the kingdom's youth—all expire. Zóphiël is the cause of most of these deaths. In many ways the hero, he is a fallen angel who, out of loyalty to Lucifer, fell with him, but who yet retains certain exalted angelic qualities. Zóphiël is in love with Egla but his success is thwarted by his betrayer Lucifer, also called here Oriel. After the death of Altheëtor, Zóphiël (who is innocent of this death) mourns with Egla. When she retreats to her grove, Zóphiël accompanies her and, in the cantos following, the angel educates Egla in music and poetry. She accepts his friendship and grows to trust him. While Zóphiël goes on a journey to obtain the elixir of life for her, Egla finds herself once more the innocent cause of another's death, this time that of Zameia, a woman who attempts to kill her out of a mistaken belief that Egla has caused Meles's death. When Zameia dies, Egla surrenders to despair and attempts suicide. Zóphiël, meanwhile, is once again prevented from achieving his desires by his nemesis, Lucifer. He returns, only to find that Egla has at last been united with her predestined lover Helon, a young Hebrew from Babylon to whose image she has remained faithful. Zóphiël attempts Helon's death but is prevented and subsequently exiled. With Egla at last united to her chosen husband, Brooks seems to suggest that perseverance and fidelity are rewarded in the end.*

Canto the Second

Death of Altheëtor

I

Soon over Meles' grave the wild flower dropt
    Its brimming dew; nor far, where Tigris' spray
Leaps to the beam, in life's sweet blossom cropt,
    Four others, fair as he, were snatched from day.

Bridegrooms like him, they knew his fate; yet, bent
    On their desires, resolved that fate to brave;
So, in succession, each a victim went,
    Borne from the bridal chamber to the grave.

II

Low liest thou, Meles! and 'tis mine to know,
　　By light of song, the darkly-hidden power
That closed thy bland, but wily lip; and show,
　　In flowing verse, what followed thy death-hour.

III

Noon slept upon thy grave, and Medea's king
　　Had sat him down, from court and harem far,
With a young boy who knew to touch the string
　　Of the sweet harp, and wage the ivory war

On painted field. The fainting breezes played
　　Among the curling clusters of his hair;
Thro' myrtle blooms and berries, white and red,
　　O'er the cool space of a pavilion, fair

As fond Ionian artist might devise:
　　Twelve columns, ivory white, support a dome,
Painted to emulate the dark blue skies,
　　When seamen watch the stars, and sigh, and think of home.

IV

And, in the midst, Night's goddess (to the sight
　　More softly beauteous for a pictured moon
That mantles her, in pale mysterious light,)
　　Comes stealing to the arms of her Endymion.[1]

[. . . . .]

---

1. In Greek myth the moon goddess Selene fell in love with a sleeping shepherd Endymion and lay down by him.

VIII

Beneath that dome, reclined the youthful king,
   Upon a silver couch; and soothed to mood
As free and soft as perfumes from the wing
   Of bird that shook the jasmines as it wooed,

Its fitful song the mingling murmur meeting
   Of marble founts of many a fair device;
And bees that banquet, from the sun retreating,
   In every full, deep flower, that crowns his paradise.

IX

While gemmy diadem thrown down beside,
   And garment, at the neck plucked open, proved
His unconstraint, and scorn of regal pride,
   When thus apart retired, he sat with those he loved.

X

One careless arm around the boy was flung,
   Not undeserving of that free caress;
But warm and true, and of a heart and tongue
   To heighten bliss or mitigate distress.

XI

Quick to perceive in him no freedom rude
   Reproved full confidence, friendship, the meat
His soul had starved without, with gratitude
   Was ta'en; and her rich wine crowned high the banquet sweet.

What sire Altheëtor owned 'twere hard to trace;
   A beautiful Ionian was his mother;
Some found to Sardius semblance, in his face,
   Who never better could have loved a brother.

XII

But now, the ivory battle at its close,
    "Go to thy harp," said Sardius, " 'twere severe
To keep thee longer, thus;" then, as he rose,
    "Where's our ambassador? Call Meles here."

XIII

Altheëtor said: "Alas! my prince, the chase
    Detains him long; and yet from peril sure
'Tis deemed he fares: nay, those there are who trace
    His absence to some silvan paramour."

XIV

"Let him be sought," said Sardius. No delay
    Mocked that command; but vestige, glimpse, nor breath
Was gleaned, till, sadly, on the seventh day,
    A band returned with tidings of his death.

[. . . . .]

"We've traced Lord Meles to that serpent's den,
    And seen him in the vile earth murdered lie;
Yet wherefore grieves the greatest king of men?
    This only is the fruit of clemency."

XVI

Then Sardius spoke, (as on the earth he cast,
    While grief gave anger place, his full dark eye):
"Whoe'er has done this deed has done his last!
    Soldier, priest, Jew, or Mede, By Belus he shall die."

XVII

Then brought they Zoroh in, misfortune's pride,
    His venerable locks with age were white;

He cheered his trembling partner, at his side,
   Reposing on his God, befall him as it might.

XVIII

Young Egla marked him stand so firm and pale;
   Looked in her mother's face—'twas anguish there;
Then gently threw aside her azure veil,
   And in an upward glance sent forth to heaven a prayer.

XIX

Then prostrate thus: "Oh, monarch, seal my doom!
   Thy sorrow for Lord Meles' death I know;
Take then thy victim, drag me to his tomb,
   And to his manes² let my life-blood flow!

XX

"Oh! by the God who made you glowing sun,
   And warmed cold dust to beauty with his breath;
By all the good that e'er was caused or done,
   Nor I, nor mine, have wrought thy subject's death.

XXI

"Yet think not I would live; alas! to me
   No warrior of my country e'er shall come;
And forth with dance, and flowers, and minstrelsy,
   I go to bid no brother welcome home.

XXII

"Sad from my birth, nay,—born upon that day
   When perished all my race, my infant ears

---

2. The manes are the appeased spirit of a dead person.

Were opened first with groans; and the first ray
    I saw came dimly through my mother's tears.

"Pour forth my life, a guiltless offering
    Most freely given! But let me die alone!
Destroy not those who gave me birth! oh, king!
    I've blood enough: let it for all atone!"

[.   .   .   .   .]

XXIV

Egla had ceased: her pure cheeks heightened glow;
    Her white hands clasped; blue veil, half fallen down;
Fair locks and gushing tears, stole o'er him so,
    That Sardius had not harmed her for his crown.

Yet, serious, thus fair justice' course pursued;
    As if to hide what look and tone revealed;
"What lured a Median to thy solitude?
    How came his death? and who his corse concealed?"

XXV

'Twas thus she told her tale: "A truant dove
    Had flown; I strayed a little from the track
That winds in mazes to my lonely grove,
    But heard a hunter's voice and hastened back.

XXVI

"Lord Meles saw; and with a slender dart,
    Fastened the little flutterer to a tree
By the white wing, with such surpassing art,
    'Twas scarcely wounded when returned to me.

XXVII

"Thankful I took; but taught to be afraid
   Of stranger's glance, retired: my mother sighed
And trembling saw; yet soon our dwelling's shade
   The Median sought, and claimed me for a bride.

XXVIII

"But when reluctant to my humble room
   I had retired, was spread a fragrance there,
Like rose and lotus shaken in their bloom;
   And something came and spoke, and looked so fair,

XXIX

"It seemed all fresh from heaven; but soon the thought
   Of things that tempt to sorcery in the night
Made me afraid. It fled; and Meles sought
   His bridal bed; the moon was shining bright;

XXX

"I saw his bracelets gleam, and knew him well;
   But, ere he spoke, was breathed a sound so dread,
That fear enchained my senses like a spell,
   And when the morning came, my lord was dead.

XXXI

"And then my mother, in her anxious care,
   Concealed me in a cave, that long before
Saved her from massacre; and left me there,
   To live in darkness, till the search was o'er

"Her fears foretold. So, in that cavern's gloom
   Alone upon the damp bare rock I lay,
Like a deserted corse; but that cold tomb
   Soon filled with rosy mists, like dawn of day,

"Which, half dispersing, showed the same fair thing
　　I saw before; and with it came another,
More gentle than the first, and helped it bring
　　Fresh flowers and fruits, in semblance like a brother.

XXXII

"They spread, upon the rock, a flowery couch;
　　And of a sparkling goblet bade me sip,—
For that they saw me cold; I dared not touch,
　　But, mid the sweet temptation, closed my lip;

"And from their grateful warmth and looks so fair
　　I turned away and shrank. Of their intent,
I do not know to tell, or what they were—
　　But feared and doubted both; and when they went,

"Fled trembling to my home; content to meet
　　The sternest death injustice might prepare,
Ere trust my weakness, in that dark retreat,
　　To such strange peril as assailed me there."

XXXIII

She ceased: and now, in palace bade to stay,
　　Awaits the royal pleasure; but no more,
Though strictly watched and guarded, all the day.
　　To that stern warrior's threats was given o'er.

[. 　.　 .　 .　 .　 .　 .　 .　 .　 .　 .　 .　 .　 .　 .　 .　 .]

XLVI

Day o'er, the task was done; the melting hues
　　Of twilight gone, and reigned the evening gloom
Gently o'er fount and tower; she could refuse
　　No more; and, led by slaves, sought the fair banquet-room.

Maria Gowen Brooks

XLVII

With unassured yet graceful step advancing,
    The light vermilion of her cheek more warm
For doubtful modesty; while all were glancing
    Over the strange attire that well became such form.

XLVIII

To lend her space the admiring band gave way;
    The sandals on her silvery feet were blue;
Of saffron tint her robe, as when young day
    Spreads softly o'er the heavens, and tints the trembling dew.

XLIX

Light was that robe, as mist; and not a gem
    Or ornament impedes its wavy fold,
Long and profuse; save that, above its hem,
    'Twas 'broidered with pomegranate-wreath, in gold.

L

And, by a silken cincture, broad and blue,
    In shapely guise about the waist confined,
Blent with the curls that, of a lighter hue,
    Half floated, waving in their length behind;
The other half, in braided tresses twined,
    Was decked with rose of pearls, and sapphires azure too,

Arranged with curious skill to imitate
    The sweet acacia's blossoms; just as live
And droop those tender flowers in natural state;
    And so the trembling gems seemed sensitive;

And pendant, sometimes, touch her neck; and there
    Seem shrinking from its softness as alive.

And round her arms flower-white, and round, and fair,
   Slight bandelets were twined of colours live;

Like little rainbows seemly on those arms;
   None of that court had seen the like before;
Soft, fragrant, bright,—so much like heaven her charms,
   It scarce could seem idolatry t' adore.

LI

He who beheld her hand forgot her face;
   Yet in that face was all beside forgot;
And he, who as she went, beheld her pace,
   And locks profuse, had said, "nay, turn thee not."

LII

Placed on a banquet-couch beside the king,
   'Mid many a sparkling guest no eye forbore;
But, like their darts, the warrior-princes fling
   Such looks as seemed to pierce, and scan her o'er and o'er:

Nor met alone the glare of lip and eye—
   Charms, but not rare:—the gazer stern and cool,
Who sought but faults, nor fault or spot could spy;
   In every limb, joint, vein, the maid was beautiful.

LIII

Save that her lip, like some bud-bursting flower,
   Just scorned the bounds of symmetry, perchance,
But by its rashness gained an added power;
   Heightening perfection to luxuriance.

[.   .   .   .   .]

LVIII

"Thy fragrant form, as the tall lily white,
  Looks full and soft; yet supple as the reed
Kissing its image in the fountain light,
  Or ostrich' wavy plume." So speaks the Mede;

While bending o'er her banquet-couch, he breathes
  Her breath, whose fragrance woos that near advance;
Plays with her silken tresses' wandering wreaths,
  And looks, and looks again with renovated glance.

LIX

But, ever watchful, to his prince's side
  Came old Idaspes; he, alone, might dare
To check the rising transport, ere its tide
  Arose too high to quell;—and thus, expressed his care,

Whispering in murmurs first: "At last, O king!
  Thy subjects breathe; the cries of slaughter cease;
And happy labourers bless thee, as they bring
  Forth from thy smiling fields, the fruits of peace.

"Their wounds just healing over, wouldst thou rush
  Upon thy doom and theirs? What bitter tears
Must flow, if thou shouldst fall! what blood must gush!
  Wait, till the cause of Meles' fate appears.

"And ere this dangerous beauty be thy bride,
  Let him who loves thee best come forth and prove
The peril first." Alcestes rose beside,
  And said, "Oh prince! to prove my faith and love,

"I'll dare as many deaths as on the sod
  Without, the falling rose of leaves has strown!

And if bland Meles fell by rival god,
    So let me fall; and live the pride of Medea's throne!"

LX

Egla, o'erwhelmed with shame, distaste, and fear,
    Could, of remonstrance, utter not a breath;
Ere fixed Idaspes' whisper met her ear:
    "One word impassive seals thy father's death."

[. . . . .]

LXXX

When Medea's last king died, a tumult rose,
    And all Idaspes' prudence scarce procured
To keep the youthful Sardius from his foes,
    And, ere his father's throne was yet secured,

Upon a terrace while Altheëtor hung
    About the prince, who carelessly carest,
A well-aimed arrow glanced; the stripling sprung,
    Stood like a shield, and let it pierce his breast.

LXXXI

But sage Pithoës knew the healing good
    Of every herb; he pluck'd the dart away;
And stopp'd the rich effusion of his blood
    As at his monarch's feet the boy exulting lay;

LXXXII

Drew forth from scrip, an antidotal balm;
    And ere the venom through life's streams could creep,
Bestowed for death's convulsions dewy calm,
    And steep'd each throbbing vein in salutary sleep.

LXXXIII

But now Altheëtor's sick. The kindly draught,
   The bath of bruised herbs were vainly tried;
While his young breath seem'd as it fain would waft
   His soul away;—so piteously he sighed.

LXXXIV

Above his couch were hung his sword and lyre,
   His polish'd bow, and javelin often proved
In the far chase, where once in faith and fire
   He fared beside to guard and watch the prince he loved.

LXXXV

His fragrant locks, thrown backward from his brow,
   Displayed its throbbing pulse; ah! how rebell'd
That heart, the seat of truth! Beside him now
   One languid hand the good Pithoës held;

LXXXVI

And look'd, and thought, and bent his brow in vain;
   Then, in the sadness of his baffled skill,
Resign'd the boy to fate; then thought again,—
   Was there no hidden cause for such consuming ill?

LXXXVII

Still o'er the couch he casts his gentle eyes,
   And brought fresh balm; but all was unavailing.
Altheëtor faintly breathes his thanks, and sighs,
   As if his guiltless life that moment were exhaling.

LXXXVIII

'Twas long he had not spoke; now heaved his breast,
   And now, despite of shame, a tear was straying

From the closed, quivering lid. Some grief supprest,
  Some secret care upon his life was preying.

LXXXIX

So came a glimpse across Pithoës' thought;
  And, in obedience to the doubt, he said,
" 'Tis strange, Altheëtor, thou has never aught
  Ask'd, or express'd, of the fair captive maid,

"For it was thou who forced the crowd to yield,
  When she was rudely dragg'd, on audience day,
And gently loosed, from Philomare's shield,
  A lock of her fair hair he else had torn away.

XC

"Sardius believed and loved her, would have wed,
  But old Idaspes, doubtful 'twas some god
That, amorous of her charms, laid Meles dead,
  Awhile restrain'd the King, who saw, unawed,

"The gay Alcestes, from her chamber fair
  Thrown dead and black. Ripheus, too, lies low;
Old Philomars spoke his last curses there;
  And young Rosanes ne'er his silver bow

"Shall draw again; and yet the King is fix'd
  In his resolve to wed; some power divine,
Envying our peace, impels; or she has mix'd,
  By magic skill, some philtre with his wine.

XCI

"Or there's in her blue eye some wicked light,
  That steadily allures him to his doom:

She's bidden to the feast again to-night,
 And good Idaspes' countenance in gloom

"Is fall'n:—in vain he strives;—his silver hairs
 Rise with the anguish at his heart's true core;
While the impatient, reckless Sardius swears
 By Baal, whate'er betides, to wait but three days more.

XCII

"Nor soldier, prince, or satrap, more appear
 Vaunting their fealty firm with fluttering breath,
But each speak low, as if some god were near,
 In silent anger singling him for death."

XCIII

Now o'er Altheëtor's face what changes glisten'd
 As ear and open lip drank every word;
He raised him from his couch, he looked, he listen'd,
 Reviving—renovating—as he heard.

XCIV

O'er cheek and brow a lively red was rushing,
 While half he felt his dark eye could not tell;
Then (spent the pang of hope) cold dews were gushing
 From brow again turned pale. He droop'd—he fell

Faint on his pillow. Unsurprised and calm
 Soon to restore the good Pithoës knew;
He saw what fever raged, and knew its balm;
 Spoke comfort to his charge; and for awhile withdrew.

XCV

What in his breast revolved, I cannot tell;
 To seek Idaspes' aid his steps were bent;

And when 'twas midnight, as by sudden spell
   Restored, to bridal room Altheëtor went.

XCVI

Touching his golden harp to prelude sweet
   Entered the youth, so pensive, pale, and fair;
Advanced respectful to the virgin's feet,
   And, lowly bending down, made tuneful parlance there.

XCVII

Like perfume soft his gentle accents rose,
   And sweetly thrill'd the gilded roof along;
His warm devoted soul no terror knows,
   And truth and love lend fervour to his song.

XCVIII

She hides her face upon her couch, that there
   She may not see him die. No groan, she springs
Frantic between a hope-beam and despair,
   And twines her long hair round him as he sings.

XCIX

Then thus:—"Oh! Being! who unseen but near
   Art hovering now, behold and pity me!
For love, hope, beauty, music,—all that's dear,
   Look,—look on me,—and spare my agony!

C

"Spirit! in mercy, make me not the cause,
   The hateful cause, of this kind being's death!
In pity kill me first!—He lives—he draws—
   Thou wilt not blast?—he draws his harmless breath."

Maria Gowen Brooks

CI

Still lives Altheëtor;—still unguarded strays
   One hand o'er his fall'n lyre; but all his soul
Is lost,—given up;—he fain would turn to gaze,
   But cannot turn, so twined. Now, all that stole

Through every vein, and thrilled each separate nerve,
   Himself could not have told,—all wound and clasped
In her white arms and hair. Ah! can they serve
   To save him?—"What a sea of sweets!"—he gasped,

But 'twas delight:—sound, fragrance, all were breathing.
   Still swell'd the transport, "Let me look and thank:"
He sighed (celestial smiles his lip enwreathing),
   "I die—but ask no more," he said and sank;

Still by her arms supported—lower—lower—
   As by soft sleep oppress'd;—so calm, so fair—
He rested on the purple tap'stried floor,
   It seemed an angel lay reposing there.

CII

Egla bent o'er him, all amazed;—awhile
   Thank'd God, the Spirit, and her stars (so much
Like life his gently closing lids and smile);—
   Then felt upon his heart. Ah! to that touch

Responds no quivering pulse;—'tis past. Then burst
   Her grief thus from her inmost heart, that bleeds:—
"Nay, finish! fiend, unpitying and accurst!
   Finish, and rid me too, of life, and of thy deeds!"

CIII

She hid her face in both her hands; and when,
    At length, look'd out, a form[3] was bending o'er
The good, the beauteous boy. With piteous ken
    It sought her eye, but still to speak forbore.

CIV

A deep unutterable anguish kept
    The silence long;—then from his inmost breast
The Spirit spoke, "Oh! were I him so wept,
    Daughter of earth, I tell thee I were blest:

CV

"Couldst thou conceive but half the pain I bear,
    Or agent of what good I fain would be,
I had not added to my deep despair
    And heavy curse, another curse—from thee.

CVI

"I've loved the youth; since first to this vile court
    I followed thee, from the deserted cave;—
I saw him—in thy arms—and did not hurt;
    What could I more?—alas! I could not save!

CVII

"He died of love; or the o'erperfect joy
    Of being pitied,—prayed for,—prest by thee.
Oh! for the fate of that devoted boy
    I'd sell my birth-right to eternity.

---

3. This "form" identifies the second entrance of Zóphiël.

CVIII

"I am not the cause of this thy last distress.
　　Nay! look upon thy Spirit ere he flies!
Look on me, once, and learn to hate me less!"
　　He said: and tears fell fast from his immortal eyes.

CIX

Her looks were on the corse; no more he said;
　　Deeper the darkness grew: 'twas near the dawn,
And chilled and sorrowing through the air he sped,
　　And in Hircania's deepest shades, ere morn,

Was hidden 'mid the leaves. Low moan'd the blast,
　　And chilly mists obscured the rising sun;
So bitter were his tears, that, where he passed,
　　Was blighted every flower they fell upon.

CX

Wild was the place, but wilder his despair:
　　Low shaggy rocks that o'er deep caverns scowl
Echo his groans: the tigress, in her lair,
　　Starts at the sound, and answers with a growl.

CXI

The day wore on; the tide of transport through
　　He listened to the forest's murmuring sound;
Until his grief alleviation drew,
　　From the according horrors that surround.

CXII

And thus, at length his plaintive lip expressed
　　The mitigated pang; 'tis sometimes so

When grief meets genius in the mortal breast,
    And words, most deeply sweet, betray subsided woe.

CXIII

"Thou'rt gone, Altheëtor; of thy gentle breath
    Guiltless am I, but bear the penalty!
Oh! is there one to whom thine early death
    Can cause the sorrow it has caused to me?

CXIV

"Cold, cold, and hush'd, is that fond, faithful breast;
    Oh! of the breath of God too much was there!
It swelled, aspired, it could not be compressed—
    But gained a bliss frail nature could not bear.

CXV

"Oh! good and true beyond thy mortal birth!
    What high-soul'd angel helped in forming thee?
Haply thou wert what I had been, if earth
    Had been the element composing me.

CXVI

"Banish'd from heaven so long, what there transpires,
    This weary exiled ear may rarely meet.
But it is whispered that the unquelled desires
    Another spirit for each forfeit seat,

"Left vacant by our fall. That spirit placed
    In mortal form, must every trial bear,
Midst all that can pollute: and, if defaced
    But by one stain, it may not enter there.

CXVII

"Though all the earth is wing'd, from bound to bound;
    Though heaven desires, and angels watch, and pray
To see their ranks with fair completion crowned;
So few to bless their utmost search are found,
    That half in heaven have ceased to hope the day;
And pensive seraphs' sighs o'er heavenly harps resound.

[.   .   .   .   .]

CXXII

"And I will steal thee, when the perfumes rise
    Around the cassia wood in smoky wave;
I'll shroud thee in a mist from mortal eyes,
    And gently lay thee in some sparry cave

"Of Paros; there, seek out some kindly Gnome
    And see him ('mid his lamps of airy light),
By wonderous process, done in earth's dark womb,
    Change thee, smile, lip, hair, all, to marble pure and white.

CXXIII

"Oh! my loved Hyacinth! when as a god
    I hurled the disk; and from thy hapless head
The pure sweet blood made flowers upon the sod;
    'Twas thus I wept thee! beautiful but dead,

"Like all I've loved. Oriel, false fiend, thy breath
    Guided my weapon: come! most happy thou
If my pain please. I mourn another death:
    Come, with thy insect wings, I'll hear thy mockery now.

CXXIV

"Thou didst not change his blood to purple flowers:
    Thy poisonous breath can blight but not create!
Thou canst but hover o'er Phraërion's bowers,
    And claim of men the honours of his state.

CXXV

"Thou kill'st my Hyacinth; but yet a beam
    Of comfort still was mine: I saw preserved
His beauty all entire; and gave a gleam
    Of him to a young burning Greek;—so served

"Thy crime a worthy cause; for long inspired,
    With a consuming wish, that Grecian's heart,
Lost to repose, so caught what it desired;
    And soon the chiselled stone glowed with a wondrous art."

CXXVI

While thus, the now half-solaced Zophiël brings
    Food to his soul, past o'er his gloomier mood:
He shakes his ringlets, spreads his pinions, springs
    From that rude seat, and leaves the mazy wood.

CXXVII

That morn o'er Ecbatane rose pale and slow;
    Thick lingering night-damps clog the morning's breath,
And veil'd the sun that rose with bloody glow,
    As if great nature's heart bled for the recent death.

CXXVIII

White-haired Idaspes from the fatal room
    Bade his own slaves love's loveliest victim bring,

Fresh, fair, but cold;—and in that lurid gloom
    Set forth the funeral couch, and show'd him to the king.

CXXIX

And drew away the tunic from the scar
    Seen on his cold white breast;—"And is it thou?"—
He said, "when treachery wings her darts afar,
    What faithful heart will be presented now!

CXXX

"Alas! alas! that ever these old eyes
    Should see Altheëtor thus! where is there one,
When lowly in the earth Idaspes lies,
    Will love and guard his prince as thou hast done?"

CXXXI

Sardius believed he slept: but undeceived,
    Soon as he found that faithful heart was cold,
He turned away his radiant brow and grieved,
    And, at that moment, freely would have sold

CXXXII

The diadem, that from his locks he tore,
    For that one life. Idaspes watched his mood,
And (ere the first fierce burst of grief was o'er—
    While lost Altheëtor's every pulse) pursued

With guardian skill, the kindly deep design,
    He probed the king's light changeful heart; and gained
A promise that the maid of Palestine,
    Until twelve moons had o'er his garden waned,

Should live in banishment from court. So sent
  To muse, in peace, upon her unknown love
(So long announced) dejected Egla went
  With all her house; and seeks her own acacia grove.

Canto the Sixth

Bridal of Helon

I

Sweet is the evening twilight; but, alas!
  There's sadness in it: day's light tasks are done,
And leisure sigh to think how soon must pass
  Those tints that melt o'er heaven, O setting sun,

And look like heaven dissolved. A tender flush
  Of blended rose and purple light, o'er all
The luscious landscape spreads, like pleasure's blush,
  And glows o'er wave, sky, flower, cottage, and palm-tree tall.

II

'Tis now that solitude has most of pain:
  Vague apprehensions of approaching night
Whisper the soul, attuned to bliss, and fain
  To find in love equivalent for light.

III

The bard has sung. God never formed a soul
  Without its own peculiar mate, to meet
Its wandering half, when ripe to crown the whole
  Bright plan of bliss, most heavenly, most complete!

IV

But thousand evil things there are that hate
    To look on happiness; these hurt, impede,
And leagued with time, space, circumstance, and fate,
    Keep kindred heart from heart to pine and pant and bleed.

And as the dove to far Palmyra flying
    From where her native founts of Antioch beam,
Weary, exhausted, longing, panting, sighing.
    Lights sadly at the desert's bitter stream,—

So many a soul o'er life's drear desert faring,
    Love's pure congenial spring unfound—unquaff'd—
Suffers—recoils—then, thirsty and despairing
    Of what it would, descends and sips the nearest draught.

V

'Tis twilight in fair Egla's grove, her eye
    Is sad and wistful; while the hues that glint
In soft profusion o'er the molten sky,
    O'er all her beauty spread a mellower tint.

VI

And form'd, in every fibre, for such love
    As heaven not yet had given her to share,
Through the deep shadowy vistas of her grove
    Sent looks of wistfulness; no Spirit there

Appears as wont; for many a month so long
    He had not left her; what could so detain?
She took her lute and tuned it for a song,
    The while spontaneous words accord them to a strain.

Taught by enamoured Zophiël; softly heaving
   The while her heart, thus from its inmost core
Such feelings gush'd, to Lydian numbers weaving,
   As never had her lip express'd before.

VII

Song

Day, in melting purple dying,
Blossoms, all around me sighing,
Fragrance, from the lilies straying,
Zephyr, with my ringlets playing,
      Ye but waken my distress:
      I am sick of loneliness.

Thou to whom I love to hearken,
Come, ere night around me darken:
Though thy softness but deceive me,
Say thou'rt true and I'll believe thee:
      Veil, if ill, thy soul's intent.
      Let me think it innocent!

Save thy toiling, spare thy treasure:
All I ask is friendship's pleasure:
Let the shining ore lie darkling,
Bring no gem in lustre sparkling:
      Gifts and gold are nought to me:
      I would only look on thee!

Tell to thee the high-wrought feeling.
Ecstacy but in revealing;
Paint to thee the deep sensation,
Rapture in participation,
      Yet but torture, if comprest
      In a lone unfriended breast.

Absent still? Ah! come and bless me!
Let these eyes again caress thee:
Once, in caution, I could fly thee:
Now, I nothing could deny thee:
   In a look if death there be,
   Come and I will gaze on thee!

SARAH HELEN WHITMAN

(1803–1878)

※※※※※※

SARAH HELEN POWER was born in Rhode Island into an old and distinguished family. When her father deserted the family, she was educated by her aunts. Helen was an eager reader of the classics, as well as French and German literature. In 1828 she married a Boston writer, editor, and attorney, John Winslow Whitman. They had no children.

Whitman published her first poem in the *American Ladies Magazine* in 1829. The editor, Sarah Josepha Hale, encouraged the poet to contribute other pieces. So began a long career in which Whitman wrote scholarly essays on the Romantics—such as Goethe, Shelley, and Emerson—translated German literature, and contributed essays and poems to several different journals.

Her husband died in 1833. Returning to Rhode Island to live with her mother, Whitman continued to write and also to support the causes she felt strongly about: educational reform, divorce, Fourierism, women's rights, universal suffrage, and the prevention of cruelty to animals. Like Elizabeth Oakes-Smith, Sarah Helen Whitman was a mystic, a follower of Transcendentalism, and a believer in psychic phenomena. "To E. O. S." and "Remembered Music" demonstrate her interest in mystical transcendence.

In 1848 she met Edgar Allan Poe. After an intense courtship, Helen became engaged to him, but the marriage never took place. Poe died in 1849, but Whitman made it her life's work to try to repair the damage his reputation suffered after his death. She published *Edgar Poe and His Critics* in 1860, an informed and persuasive defense based on personal knowledge of the man and giving serious attention to his work. "The Raven" and "To ———" celebrate Whitman's love for Poe and her appreciation of his work.

Her book of poetry, *Hours of Life and Other Poems,* was first published in 1848 and went through several editions. In 1879 Houghton Osgood published an enlarged collection called simply *Poems.* During her lifetime, Whitman's poetry was praised for its purity, its feeling for nature, and its fervent idealism. Though the muted tones of "A November Landscape" and "The Past" may strike some readers as overly melancholy, "A Pat of Butter" is a delightful exception to this mood. Furthermore, "Science" (written in 1877) is notable for the way it plays off Poe's sonnet "Science" to reflect a later generation's resistance to the spread of Darwinism.

Whitman was obviously a talented and thoughtful woman. In her day she was regarded as the epitome of the "poetess." Her beauty, magnetism, and intense, deep-set eyes were widely admired, and her contemporaries claimed that she appeared to age very little. Though Whitman's poetic range was limited, her interests were broad, and she was both well educated and well read. Her deeply romantic spirit— conveyed by her personal motto "break all bonds"—made her the voice of a longing for transcendence shared by many of her contemporaries.

Selected Criticism: Miller, J. C. *Poe's Helen Remembers.* Charlottesville: UP of Virginia, 1979; Ticknor, Caroline. *Poe's Helen.* New York: Scribner's, 1916; Unsigned Intro. to *Poems.* 1879.

THE MORNING-GLORY

When the peach ripens to a rosy bloom,
When purple grapes glow through the leafy gloom
Of trellised vines, bright wonder, thou dost come,
Cool as a star dropt from night's azure dome,

To light the early morning, that doth break
More softly beautiful for thy sweet sake.

Thy fleeting glory to my fancy seems
Like the strange flowers we gather in our dreams;
Hovering so lightly o'er the slender stem,
Wearing so meekly the proud diadem
Of penciled rays, that gave the name you bear
Unblamed amid the flowers, from year to year.
The tawny lily, flecked with jetty studs,
Pard-like, and dropping through long, pendent buds,
Her purple anthers; nor the poppy, bowed
In languid sleep, enfolding in a cloud
Of drowsy odors her too fervid heart,
Pierced by the day-god's barbed and burning dart;
Nor the swart sunflower, her dark brows enrolled
With their broad carcanets[1] of living gold,—
A captive princess, following the car
Of her proud conqueror; nor that sweet star,
The evening primrose, pallid with strange dreams
Born of the wan moon's melancholy beams;
Nor any flower that doth its tendrils twine
Around my memory, hath a charm like thine.
Child of the morning, passionless and fair
As some ethereal creature of the air,
Waiting not for the bright lord of the hours
To weary of thy bloom in sultry bowers;
Nor like the summer rose, that one by one,
Yields her fair, fragrant petals to the sun,
Faint with the envenomed sweetness of his smile,
That doth to lingering death her race beguile;
But, as some spirit of the air doth fade

---

1. A carcanet is an ornamental necklace or headband.

Into the light from its own essence rayed,
So, Glory of the morning, fair and cold,
Soon in thy circling halo dost thou fold
Thy virgin bloom, and from our vision hide
That form too fair, on earth, unsullied to abide[2]

A NOVEMBER LANDSCAPE

How like a rich and gorgeous picture hung
In memory's storied hall seems that fair scene
O'er which long years their mellowing tints have flung!
The way-side flowers had faded one by one,
Hoar were the hills, the meadows drear and dun,
When homeward wending, 'neath the dusky screen
Of the autumnal woods, at close of day,
As o'er a pine-clad height my pathway lay,
Lo! at a sudden turn, the vale below
Lay far outspread, all flushed with purple light;
Gray rocks and umbered woods gave back the glow
Of the last day-beams, fading into night;
While down a glen where dark Moshassuck flows,
With all its kindling lamps the distant city rose.

---

2. "The disk of the Convolvulus, after remaining expanded for a few hours, gathers itself up within the five star-like rays that intersect the corolla until it is entirely concealed from sight" (Whitman's note).

Sarah Helen Whitman

TO E. O. S.

"Eos, fair Goddess of the Morn! whose eyes
Drive back Night's wandering ghosts."—Horne's *Orion*[1]

When issuing from the realms of "Shadow Land"
   I see thee mid the Orient's kindling bloom,
With mystic lilies gleaming in thy hand,
   Gathered by dream-light in the dusky gloom
Of bowers enchanted—I behold again
   The fabled Goddess of the Morning, veiled
   In fleecy clouds. Thy cheek, so softly paled
With memories of the Night's mysterious reign,
   And something of the starlight, burning still
   In thy deep, dreamy eyes, do but fulfill
The vision more divinely to my thought:
   While all the cheerful hopes enkindling round thee—
   Warm hopes, wherewith thy prescient soul hath crowned thee—
Are with the breath of morning fragrance fraught.

The initials of the title are those of Elizabeth Oakes-Smith, author of *Shadow Land.*
  1. Richard Henry Horne (1802–84) published the allegorical epic *Orion* in 1843. An unconventional British poet and friend of E. B. Browning, he was much admired for *Orion.* Poe thought the poem one of the noblest of the age.

Sarah Helen Whitman

THE PAST

"So fern, und doch so nah."—Goethe[1]

Thick darkness broodeth o'er the world:
　　The raven pinions of the Night,
Close on her silent bosom furled,
　　Reflect no gleam of Orient light.
E'en the wild Norland fires that mocked
　　The faint bloom of the eastern sky,
Now leave me, in close darkness locked,
　　To-night's weird realm of fantasy.

Borne from pale shadow-lands remote,
　　A morphean music, wildly sweet,
Seems, on the starless gloom, to float,
　　Like the white-pinioned Paraclete.
Softly into my dream it flows,
　　Then faints into the silence drear;
While from the hollow dark outgrows
　　The phantom Past, pale gliding near.

The visioned Past; so strangely fair!
　　So veiled in shadowy, soft regrets.
So steeped in sadness, like the air
　　That lingers when the day-star sets!
Ah! could I fold it to my heart,
　　On its cold lip my kisses press,
This waste of aching life impart,
　　To win it back from nothingness!

---

1. Ger., so far and yet so near. Probably a misquotation of similar lines from Goethe's poem "Nähe des Geliebten" (Nearness of the Loved One), which was set to music by Franz Schubert.

Sarah Helen Whitman

I loathe the purple light of day,
    And shun the morning's golden star,
Beside that shadowy form to stray,
    Forever near, yet oh how far!
Thin as a cloud of summer even,
    All beauty from my gaze it bars;
Shuts out the silver cope of heaven,
    And glooms athwart the dying stars.

Cold, sad, and spectral, by my side,
    It breathes of love's ethereal bloom,—
Of bridal memories, long affied
    To the dread silence of the tomb:
Sweet, cloistered memories, that the heart
    Shuts close within its chalice cold;
Faint perfumes, that no more dispart
    From the bruised lily's floral fold.

"My soul is weary of her life;"
    My heart sinks with a slow despair;
The solemn, star-lit hours are rife
    With fantasy; the noontide glare,
And the cool morning, fancy free,
    Are false with shadows; for the day
Brings no blithe sense of verity,
    Nor wins from twilight thoughts away.

Oh, bathe me in the Lethean stream,
    And feed me on the lotus flowers;
Shut out this false, bewildering dream,
    This memory of departed hours!
Sweet haunting dream! so strangely fair—
    So veiled in shadowy, soft regrets—
So steeped in sadness, like the air
    That lingers when the day-star sets!

The Future can no charm confer,
    My heart's deep solitudes to break;
No angel's foot again shall stir
    The waters of that silent lake.
I wander in pale dreams away,
    And shun the morning's golden star,
To follow still that failing ray,
    Forever near, yet oh how far!
Feb., 1846.

TO ——

Vainly my heart had with thy sorceries striven:
It had no refuge from thy love,—no Heaven
But in thy fatal presence;—from afar
It owned thy power and trembled like a star
O'erfraught with light and splendor. Could I deem
How dark a shadow should obscure its beam?—
Could I believe that pain could ever dwell
Where thy bright presence cast its blissful spell?
Thou wert my proud palladium;—could I fear
The avenging Destinies when thou wert near?—
Thou wert my Destiny;—thy song, thy fame,
The wild enchantments clustering round thy name,
Were my soul's heritage, its royal dower;
Its glory and its kingdom and its power!

Sarah Helen Whitman

"THE RAVEN"

Raven, from the dim dominions
　　On the Night's Plutonian shore,
Oft I hear thy dusky pinions
　　Wave and flutter round my door—
See the shadow of thy pinions
　　Float along the moon-lit floor;

Often, from the oak-woods glooming
　　Round some dim ancestral tower,
In the lurid distance looming—
　　Some high solitary tower—
I can hear thy storm-cry booming
　　Through the lonely midnight hour.

When the moon is at the zenith,
　　Thou dost haunt the moated hall,
Where the marish flower greeneth
　　O'er the waters, like a pall—
Where the House of Usher leaneth,
　　Darkly nodding to its fall:

There I see thee, dimly gliding,—
　　See thy black plumes waving slow,—
In its hollow casements hiding,
　　When their shadow yawns below,
To the sullen tarn confiding
　　The dark secrets of their woe:—

The title of this poem and the references to the House of Usher, Ligeia, Mo-
rella, Ulalume, and others refer to works by Edgar Allan Poe.

Sarah Helen Whitman

See thee, when the stars are burning
   In their cressets, silver clear,—
When Ligeia's spirit yearning
   For the earth-life, wanders near,—
When Morella's soul returning,
Weirdly whispers "I am here."

Once, within a realm enchanted,
   On a far isle of the seas,
By unearthly visions haunted,
   By unearthly melodies,
Where the evening sunlight slanted
   Golden through the garden trees,—

Where the dreamy moonlight dozes,
   Where the early violets dwell,
Listening to the silver closes
   Of a lyric loved too well,
Suddenly, among the roses,
   Like a cloud, thy shadow fell.

Once, where Ulalume lies sleeping,
   Hard by Auber's haunted mere,
With the ghouls a vigil keeping,
   On that night of all the year,
Came thy sounding pinions, sweeping
   Through the leafless woods of Weir!

Oft, with Proserpine I wander
   On the Night's Plutonian shore,
Hoping, fearing, while I ponder
   On thy loved and lost Lenore—
On the demon doubts that sunder
   Soul from soul for evermore;

Trusting, though with sorrow laden,
 That when life's dark dream is o'er,
By whatever name the maiden
 Lives within thy mystic lore,
Eiros, in that distant Aidenn,
 Shall his Charmion meet once more.

REMEMBERED MUSIC

Oh, lonely heart! why do thy pulses beat
 To the hushed music of a voice so dear,
That all sweet, mournful cadences repeat
 Its low, bewildering accents to thine ear.
Why dost thou question the pale stars to know
 If that rich music floats upon the air,
In those far realms where, else, their fires would glow
 Forever beautiful to thy despair?
Trust thou in God; for, far within the veil,
 Where glad hosannas through the empyrean roll,
And choral anthems of the angel's hail
 With hallelujah's sweet the enfranchised soul,—
The voice that sang earth's sorrow through earth's night,
Shall with glad seraphs sing, in God's great light.

Sarah Helen Whitman

"A PAT OF BUTTER"

To Emilia

Yellow as the cups of gold,
Peering through the springtime mold,
Sweeter than a breath of clover
Blowing the June meadows over.—
Butter, such as Goethe said
Werther saw his Charlotte spread
For her sisters and her brothers,
And, perhaps, for a few others,
Till it turned her lover's head;[1]
Such as sweet Red Riding Hood,
By that wicked wolf pursued,
Through the enchanted forest bore
To her grandam's fatal door.
'T is the ashen time of Lent.
Well, I know some fairy sent
This, for my soul's nourishment:
Well I know a fairy churned
The creamy lactage till it turned
To golden gobbets; that a dame
Of gracious presence, known to fame
By her sweet baptismal name
Of Emilia (Emily),
Pressed it into shape for me
With her jeweled fingers.
                Say you:
"This is all a dream?" I pray you,
Then, in sober truth to tell me
Has your huckster some to sell me?

---

1. The reference is to *The Sorrows of Young Werther* by Goethe (1774, 1787) in which Werther falls hopelessly in love with a simple girl named Charlotte.

Sarah Helen Whitman

Tell me, tell me, I implore,
What's his number? Where's his store?

"SCIENCE"

*"The words 'vital force,' 'instinct,' 'soul,' are only expressions of our
ignorance."*—Buchner.[1]

While the dull Fates sit nodding at their loom,
Benumbed and drowsy with its ceaseless boom,
I hear, as in a dream, the monody
Of life's tumultuous, ever-ebbing sea;
The iron tramp of armies hurrying by
Forever and forever but to die;
The tragedies of time, the dreary years,
The frantic carnival of hopes and fears,
The wild waltz-music wailing through the gloom,
The slow death-agonies, the yawning tomb,
The loved ones lost forever to our sight,
In the wide waste of chaos and old night;
Earth's long, long dream of martyrdom and pain;
No God in heaven to rend the welded chain
Of endless evolution!
                                        Is this *all?*
And mole-eyed "Science," gloating over bones,
The skulls of monkeys and the Age of Stones,
Blinks at the golden lamps that light the hall
Of dusty death, and answers: "It is all."
    1877.

---

1. This quotation, which I have not been able to locate, is probably from Georg
Büchner (1813–37), a German dramatist inspired by socialism and in some works
such as *Woyzeck* an early creator of brutally realistic depictions of lower-class life.

ELIZABETH OAKES-SMITH

(1806–1893)

🐛🐛🐛🐛🐛

ELIZABETH OAKES-SMITH is unusual among the women in this anthology in that she left behind a detailed personal record of her life and its frustrations. Married at the age of sixteen to a much older man (humor writer Seba Smith), Elizabeth was suddenly snatched from the intellectual and spiritual empyrean of her dreams and "engulfed," as she put it, "in the tasteless actual." Her mother felt that her daughter needed a steadying influence in her life. Unfortunately, life with Seba Smith hardly provided that sense of stability.

Oakes-Smith bore five sons in this marriage, four of whom survived to adulthood; she later confessed that she was grateful not to have had any daughters who might suffer as she had. Though she never dissolved her marriage, Oakes-Smith did find relief in her writing which contributed considerably to the family's income. She also gained a wide reputation as a lyceum lecturer in support of women's rights. Emma Embury thought her ideas dangerously radical, and Seba Smith was bitter about her popularity, but she persisted despite their objections.

Her first major success as a poet came with *The Sinless Child* (1842), a long poem about a spiritual maiden, Eva, whose purity wins out over adverse circumstances. Today this early poem seems sickly sweet, but a comment from a contemporary review in the *Boston Notion* (quoted in Tuckerman's preface) suggests the effect it had at the time: "The whole poem breathes the very air of purity, and is instinct with the life and soul of poetry. It is one of those productions which, without dazzling by brilliant points of expression or imagery, still wins upon the heart by the pure force of the sentiment embodied, and the naturalness and beauty of the language in which it is clothed" (xxxii).

Oakes-Smith had a strong mystical streak in her nature and felt that she could sense coming events before they happened. Her connection to the occult is discussed in *Shadow Land,* and in 1887 she spent one year as a minister to an independent congregation in Canastota, N.Y. "Strength from the Hills" forcibly conveys her spirituality and illustrates its alliance with Nature.

Oakes-Smith's frustrations with the limitations enforced upon women are passionately expressed in her poems and in her autobiography. *Woman and Her Needs* (1851), a series of feminist lectures reprinted in 1974, is still of interest. Oakes-Smith was a feminist and an abolitionist, did social work in New York City, and preceded Horatio Alger with her eye-opening account of juvenile life called *The Newsboy* (1854). Poems such as "An Incident," however, convey the ambivalence toward freedom she and others like her struggled to resolve.

Selected Works: The Western Captive. 1842; *Shadow Land.* 1853; *Bertha and Lily.* 1854; *Selections from the Autobiography of Elizabeth Oakes Smith.* Ed. Mary Alice Wyman. Lewiston, MD: Lewiston Journal, 1924.

Selected Criticism: Riegel, Robert E. *American Feminists.* Lawrence: U of Kansas P, 1963; Tuckerman, H. T. Preface to *The Sinless Child.* Ed. John Keese. New York: Wiley & Putnam, 1842; Watts; Wiltenberg, Joy. "Excerpts from the Diary of Elizabeth Oakes Smith." *Signs* 9 : 3 (1984): 534–48; Wyman, M. A. *Two American Pioneers: Seba Smith and Elizabeth Oakes Smith.* New York: Columbia UP, 1927.

INSCRIPTION

(From *The Sinless Child*)

Sweet Eva! shall I send thee forth,
To other hearts to speak?

Elizabeth Oakes-Smith

With all thy timidness and love,
　　Companionship to seek?
Send thee with all thy abstract ways,
　　Thy more than earthly tone—
An exile, dearest, send thee forth,
　　Thou, who art all mine own!

Thou art my spirit's cherished dream,
　　Its pure ideal birth;
And thou hast nestled in my heart,
　　With love that's not of earth.
Alas! for I have failed, methinks,
　　Thy mystic life to trace;
Thy holiness of thought and soul,
　　Thy wild enchanting grace.

With thee I've wandered, cherished one,
　　At twilight's dreamy hour
To learn the language of the bird,
　　The mystery of the flower;
And gloomy must that sorrow be,
　　Which then could'st not dispel,
As thoughtfully we loitered on
　　By stream or sheltered dell.

Thou fond Ideal! vital made,
　　The trusting, earnest, true;
Who fostered, sacred, undefiled
　　My hearts pure, youthful dew;
Thou woman—soul, all tender, meek,
　　Thou wilt not leave me now
To bear alone the weary thoughts
　　That stamp an aching brow!

Yet go! I may not say farewell,
　　For thou wilt not forsake,

Thou'lt linger, Eva, wilt thou not,
    All hallowed thoughts to wake?
Then go; and speak to kindred hearts
    In purity and truth;
And win the spirit back again,
    To Love, and Peace, and Youth.

ATHEISM

Faith

Beware of doubt—faith is the subtle chain
    Which binds us to the Infinite: the voice
Of a deep life within, that will remain
    Until we crowd it thence. We may rejoice
With an exceeding joy, and make our life,
    Ay, this external life, become a part
Of that which is within, o'erwrought and rife
    With faith, that childlike blessedness of heart.
The order and the harmony inborn
    With a perpetual hymning crown our way,
Till callousness, and selfishness, and scorn,
    Shall pass as clouds where scatheless lightnings play.
Cling to thy faith—'tis higher than the thought
That questions of thy faith, the cold external doubt.

Reason

The Infinite speaks in our silent hearts,
    And draws our being to himself, as deep

Calleth unto deep. He, who all thought imparts,
    Demands the pledge, the bond of soul to keep;
But reason, wandering from its fount afar,
    And stooping downward, breaks the subtle chain
That binds it to itself, like star to star,
    And sun to sun, upward to God again:
Doubt, once confirmed, tolls the dead spirit's knell,
    And man is but a clod of earth, to die
Like the poor beast that in his shambles fell—
    More miserable doom than that, to lie
In trembling torture, like believing ghosts,
Who, though divorced from good, bow to the Lord of Hosts.

Annihilation

Doubt, cypress crowned, upon a ruined arch
    Amid the shapely temple overthrown,
Exultant, stays at length her onward march:
    Her victim, all with earthliness o'ergrown,
Hath sunk himself to earth to perish there;
    His thoughts are outward, all his love a blight,
Dying, deluding, are his hopes, though fair—
    And death, the spirit's everlasting night.
Thus, midnight travellers, on some mountain steep
    Hear far above the avalanche boom down,
Starting the glacier echoes from their sleep,
    And lost in glens to human foot unknown—
The death-plunge of the lost come to their ear,
And silence claims again her region cold and drear.

Elizabeth Oakes-Smith

AN INCIDENT

A simple thing, yet chancing as it did,
  When life was bright with its illusive dreams,
A pledge and promise seemed beneath it hid;
  The ocean lay before me, tinged with beams
That lingering draped the west, a wavering stir,
  And at my feet down fell a worn, gray quill;
An eagle, high above the darkling fir,
  With steady flight, seemed there to take his fill
Of that pure ether breathed by him alone.
  O noble bird! why didst thou loose for me
Thy eagle plume? still unessayed, unknown
  Must be that pathway fearless winged by thee;
I ask it not, no lofty flight be mine,
I would not soar like thee, in loneliness to pine!

THE UNATTAINED

And is this life? and are we born for this?
  To follow phantoms that elude the grasp,
  Or whatsoe'er secured, within our clasp,
  To withering lie, as if each earth'y kiss
  Were doomed Death's shuddering touch alone to meet.
O Life! hast thou reserved no cup of bliss?
  Must still the UNATTAINED beguile our feet?
The UNATTAINED with yearnings fill the breast,
That rob, for ay, the spirit of its rest?
  Yes, this is Life; and everywhere we meet,
  Not victor crowns, but wailings of defeat;
Yet faint thou not, thou dost apply a test
  That shall incite thee onward, upward still,
  The present can not sate nor e'er thy spirit fill.

Elizabeth Oakes-Smith

THE BARD

It can not be, the baffled heart, in vain,
   May seek, amid the crowd, its throbs to hide;
   Ten thousand other kindred pangs may bide,
Yet not the less will our own griefs complain.
Chained to our rock, the vulture's gory stain
   And tearing beak is every moment rife,
   Renewing pangs that end but with our life.
Thence bursteth forth the gushing voice of song,
   The soul's deep anguish thence an utterance finds,
   Appealing to all hearts: and human minds
Bow down in awe: thence doth the Bard belong
Unto all times: the laurel steeped in wrong
Unsought is his: his soul demanded bread,
And ye, charmed with the voice, gave but a stone instead.

THE DREAM

I dreamed last night, that I myself did lay
   Within the grave, and after stood and wept,
   My spirit sorrowed where its ashes slept!
'T was a strange dream, and yet methinks it may
   Prefigure that which is akin to truth.
   How sorrow we o'er perished dreams of youth,
High hopes and aspirations doomed to be
Crushed and o'ermastered by earth's destiny!
   Fame, that the spirit loathing turns to truth—
And that deluding faith so loath to part,
That earth will shrine for us one kindred heart!
   Oh, 't is the ashes of such things that wring
Tears from the eyes—hopes like to these depart,
   And we bow down in dread, o'ershadowed by Death's wing!

Elizabeth Oakes-Smith

TO THE HUDSON

Oh, river! gently as a wayward child
   I saw thee mid the moonlight hills at rest;
Capricious thing, with thine own beauty wild,
   How didst thou still the throbbings of thy breast?
Rude headlands were about thee, stooping round,
   As if amid the hills to hold thy stay;
But thou didst hear the far-off ocean sound,
   Inviting thee from hill and vale away,
To mingle thy deep waters with its own;
   And, at that voice, thy steps did onward glide,
Onward from echoing hill and valley lone.
   Like thine, oh, be my course—nor turned aside,
While listing to the soundings of a land,
That like the ocean call invites me to its strand.

ODE TO SAPPHO

Bright, glowing Sappho! child of love and song.
   Adown the blueness of long-distant years
Beams forth thy glorious shape, and steal along
   Thy melting tones, beguiling us to tears.
      Thou priestess of great hearts,
       Thrilled with the secret fire
      By which a god imparts
       The anguish of desire—
   For meaner souls be mean content—
   Thine was a higher element.
Over Leucadia's rock[1] thou leanest yet,

---

1. According to legend, Sappho leapt from Leucadia's rock when Phaon did not reciprocate her love.

With thy wild song, and all thy locks outspread;
The stars are in thine eyes, the moon hath set—
    The night dew falls upon thy radiant head;
        And thy resounding lyre—
            Ah! not so wildly sway:
        Thy soulful lips inspire
            And steal our hearts away!
        Swanlike and beautiful, thy dirge
        Still moans along the Ægean surge.
No unrequited love filled thy lone heart,
    But thine infinitude did on thee weigh,
And all the wildness of despair impart,
    Stealing the down from Hope's own wing away.
            Couldst thou not suffer on,
                Bearing the direful pang,
            While thy melodious tone
                Through wondering cities rang?
        Couldst thou not bear thy godlike grief?
        In godlike utterance find relief?
Devotion, fervor, might upon thee wait:
    But what were these to thine? all cold and chill,
And left thy burning heart but desolate;
    Thy wondrous beauty with despair might fill
            The worshipper who bent
                Entranced at thy feet:
            Too affluent the dower lent
                Where song and beauty meet!
        Consumed by a Promethean fire
        Wert thou, O daughter of the lyre!
Alone, above Leucadia's wave art thou,
    Most beautiful, most gifted, yet alone!
Ah! what to thee the crown from Pindar's [2] brow!
    What the loud plaudit and the garlands thrown

---

2. Greek lyric poet (c. 522–c. 438 BC) famous for his odes celebrating victors in the national games.

By the enraptured throng,
    When thou in matchless grace
Didst move with lyre and song,
    And monarchs gave thee place?
What hast thou left, proud one? what token?
Alas! a lyre and heart—both broken!

THE POET

Non Vox Sed Votum[1]

*It is the belief of the vulgar that when the nightingale sings, she leans her breast
    upon a thorn.*

Sing, sing—Poet, sing!
With the thorn beneath thy breast,
Robbing thee of all thy rest;
Hidden thorn for ever thine,
Therefore dost thou sit and twine
    Lays of sorrowing—
Lays that wake a mighty gladness,
Spite of all their mournful sadness.
    Sing, sing—Poet sing!
It doth ease thee of thy sorrow—
"Darkling" singing till the morrow;
Never weary of thy trust,
Hoping, loving as thou must,
    Let thy music ring;
Noble cheer it doth impart,

---

1. Lat., not the voice but the vow.

Strength of will and strength of heart.
Sing, sing—Poet, sing!
Thou art made a human voice;
Wherefore shouldst thou not rejoice
That the tears of thy mute brother
Bearing pangs he may not smother,
Through thee are flowing—
For his dim, unuttered grief
Through thy song hath found relief?
Sing, sing—Poet, sing!
Join the music of the stars,
Wheeling on their sounding cars;
Each responsive in its place
To the choral hymn of space—
Lift, oh lift thy wing—
And the thorn beneath thy breast.
Though it pierce, shall give thee rest.

STRENGTH FROM THE HILLS

Come up unto the hills—thy strength is there.
Oh, thou hast tarried long,
Too long, amid the bowers and blossoms fair,
With notes of summer song.
Why dost thou tarry there? what though the bird
Pipes matin in the vale—
The plough-boy whistles to the loitering herd,
As the red daylights fail—

Yet come unto the hills, the old strong hills,
And leave the stagnant plain;
Come to the gushing of the newborn rills,
As sing they to the main;

And thou with denizens of power shalt dwell,
    Beyond demeaning care;
Composed upon his rock, mid storm and fell,
    The eagle shall be there.

Come up unto the hills: the shattered tree
    Still clings unto the rock,
And flingeth out his branches wild and free,
    To dare again the shock.
Come where no fear is known: the seabird's nest
    On the old hemlock swings,
And thou shalt taste the gladness of unrest,
    And mount upon thy wings.

Come up unto the hills. The men of old,
    They of undaunted wills,
Grew jubilant of heart, and strong, and bold,
    On the enduring hills—
Where came the soundings of the sea afar,
    Borne upward to the ear,
And nearer grew the moon and midnight star,
    And God himself more near.

EMMA EMBURY

(1806–1863)

BEST KNOWN IN NEW YORK CIRCLES for her extremely successful literary salons, Emma Embury is one of the few women poets included here who seems to have been happily married. Her husband, Daniel Embury, whom she wed in 1828, was president of the Atlantic Bank of Brooklyn and has been described as a man of courtly manners, gentlemanly refinement, and extensive reading. According to the preface of the 1869 *Poems,* he "appreciated fully the peculiar talents of his wife, and in every way encouraged their development."

Emma Embury was a precocious child, well read and well educated, growing up in a privileged household as the daughter of an eminent physician, Dr. James Manly of New York City. In the style of those years, Embury's first major poem was an exotic narrative entitled *Guido, a Tale* which she published along with some persona poems (called "sketches from history") in 1828. She was an active contributor to the periodicals of the day and served on the editorial staffs of *Godey's Lady's Book, Graham's Magazine,* and *The Ladies' Companion.*

A woman of considerable warmth and wit, Emma Embury's best poetry shows a degree of sophistication about life and letters often missing in other popular women poets of her day. Though she was saddled with the title "the American Hemans" and wrote a great many poems about silent suffering, Embury was active and productive until she was struck down by illness in 1848. She lived another fifteen years, but the end of her life was marred by ill health, and the once active hostess withdrew into the life of a recluse. "The Garden" alludes to her invalidism.

In addition to her poetry, Embury published short stories and essays. These reveal that combination of independence and conservativism so characteristic of women writers of her day. Embury was highly critical of Mary Wollstonecraft, for instance, because she felt women's highest aspirations should never conflict with the roles of wife and mother she considered primary. Her poem "Stanzas," however, makes clear the special value she attributed to female artists who could capture a woman's secret sorrows. Embury was a great admirer of Madame de Staël whose talents she called "far higher, holier gifts" than the "charms that make a woman's pride." Embury's poetry, which virtually ignores American culture, gives a lively account of the attitudes a cultured, talented, intelligent woman of her time was apt to have. In her "Lament (of One of the Old Régime)" she has left an amusing parody of those who were not so inclined to celebrate the arrival of talented women like herself on the literary scene.

Selected Works: Guido, A Tale: Sketches from History and Other Poems. 1828; *Constance Latimer, or the Blind Girl, with Other Tales.* 1838; *Glimpses of Home Life, or Causes and Consequences.* 1848; *The Poems of Emma Catherine Embury.* 1869; *Selected Prose Writings of Mrs. Emma Catherine Embury.* 1893.

Selected Criticism: Poe, Edgar Allan. Article in *Godey's Lady's Book.* Aug. 1846; Rollins, J. A. "Mrs. Emma Catherine Embury's Account Book: A Study of Some of Her Periodical Contributions." *Bulletin of the New York Public Library* 51 (Aug. 1947): 479–85; Unsigned Preface to *The Poems of Emma Catherine Embury.* New York: Hurd and Houghton, 1869.

MADAME DE STAËL

There was no beauty on thy brow,
No softness in thine eye,

Thy cheek wore not the rose's glow,
    Thy lip the ruby's dye;
The charms that make a woman's pride
    Have never been thine own;
Heaven had to thee these gifts denied,
    In which earth's bright ones shone.

Far higher, holier gifts were thine—
    Mind, intellect were given,
Till thou wert as a holy shrine,
    Where men might worship Heaven.
Yes; woman as thou wert, thy word
    Could make the strong man start,
And thy lip's magic power has stirred
    Ambition's iron heart.

The charm of eloquence; the skill
    To wake each secret string,
And from the bosom's chords at will
    Life's mournful music bring;
The o'ermastering strength of mind, which sways
    The haughty and the free,
Whose might earth's mightiest one obeys,—
    These—these were given to thee.

Thou hadst a prophet's eye to pierce
    The depths of man's dark soul,
And bring back tales of passions fierce,
    O'er which its dim waves roll;
And all too deeply hadst thou learned
    The lore of woman's heart;
The thoughts in thine own breast that burned,
    Taught thee that mournful part.

Thine never was a woman's dower
    Of tenderness and love;

Thou couldst tame down the eagle's power,
    But couldst not chain the dove.
O! love is not for such as thee;
    The gentle and the mild,
The beautiful thus blest may be,
    But never Fame's proud child.

When 'mid the halls of state alone,
    In queenly "pride of place,"
The majesty of mind thy throne,
    Thy sceptre, mental grace,—
Then was thy glory felt; and thou
    Didst triumph in that hour,
When men could turn from Beauty's brow
    In tribute to thy power.

And yet a woman's heart was thine;
    No dream of fame can fill
The bosom which must vainly pine
    For sweet Affection's thrill;
And O! what pangs thy spirit wrung
    E'en in thine hour of pride,
When all could list Love's wooing tongue
    Save thee, bright Glory's bride.

Corinna![1] thine own hand has traced
    Thy melancholy fate;
Though by earth's noblest triumphs graced,
    Bliss waits not on the great;
Only in lowly places sleep
    Life's flowers of sweet perfume,

---

1. Anne-Louïse-Germaine de Staël (1766–1817), a leading French woman writer, was the author of a Romantic novel entitled *Corinne* (1807) and therefore was sometimes known as Corinna.

Emma Embury

And they who climb Fame's mountain steep
Must mourn their own high doom.

THE CONSUMPTIVE

Bring flowers, fresh flowers, the fairest spring can yield—
The poetry of earth, o'er every field
   Scattered in rich display;
Bring flowers, fresh flowers, around my dying bed,
The sweetness of the sunny south to shed,
   Ere I am called away.

Bring flowers, fresh flowers, from every sheltered glade;
I know their brilliant beauties soon will fade
   Beneath my feverish breath,
But their bright hues seem to my wondering thought
With promises of bliss and beauty fraught,
   Winning my heart from death.

Bring flowers, fresh flowers; ere they again shall bloom
I shall be lying in the narrow tomb,
   Mouldering in cold decay.
Bring flowers, fresh flowers, that I may cheer my heart
With pleasant images, ere I depart
   To tread the grave's dark way.

Bring fruits, rich fruits, that blush on every bough
Bending above the traveller's weary brow,
   And wooing him to taste;
Bring fruits; methinks I never knew how sweet
The joys that every day our senses greet,
   Till now, in life's swift waste.

Bring fruits, rich fruits; earth's fairest gifts are vain
To minister relief to the dull pain
   That steals upon my heart.
Yet bring me fruits and flowers; they still have power
To cheer, if not prolong life's little hour;
   Bring flowers ere I depart.

STANZAS

Written after the Second Reading of "Corinna" [1]

Childhood's glad smile was on my lip, life's sunshine on my brow,
When first I looked upon the page that lies before me now;
'Twas mystery all—I had not learned the love of woman's heart,
No meaning to my spirit could its thrilling words impart.

Years fleeted on; the sunny smile had faded from my face,
Upon my brow was graved the sign which pain alone can trace;
Youth still was mine, but not the youth of childhood's laughing day,
Youth still was mine, but early hope and joy had passed away.

O, then no mystery was the page that told Corinna's woe,
Too deeply had my spirit learned such bitter truth to know;
Mine own wild heart! did I not read thy secret sorrow there,
Thy lofty dreams, thy fervent love, thy bliss, and thy despair?

Feelings that long had wrestled on within my inmost soul,
Thoughts that had ne'er found voice, and dreams that spurned at truth's
    control,
Love far too pure and deep to pour on aught of mortal mould,
All that my heart so long had hid, Corinna's passion told.

---

1. Mme de Staël's novel tells of a Romantic woman poet who refuses a marriage she feels might require the sacrifice of her free style of life.

O! none but woman's tongue such tales of woman's heart could tell,
Its varied perils when the tides of passion wildly swell,
Its hopes, its fears, its visions wild, its weakness, and its power—
The reed when wooed by zephyr's breath, the oak when tempests lower.

TO MY FIRST-BORN

My own, my child, with strange delight I look upon thy face,
And press thee to my throbbing heart in a mother's fond embrace;
Each breath that stirs thy little frame can a thrill of joy impart,
And the clasp of thy tiny hand is felt like a pulse within my heart.
Thy little life lies but within the compass of a dream,
And yet how changed does every scene of my existence seem!
For over e'en its dreariest path in freshening gushes roll
Feelings that long, like hidden springs, slept darkly in my soul.

My own, my child, what magic power is in that simple word!
The very depths of tenderness by its sweet sound are stirred,
And, like Bethesda's heaven-blessed pool,[1] give out a healing power;
For how can sorrow dwell with thee, fair creature of an hour?
Though from my breast had died away each spark of hope's pure flame,
Though pain and anguish wrung my heart as erst they racked my frame,
Yet would each pang seem light compared with the deep rapturous glow
That thrilled each nerve when first I gazed upon thy baby brow.

My own, my child, fain would I draw the shadowy veil that shrouds
The future from my view, with all its sunshine and its clouds,
To learn what storms must gather yet around thy sinless head,

---

1. Bethesda's pool was in Biblical Jerusalem believed to have healing powers
(John 5.2−4)

And gaze upon the varied path which thou through life must tread.
It may not be! no human skill these mysteries may divine,
The God who led my erring steps will surely watch o'er thine;
Enough if to thy mother's hand the blessed power be given,
To shield thy heart from passion's strife and fix its hope on Heaven.

STANZAS

Addressed to a Friend on Her Marriage

No voice but that of gladness
   Should meet thine ear to-day,
Yet only in deep sadness
   Can I love's tribute pay;
Unbidden tears are springing,
   Their source thy heart can tell:
Of joy I should be singing,
   I can but sigh—Farewell!

When from life's fairy garland
   Has fallen a precious gem,
Can I smile to see it glisten
   In another's diadem?
Could I hear thy deep vow spoken
   Without a thought of pain,
When I felt the best link broken
   In friendship's golden chain?

Yet mine is selfish sorrow,
   Which love should hush to rest,
And my heart should solace borrow
   From the thought that thou art blest;

Emma Embury

Where hope once claimed dominion,
   Joy holds his revel bright,
And thy spirit's drooping pinion
   Waxes strong in love's pure light.

I know that thou art happy!
   O may affection's glass
With its diamond sparkles measure
   Life's changes as they pass.
Could friendship's gentle magic
   Rule thy horoscope of doom,
Not a moment e'er should meet thee
   In sadness or in gloom.

Farewell, farewell, beloved one,
   Though destined far to roam,
When thoughts come crowding on thee
   Of thy distant native home—
The home from whence has vanished
   One dear familiar face,
And the hearth whence joy was banished
   When thou left a vacant place—

When memory's mournful music
   Awakes thy pleasant tears,
O! let one chord still vibrate
   To the friend of early years.
I've loved thee in thy sorrow,
   I'll love thee still in joy:
Time could not change our friendship,—
   Shall absence it destroy?

Emma Embury

LINES

Come to the vintage feast!
The west wind sighs 'mid the stately flowers
That deck so brightly our garden bowers,
Flowers which awoke as the summer died,
To rival her many-colored pride,
Flowers whose rich tint and gorgeous dye
An eastern monarch's pomp outvie.

Come to the vintage feast!
The sun shines out, but a soft mist lies
Like a gossamer veil o'er the autumn skies,
The air has stolen its sweet perfume
From the crimson clover's rich beds of bloom,
And the insect hum is as musical still
As if summer yet ruled over valley and hill.

Come to the vintage feast!
The vine bends down with its purple fruit,
The foliage lies thick round its gnarled root,
For the leaves are dropping as if to show
The purple clusters that lie below,
And the tendrils close round the lattice twine,
As if asking support for the burdened vine.

Come to the vintage feast!
In Hebe's temple is spread the board
With the golden treasures of autumn stored;
The sun of our native skies has shed
O'er the ripened fruitage its glowing red;
But the grapes that grow 'neath a warmer heaven
The sparkling wine to our feast has given;
Then come and awaken the choral hymn,
While the bead-drop foams on the beaker's brim.

Emma Embury

LAMENT (OF ONE OF THE OLD RÉGIME)

O the times will never be again
    As they were when we were young:
When Scott was writing "Waverleys,"
    And Moore and Byron sung;
When Harolds, Giaours, and Corsairs[1] came
    To charm us every year,
And "Loves" of "Angels" kissed Tom's cup,[2]
    While Wordsworth sipped small beer;

When Campbell[3] drank of Helicon,
    And didn't mix his liquor;
When Wilson's[4] strong and steady light
    Had not begun to flicker;
When Southey, climbing piles of books,
    Mouthed "Curses of Kehama,"[5]
And Coleridge in his dreams began
    Strange oracles to stammer;

When Rogers sent his "Memory,"[6]
    Thus hoping to delight us,

---

1. Harold probably refers to *Harold the Dauntless* published by Sir Walter Scott in 1817. *The Giaour* (1813) and *The Corsair* (1814) are romantic poems of Lord Byron. Both pit an evil Turkish pacha against a Byronic hero who saves an innocent maiden.

2. Thomas Moore (1779–1852), a close friend of Byron, was the author of *The Loves of Angels* (1823), a scandalous poem of romance between angels and mortal maidens.

3. Thomas Campbell (1777–1844), a popular Scottish poet.

4. John Wilson (1785–1854) an early friend of the Romantic poets and energetic critic of them in later life.

5. *The Curse of Kehama* was published by the poet Robert Southey in 1810. Like other poems mentioned here, it was an oriental tale.

6. Samuel Rogers (1763–1855) was a highly successful poet and art collector, whose *The Pleasures of Memory* sold over 23,000 copies.

Before he learned his mission was
    To give feeds and invite us;
When James Montgomery's "weak tea" strains
    Enchanted pious people,
Who didn't mind poetic haze,
    If through it loomed a steeple;[7]

When first reviewers learned to show
    Their judgment without mercy;
When "Blackwood"[8] was as young and lithe
    As now he's old and pursy;
When Gifford, Jeffrey, and their clan[9]
    Could fix an author's doom,
And Keats was taught how well they knew
    To kill, "à coup de plume."[10]

No women folk were rushing then
    Up the Parnassian mount,
And seldom was a teacup dipped
    In the Castalian fount;
Apollo kept no pursuivant
    To cry out, "Place aux Dames!"[11]
In life's round game they held good hands,
    And didn't strive for palms.

---

7. James Montgomery (1771–1854) was often confused with the popular religious writer, Robert Montgomery. He did write religious poetry but was highly regarded by the Romantics, especially Byron. His poetry was not "weak tea" to them.

8. "Blackwood" here no doubt refers to the magazine founded by William Blackwood (1776–1834), a Scotsman. *Blackwood's Magazine* was known for its venomous reviews, and it specifically attacked Keats.

9. William Gifford and Francis Jeffrey were known for their attacks on young British Romantic poets.

10. Fr., at the stroke of the pen.

11. Fr., Make way for the women.

O, the world will never be again
   What it was when we were young,
And shattered are the idols now
   To which our boyhood clung;
Gone are the giants of those days
   For whom our bays we twined,
And pigmies now kick up a dust
   To show the "march of mind."

THE GARDEN

O what a world of beauty lies within
The narrow space on which mine eye now rests!
And yet how cold and tintless seem the words
That fain would picture to another's sense
Those tall, dark trees, whose young, fresh-budded leaves
Give out their music to the summer wind;
Or that green turf, with golden drops besprent,
As if Aurora,[1] bending down to gaze
On scene so lovely, from her saffron crown
Had dropped some blossoms as she sped along!
What joyous language could be found to paint
Yon vine with its lithe tendrils dancing wild,
As if inebriate with th' inspiring blood
That courses through its old and sturdy heart?
What rainbow-tinted words could sketch the flowers
Which through the copse-like leafiness gleam out?
First in her beauty stands the festal rose,
Wearing with stately pride night's dewy pearls
Yet fresh upon her brow, as if to show

---

1. The Roman goddess of dawn.

That none might woo her, save the evening-star,
Yet e'en now hiding in her heart of hearts
The bee that lives on sweetness.
                              At her feet,
With eye scarce lifted from earth's mossy bed,
The pansy wears her purple robe and crown,
As modestly as a young maiden queen,
Abashed at her own state.
                              The hoyden pink
(Like some wild beauty scorning fashion's garb),
In her exuberant loveliness, breaks loose
From the green bodice by Dame Nature laced,
And bares her fragrant bosom to the winds.
The honeysuckle, climbing high in air,
Swings her perfumed censer toward heaven,
Giving forth incense such as never breathed
From gemmed and golden chalice, or carved urn
In dim cathedral aisles.
                              All things around
Are redolent of sweetness and of beauty,
And, as beside the casement I recline,
Prisoned by sickness to the couch of pain,
Their mingled odors to my senses come,
Like the spice-scented breath of Indian isles
To the sick sailor, who, 'mid watery wastes,
Pines for one glimpse of the green-earth again,
And sees the cheating calenture [2] arise
To mock his yearning dreams.
                              Yet thus to lie,
With such a glimpse of Eden spread before me,
And such a blue and lucid sky above,
As might have stretched its interposing veil
'Twixt sinless man and heaven's refulgent host,

---

2. This is a disease suffered by sailors in the tropics causing delirium. The
sailors hallucinate, seeing the sea as green fields they long to jump into.

Emma Embury

When heaven seemed nearer to the earth than now,
And the Almighty talked amid the trees
With his last, best creation,—thus to lie,
E'en though in bondage to bewildering pain,
And fettered by unnerving feebleness
To one small spot, is happiness so much
Beyond my poor deservings, that each breath
Goes forth like a thanksgiving from my lips.

Hark! merry voices now are on the breeze,
While glad young faces smile through leafy screens,
And where the arrowy sunbeams pierce their way
Like random shafts sent 'mid the clustering boughs,
The sheen of snowy robes is gleaming out;
Thus by her own pure brightness I can trace
The fleeting footsteps of that blessed one
Who to my glad youth like an angel came,
Folded her pinions in my happy home,
And called me "Mother."
                                    To my o'erfraught soul
These images of all my home joys come
Like rose-leaves strewn upon a brimming cup,
And in its very fullness of content
My heart grows calm, while every pulse is hushed
With a most tremulous stillness.

LUCRETIA DAVIDSON

(1808–1825)

❧❧❧❧❧

DAVIDSON is the outstanding example in this anthology of a type: the precocious female poet who died young and afterward became a legend. She wrote all her poetry before the age of seventeen. Through her mother's efforts, *Amir Kahn and Other Poems* was published in 1829 (after her death) and subsequently went through fifteen editions, eventually including translations into German (1844) and Italian (1906).

One biographical introduction, by Catharine Sedgwick, emphasizes that Lucretia was addicted to writing poetry from the time she was a young child, but that her mother insisted she learn the female arts of needlework and housekeeping to prevent her from becoming too much of an oddity. However, according to Sedgwick, Lucretia found ways of accomplishing these tasks with amazing rapidity so that she could cloister herself once again with pen and paper.

Twice she was sent away from her home in Plattsburgh, New York: once to Emma Willard's Female Academy in Troy—from which she returned desperately ill—and a second time, at the insistence of her father and against her mother's wishes, to Miss Gilbert's in Albany. An admirer, Moss Kent (for whom Lucretia wrote the poem "To My Friend and Patron"), offered to adopt the talented young woman. Before this could happen, however, she died, just before her seventeenth birthday. Lucretia's family life remains unclear, but the Sedgwick biography hints at considerable domestic friction.

Davidson's mother (often an invalid herself) undertook to put together the first edition of the poems, which included a biographical introduction by Samuel F. B. Morse, the inventor and artist. Morse sent a copy to Robert Southey who gave the volume a warm review in the *London Quarterly*. In time, Washington Irving's support was solicited on behalf of Lucretia and her sister Margaret, who also died very young. He offered an emotional tribute to both these young poets though in not very specific terms. Poe, on the other hand, insisted that the poetry be considered on its own merits and was far less enthusiastic.

Lucretia is the better of the two poets. Though "Amir Kahn" now seems a merely derivative exotic tale, Davidson's shorter lyrics occasionally demonstrate an original sensibility, as in "Auction Extraordinary" where the poet's humor comes through. Other poems, such as those on Byron and Shakespeare, are of historical interest for the way they document nineteenth-century attitudes. Also revelatory of Davidson's culture is her poem "America," which makes a contribution to the Adamic school of nativist literature prominent at the time. "To the Vermont Cadets" suggests a bloodthirsty side to the female spirit, discordant with some stereotypes of the poetess. The most chilling of her lyrics, though, is probably "The Fear of Madness," a fragment left unfinished at her death.

Selected Works: Amir Kahn and Other Poems. Ed. M[argaret] Davidson with bio. by S. B. Morse. 1829—rev. ed. with bio. by C[atharine] Sedgwick. 1846;—rev. ed. with poems by Margaret M. Davidson (1857); *Poems.* Ed. M. Oliver Davidson. 1871.

Selected Criticism: Poe, Edgar Allan. *Collected Works.* Vol. 8 (1895).

AN ACROSTIC

The Moon

Lo! yonder rides the empress of the night!
Unveiled she casts around her silver light;
Cease not, fair orb, thy slow majestic march,
Resume again thy seat in yon blue arch.

E'en *now,* as weary of the tedious way,
Thy head on Ocean's bosom thou dost lay;
In his blue waves thou hid'st thy shining face,
And gloomy darkness takes its vacant place.

The Sun

[In Continuation]

Darting his rays the sun now glorious rides,
And from his path fell darkness quick divides;
Vapor dissolves and shrinks at his approach.
It dares not on his blazing path encroach;
Down droops the flow'ret, and his burning ray
Scorches the workmen o'er the new-mown hay.
O, lamp of Heaven, pursue thy glorious course,
Nor till gray twilight, aught abate thy force.

LINES

Written under the Promise of Reward

Whene'er the Muse pleases to grace my dull page,
At the sight of *reward,* she flies off in a rage;
Prayers, threats, and entreaties I frequently try,
But she leaves me to scribble, to fret, and to sigh.

She torments me each moment, and bids me go write,
And when I obey her, she laughs at the sight;
The rhyme will not jingle, the verse has no sense,
And against all her insults I have no defense.

I advise all my friends, who wish me to write,
To keep their rewards and their praises from sight;
So that jealous Miss Muse won't be wounded in pride,
Nor Pegasus rear, till I've taken my ride.

BYRON

His faults were great, his virtues less,
    His mind a burning lamp of heaven;
His talents were bestowed to bless,
    But were as vainly lost as given.

His was a harp of heavenly sound,
    The numbers wild, and bold, and clear;
But ah! some demon, hovering round,
    Tuned its sweet chords to Sin and Fear.

His was a mind of giant mould,
    Which grasped at all beneath the skies;
And his a heart, so icy cold,
    That virtue in its recess dies.

SHAKESPEARE

Shakespeare! "with all thy faults (and few have more)
I love thee still," and still will con thee o'er.
Heaven, in compassion to man's erring heart,
Gave thee of virtue, then of vice a part,

Lest we, in wonder here, should bow before thee,
Break God's commandment, worship, and adore thee:
But admiration now, and sorrow join;
His works we reverence, while we pity thine.

SABRINA

A Volcanic Island, Which Appeared and Disappeared among the Azores, in 1711

Isle of the ocean, say, whence comest thou?
The smoke thy dark throne, and the blaze round thy brow;
The voice of the earthquake proclaims thee abroad,
And the deep, at thy coming, rolls darkly and loud.

From the breast of the ocean, the bed of the wave,
Thou hast burst into being, hast sprung from the grave;
A stranger, wild, gloomy, yet terribly bright,
Thou art clothed with the darkness, yet crowned with the light.

Thou comest in flames, thou hast risen in fire;
The wave is thy pillow, the tempest thy choir;
They will lull thee to sleep on the ocean's broad breast,
A slumbering volcano, an earthquake at rest.

Thou hast looked on the isle—thou hast looked on the wave—
Then hie thee again to thy deep, watery grave;
Go, quench thee in ocean, thou dark, nameless thing,
Thou spark from the *fallen one's* wide flaming wing.

Lucretia Davidson

AUCTION EXTRAORDINARY

I dreamed a dream in the midst of my slumbers,
And as fast as I dreamed it, it came into numbers;
My thoughts ran along in such beautiful metre,
I'm sure I ne'er saw any poetry sweeter.
It seemed that a law had been recently made
That a tax on old bachelors' pates should be laid;
And in order to make them all willing to marry,
The tax was as large as a man could well carry.
The bachelors grumbled, and said 'twas no use;
'Twas horrid injustice, and horrid abuse;
And declared that, to save their own hearts'-blood from spilling,
Of such a vile tax they would not pay a shilling.
But the rulers determined *them* still to pursue,
So they set the old bachelors up at vendue.
A crier was sent through the town to and fro,
To rattle his bell, and his trumpet to blow,
And to call out to all he might meet in his way,
"Ho! forty old bachelors sold here to-day!"
And presently all the old maids in the town,
Each in her very best bonnet and gown,
From thirty to sixty, fair, plain, red, and pale,
Of every description, all flocked to the sale:
The auctioneer then in his labor began,
And called out aloud, as he held up a man,
"How much for a bachelor? who wants to buy?"
In a twink, every maiden responded, "I,—I;"
In short, at a highly extravagant price,
The bachelors all were sold off in a trice;
And forty old maidens, some younger, some older,
Each lugged an old bachelor home on her shoulder.

Lucretia Davidson

TO MY FRIEND AND PATRON,

M—— K——, Esq.

And can my simple harp be strung
    To higher theme, to nobler end,
Than that of gratitude to thee,
    To thee, my father and my friend?

I may not, cannot, will not say
    All that a grateful heart would breathe;
But I may frame a simple lay,
    Nor Slander blight the blushing wreath.

Yes, I will touch the string to thee,
    Nor fear its wildness will offend;
For well I know that thou wilt be,
    What thou hast ever been—a friend.

There are, whose cold and idle gaze
    Would freeze the current where it flows;
But Gratitude shall guard the fount,
    And Faith shall light it as it flows.

Then tell me, may I dare to twine
    While o'er my simple harp I bend,
This little offering for thee,
    For thee, my father, and my friend?

Lucretia Davidson

TO THE VERMONT CADETS

Pass on! for the bright torch of glory is beaming;
  Go, wreathe round your brows the green laurels of fame;
Around you a halo is brilliantly streaming,
  And history lingers to write down each name.

Yes! ye are the pillars of liberty's throne;
  When around you the banner of glory shall wave,
America proudly shall claim you her own,
  And freedom and honor shall pause o'er each grave!

A watch-fire of glory, a beacon of light,
  Shall guide you to honor, shall point you to fame:
The heart that shrinks back, be it buried in night,
  And withered with dim tears of sorrow and shame!

Though death should await you, 'twere glorious to die
  With the glow of pure honor still warm on the brow;
With a light sparkling brightly around the dim eye,
  Like the smile of a spirit still ling'ring below.

Pass on, and when War in his strength shall arise,
  Rush on to the conflict, and conquer or die;
Let the clash of your arms proudly roll to the skies:
  Be blest if victorious—and cursed, if you fly!

HEADACHE

Headache! thou bane to Pleasure's fairy spell,
Thou fiend, thou foe to joy, I know thee well!
Beneath thy lash I've writhed for many an hour,—
I hate thee, for I've known, and dread thy power.

Even the heathen gods were made to feel
The aching torments which thy hand can deal;
And Jove, the ideal king of heaven and earth,
Owned thy dread power, which called stern Wisdom forth.

Wouldst thou thus ever bless each aching head,
And bid Minerva [1] make the brain her bed,
Blessings might then be taught to rise from wo,
And Wisdom spring from every throbbing brow.

But always the reverse to me, unkind,
Folly forever dogs thee close behind;
And from this burning brow, her cap and bell,
Forever jingle Wisdom's funeral knell.

THE YELLOW FEVER

The sky is pure, the clouds are light,
The moonbeams glitter cold and bright;
O'er the wide landscape breathes no sigh;
The sea reflects the star-gemmed sky,
And every beam of heaven's broad brow
Glows brightly on the world below.
But ah! the wing of death is spread;
I hear the midnight murderers' tread;
I hear the Plague that walks at night,
I mark its pestilential blight;
I feel its hot and withering breath,
It is the messenger of death!
And can a scene so pure and fair
Slumber beneath a baneful air?

---

1. Minerva—goddess of wisdom

And can the stealing form of death
Here wither with its blighting breath?
Yes; and the slumberer feels its power
At midnight's dark and silent hour.
He feels the wild-fire through his brain;
He wakes; his frame is racked with pain;
His eye half closed; his lip is dark;
The sword of death hath done his work!
That sallow cheek, that fevered lip,
That eye which burns but cannot sleep,
That black parched tongue, that raging brain,
All mark the monarch's baleful reign!
O! for one pure, one balmy breath,
To cool the sufferer's brow in death;
O! for one wandering breeze of heaven;
O that one moment's rest were given!
'Tis past; and hushed the victim's prayer;
The spirit *was*—but *is* not there!

AMERICA

And this was once the realm of Nature, where
Wild as the wind, though exquisitely fair,
She breathed the mountain breeze, or bowed to kiss
The dimpling waters with unbounded bliss.
Here in this Paradise of earth, where first
Wild mountain Liberty began to burst,
Once Nature's temple rose in simple grace,
The hill her throne, the world her dwelling-place.
And where are now her lakes, so still and lone,
Her thousand streams with bending shrubs o'ergrown?
Where her dark cat'racts tumbling from on high,

With rainbow arch aspiring to the sky?
Her tow'ring pines with fadeless wreaths entwined,
Her waving alders streaming to the wind?
Nor these alone,—her own,—her fav'rite child,
All fire, all feeling; man untaught and wild;
Where can the lost, lone son of Nature stray?
For art's high car is rolling on its way;
A wand'rer of the world, he flies to drown
The thoughts of days gone by and pleasures flown
In the deep draught, whose dregs are death and woe,
With slavery's iron chain concealed below.
Once through the tangled wood, with noiseless tread
And throbbing heart, the lurking warrior sped,
Aimed his sure weapon, won the prize, and turned,
While his high heart with wild ambition burned,
With song and war-whoop to his native tree,
There on its bark to carve the victory.
His all of learning did that act comprise,
But still in *nature's* volume doubly wise.

The wayward stream which once, with idle bound,
Whirled on resistless in its foaming round,
Now curbed by art flows on, a wat'ry chain
Linking the snow-capped mountains to the main.
Where once the alder in luxuriance grew,
Or the tall pine its towering branches threw
Abroad to heaven, with dark and haughty brow,
There mark the realms of plenty smiling now;
There the full sheaf of Ceres richly glows,
And Plenty's fountain blesses as it flows;
And man, a brute when left to wander wild,
A reckless creature, Nature's lawless child,
What boundless streams of knowledge rolling now
From the full hand of art around him flow!
Improvement strides the surge, while from afar

Learning rolls onward in her silver car;
Freedom unfurls her banner o'er his head,
While peace sleeps sweetly on her native bed.

The Muse arises from the wild-wood glen,
And chants her sweet and hallowed song again,
As in those halcyon days, which bards have sung,
When hope was blushing, and when life was young.
Thus shall she rise, and thus her sons shall rear
Her sacred temple *here,* and only *here,*
While Percival,[1] her loved and chosen priest,
Forever blessing, though himself unblest,
Shall fan the fire that blazes at her shrine,
And charm the ear with numbers half divine.

THE FEAR OF MADNESS

Written While Confined to Her Bed, During Her Last Illness

There is a something which I dread,
    It is a dark, a fearful thing;
It steals along with withering tread,
    Or sweeps on wild destruction's wing.

That thought comes o'er me in the hour
    Of grief, of sickness, or of sadness;
'Tis not the dread of death—'tis more,
    It is the dread of madness.

---

1. A legendary knight of questionable origins, Percival was a symbol of upward mobility, perhaps. He triumphed because he was pure, not well born.

O! may these throbbing pulses pause,
   Forgetful of their feverish course;
May this hot brain, which, burning, glows
   With all its fiery whirlpool's force,

Be cold, and motionless, and still,
   A tenant of its lowly bed,
But let not dark delirium steal—

. . . .

[Unfinished.]

1825

FRANCES SARGENT OSGOOD

(1811–1850)

꽃꽃꽃꽃꽃꽃

MUCH MYSTERY SURROUNDS the life and character of Frances Osgood, who has been treated both indulgently and contemptuously by Poe scholars in the twentieth century. John Evangelist Walsh has recently attempted to argue that Osgood had Poe's child, a little girl named Fanny Fay who died in infancy.

Most contemporary accounts of Frances Osgood, including Elizabeth Oakes-Smith's, remember her as unusually childlike, a perennial ingenue who shied away from all darker aspects of life. She was educated at home among talented siblings, married the painter Samuel Stillman Osgood in 1835, and went to live in England for five years. While there, she published *A Wreath of Wild Flowers from New England,* which established her reputation as a poet. She also gave birth to two girls, Ellen and May.

In 1840 she returned to America, publishing widely in periodicals and books, and became extremely popular. Her marriage to Osgood faltered (some poems suggest infidelity on his part), and the couple separated. Samuel went West looking for gold, but not long before Fanny's death, they were reconciled.

During her life in New York, she attended many literary salons, became involved with Poe, and cultivated a friendship with Rufus Griswold to whom her final edition of poems is dedicated. According to Walsh, Griswold was offended by Poe's treatment of the impressionable "Fanny" and, as Poe's literary executor, Griswold set out to muddy

Poe's reputation in the eyes of posterity. Osgood herself, like Sarah Helen Whitman, continued to treasure Poe's memory until her death in 1850 of tuberculosis. The following year her daughters also died of the disease.

Osgood's poetry clashes somewhat with the childlike and innocent version of her character provided by Griswold and Elizabeth Oakes-Smith. Unusually coy and flirtatious, even—in "He Bade Me Be Happy"—pointedly arch and Millayish, Osgood's persona seems anything but naïve. It is difficult in poems such as "A Flight of Fancy" and "Woman," however, to be certain of Osgood's intentions. "The Cocoa-Nut Tree" seems an example of blatant phallus worship. Her many poems about masking suggest that her sensibility was indeed complex, and her daisy poems make interesting companion pieces to some of Dickinson's deliberately infantilized projections as "daisy." Osgood's poems about her children, Ellen and May, appear both spontaneous and calculated.

The epigraph to her collected poems comes from Felicia Hemans: "I strive with yearnings vain / The Spirit to detain / Of the deep harmonies that round me roll." Still, the sensibility of Osgood's work is much more worldly than this quotation suggests. Frances Osgood remains an elusive figure: part siren, part sylph, part sycophant, part rebel—a poet well worth further study.

Selected Works: A Wreath of Wild Flowers from New England. 1838; *Poems.* 1846; *The Floral Offering.* 1847; *Osgood's Poetical Works.* 1880.

Selected Criticism: De Jong, Mary G. "Her Fair Fame: The Reputation of Frances Sargent Osgood, Woman Poet." *Studies in the American Renaissance.* 1987. 265–84; De Jong, Mary G. "Lines from a Partly Published Drama: The Romance of Frances Sargent Osgood and Edgar Allan Poe." In Marchalonis 31–58; Hunnewell, Fannie. "The Life and Writings of Frances Sargent Osgood." MA diss. U of Texas, 1924; *Memorial, The;* Ostriker; Walker, Cheryl. "Profile of Frances Osgood." *Legacy* 1:2 (1984); Walsh; Watts.

Frances Sargent Osgood

A FLIGHT OF FANCY

At the bar of Judge Conscience stood Reason arraign'd,
The jury impannell'd—the prisoner chain'd.
The judge was facetious at times, though severe,
Now waking a smile, and now drawing a tear;
An old-fashion'd, fidgety, queer-looking wight,
With a clerical air, and an eye quick as light.

"Here, Reason, you vagabond! look in my face;
I'm told you're becoming an idle scapegrace.
They say that young Fancy, that airy coquette,
Has dared to fling round you her luminous net;
That she ran away with you, in spite of yourself,
For pure love of frolic—the mischievous elf.

"The scandal is whisper'd by friends and by foes,
And darkly they hint, too, that when they propose
Any question to *your* ear, so lightly you're led,
At once to gay Fancy you turn your wild head:
And *she* leads you off in some dangerous dance,
As wild as the Polka that gallop'd from France.

"Now up to the stars with you, laughing, she springs,
With a whirl and a whisk of her changeable wings;
Now dips in some fountain her sun-painted plume,
That gleams through the spray, like a rainbow in bloom;
Now floats in a cloud, while her tresses of light
Shine through the frail boat and illumine its flight;
Now glides through the woodland to gather its flowers;
Now darts like a flash to the sea's coral bowers;
In short—cuts such capers, that with her, I ween,
It's a wonder you are not ashamed to be seen!

"Then she talks such a language!——melodious enough,
To be sure, but a strange sort of outlandish stuff!
I'm told that it licenses many a whapper,[1]
And when once she commences, no frowning can stop her;
Since it's new, I've no doubt it is very improper!
They say that she cares not for order or law;
That of you, you great dunce! she but makes a cat's-paw.
I've no sort of objection to fun in its season,
But it's plain that this Fancy is *fooling* you, Reason!"

Just then into court flew a strange little sprite,
With wings of all colours and ringlets of light!
She frolick'd round Reason, till Reason grew wild,
Defying the court and caressing the child.
The judge and the jury, the clerk and recorder,
In vain call'd this exquisite creature to order:——
"Unheard of intrusion!"——They bustled about,
To seize her, but, wild with delight, at the rout,
She flew from their touch like a bird from a spray,
And went waltzing and whirling and singing away!

Now up to the ceiling, now down to the floor!
Were never such antics in courthouse before!
But a lawyer, well versed in the tricks of his trade,
A trap for the gay little innocent laid:
He held up a *mirror,* and Fancy was caught
By her image within it,——so lovely, she thought.
What could the fair creature be!——bending its eyes
On her own with so wistful a look of surprise!
She flew to embrace it. The lawyer was ready:
He closed round the spirit a grasp cool and steady,

---

1. This is probably a variant spelling of whopper, an exaggeration.

And she sigh'd, while he tied her two luminous wings,
"Ah! Fancy and Falsehood are different things!"

The witnesses—maidens of uncertain age,
With a critic, a publisher, lawyer, and sage—
All scandalized greatly at what they had heard
Of this poor little Fancy, (who flew like a bird!)
Were call'd to the stand, and their evidence gave.
The judge charged the jury, with countenance grave:
Their verdict was "Guilty," and Reason look'd down,
As his honour exhorted her thus, with a frown:—

"This Fancy, this vagrant, for life shall be chain'd
In your own little cell, where *you* should have remain'd;
And you—for *your* punishment—jailer shall be:
Don't let your accomplice come coaxing to me!
I'll none of her nonsense—the little wild witch!
Nor her bribes—although rumour does say she is rich.

"I've heard that all treasures and luxuries rare
Gather round at her bidding, from earth, sea, and air;
And some go so far as to hint, that the powers
Of darkness attend her more sorrowful hours.
But go!" and Judge Conscience, who never was bought,
Just bow'd the pale prisoner out of the court.

'Tis said, that poor Reason next morning was found,
At the door of her cell, fast asleep on the ground,
And nothing within but one plume rich and rare,
Just to show that young Fancy's wing once had been there.
She had dropp'd it, no doubt, while she strove to get through
The hole in the lock, which she could not undo.

Frances Sargent Osgood

THE COCOA-NUT TREE

Oh, the green and the graceful—the cocoa-nut tree!
The lone and the lofty—it loves like me
The flash, the foam of the heaving sea,
    And the sound of the surging waves
    In the shore's unfathom'd caves;
With its stately shaft, and its verdant crown,
And its fruit in clusters drooping down;
Some of a soft and tender green,
And some all ripe and brown between;
And flowers, too, blending their lovelier grace
Like a blush through the tresses on Beauty's face.
      Oh, the lovely, the free,
        The cocoa-nut tree,
      Is the tree of all trees for me!

The willow, it waves with a tenderer motion,
    The oak and the elm with more majesty rise;
But give me the cocoa, that loves the wild ocean,
    And shadows the hut where the island-girl lies.

In the Nicobar islands,[1] each cottage you see
Is built of the trunk of the cocoa-nut tree,
While its leaves matted thickly, and many times o'er,
Make a thatch for its roof and a mat for its floor;
Its shells the dark islander's beverage hold—
'Tis a goblet as pure as a goblet of gold.
      Oh, the cocoa-nut tree,
        That blooms by the sea,
      Is the tree of all trees for me!

---

1. Nicobar and Anidaman are Indian islands in the Bay of Bengal.

Frances Sargent Osgood

In the Nicobar isles, of the cocoa-nut tree
They build the light shallop—the wild, the free;
They weave of its fibres so firm a sail,
It will weather the rudest southern gale;
They fill it with oil, and with coarse jaggree,
With arrack and coir, from the cocoa-nut tree.
    The lone, the free,
    That dwells in the roar
    Of the echoing shore—
  Oh, the cocoa-nut tree for me!

Rich is the cocoa-nut's milk and meat,
And its wine, the pure palm-wine, is sweet;
It is like the bright spirits we sometimes meet—
  The wine of the cocoa-nut tree:

For they tie up the embryo bud's soft wind,
From which the blossoms and nuts would spring;
And thus forbidden to bless with bloom
Its native air, and with soft perfume,
The subtle spirit that struggles there
Distils an essence more rich and rare,
And instead of a blossom and fruitage birth,
The delicate palm-wine oozes forth.

Ah, thus to the child of genius, too,
  The rose of beauty is oft denied;
But all the richer, that high heart, through
  The torrent of feeling pours its tide,
And purer and fonder, and far more true,
  Is that passionate soul in its lonely pride.
    Oh, the fresh, the free,
    The cocoa-nut tree,
  Is the tree of all trees for me!

The glowing sky of the Indian isles,
Lovingly over the cocoa-nut smiles,
And the Indian maiden lies below,
Where its leaves their graceful shadow throw:
She weaves a wreath of the rosy shells
That gem the beach where the cocoa dwells;
She winds them into her long black hair,
And they blush in the braids like rosebuds there;
Her soft brown arm and her graceful neck,
With those ocean-blooms she joys to deck.
    Oh, wherever you see
    The cocoa-nut tree,
There will a picture of beauty be!

HE BADE ME BE HAPPY

He bade me "Be happy," he whisper'd "Forget me;"
   He vow'd my affection was cherish'd in vain.
"Be happy!" "Forget me!" I would, if he'd let me—
   Why will he keep coming to say so again?

He came—it was not the first time, by a dozen—
   To take, as he said, "an eternal adieu;"
He went, and, for comfort, I turn'd to—my cousin,
   When back stalk'd the torment his vows to renew.

"You must love me no longer!" he said but this morning.
   "I love you no longer!" I meekly replied.
"Is this my reward?" he cried; "falsehood and scorning
   From her who was ever my idol, my pride!"

Frances Sargent Osgood

WOMAN

A Fragment

Within a frame, more glorious than the gem
To which Titania could her sylph condemn,
Fair woman's spirit dreams the hours away,
Content at times in that bright home to stay,
So that you let her deck her beauty still,
And waltz and warble at her own sweet will.
   Taught to restrain, in cold Decorum's school,
The step, the smile, to glance and dance by rule;
To smooth alike her words and waving tress,
And her pure *heart's* impetuous play repress;
Each airy impulse—every frolic thought
Forbidden, if by Fashion's law untaught,
The graceful houri of your heavenlier hours
Forgets, in gay saloons, her native bowers,
Forgets her glorious home—her angel-birth—
Content to share the passing joys of earth;
Save when, at intervals, a ray of love
Pleads to her spirit from the realms above,
Plays on her pinions shut, and softly sings
In low Æolian tones of heavenly things.
   Ah! *then* dim memories dawn upon the soul
Of that celestial home from which she stole;
She feels its fragrant airs around her blow;
She sees the immortal bowers of beauty glow;
And faint and far, but how divinely sweet!
She hears the music where its angels meet.
   Then wave her starry wings in hope and shame,
Their fire illumes the fair, transparent frame,
Fills the dark eyes with passionate thought the while,
Blooms in the blush and lightens in the smile:

No longer then the toy, the doll, the slave,
But frank, heroic, beautiful, and brave,
She rises, radiant in immortal youth,
And wildly pleads for Freedom and for Truth!

These captive Peris[1] all around you smile,
And one I've met who might a god beguile.
She's stolen from Nature all her loveliest spells:
Upon her cheek morn's blushing splendour dwells,
The starry midnight kindles in her eyes,
The gold of sunset on her ringlets lies,
And to the ripple of a rill, 'tis said,
She tuned her voice and timed her airy tread!
    No rule restrains *her* thrilling laugh, or moulds
Her flowing robe to tyrant Fashion's folds;
No custom chains the grace in that fair girl,
That sways her willowy form or waves her careless curl.
I plead not that she share each sterner task;
The cold reformers know not what they ask;
I only seek for our transplanted fay,
That she may have—in all *fair ways*—her way!
    I would not see the aerial creature trip,
A blooming sailor, up some giant ship,
Some man-of-war—to reef the topsail high—
Ah! reef your *curls*—and let the *canvas* fly!
    Nor would I bid her quit her 'broidery frame,
A fairy blacksmith by the forge's flame:
No! be the fires *she* kindles only those
With which man's iron nature wildly glows.
"Strike while the iron's hot," with all your art,
But strike *Love's* anvil in his yielding heart!
    Nor should our sylph her tone's low music strain,

---

1. These feminine spirits were associated with fallen angels.

A listening senate with her wit to chain,
To rival Choate[2] in rich and graceful lore,
Or challenge awful Webster[3] to the floor,
Like that rash wight who raised the casket's lid,
And set a genius free the stars that hid.

    Not thus forego the poetry of life,
The sacred names of mother, sister, wife!
Rob not the household hearth of all its glory,
Lose not those tones of musical delight,
All man has left, to tell him the sweet story
Of his remember'd home—beyond the night.

    Yet men too proudly use their tyrant power;
They chill the soft bloom of the fairy flower;
They bind the wing, that would but soar above
In search of purer air and holier love;
They hush the heart, that fondly pleads its wrong
In plaintive prayer or in impassion'd song.

    Smile on, sweet flower! soar on, enchanted wing!
Since she ne'er asks but for *one trifling thing,*
Since but *one* want disturbs the graceful fay,
Why *let* the docile darling *have—her way!*

THE STATUE TO PYGMALION

Gaze on! I thrill beneath thy gaze,
I drink thy spirit's potent rays;
I tremble to each kiss they give:
Great Jove! I *love,* and *therefore live.*

---

2. Joseph Hodges Choate (1832–1917), American laywer and diplomat.

3. Daniel Webster (1782–1852), American statesman and orator noted for his eloquence.

Frances Sargent Osgood

FORGIVE AND FORGET

"Forgive—forget! I own the wrong!"
    You fondly sigh'd when last I met you;
The task is neither hard nor long—
    I *do* forgive—I *will* forget you!

HAD WE BUT MET

Had we but met in life's delicious spring,
    When young romance made Eden of the world;
When bird-like Hope was ever on the wing,
    (In *thy* dear breast how soon had it been furl'd!)

Had we but met when both our hearts were beating
    With the wild joy—the guileless love of youth—
Thou a proud boy—with frank and ardent greeting—
    And I, a timid girl, all trust and truth!

Ere yet my pulse's light, elastic play
    Had learn'd the weary weight of grief to know,
Ere from these eyes had pass'd the morning ray,
    And from my cheek the early rose's glow;

Had we but met in life's delicious spring,
    Ere wrong and falsehood taught me doubt and fear,
Ere hope came back with worn and wounded wing,
    To die upon the heart she could not cheer;

Ere I love's precious pearl had vainly lavish'd,
    Pledging an idol deaf to my despair;

Frances Sargent Osgood

Ere one by one the buds and blooms were ravish'd
  From life's rich garland by the clasp of Care.

Ah! had we *then* but met!—I dare not listen
  To the wild whispers of my fancy now!
My full heart beats—my sad, droop'd lashes glisten—
  I hear the music of thy *boyhood's* vow!

I see thy dark eyes lustrous with love's meaning,
  I feel thy dear hand softly clasp mine own—
Thy noble form is fondly o'er me leaning—
  Love's radiant morn—but ah! the dream has flown!

How had I pour'd this passionate heart's devotion
  In voiceless rapture on thy manly breast!
How had I hush'd each sorrowful emotion,
  Lull'd by thy love to sweet, untroubled rest!

How had I knelt hour after hour beside thee,
  When from thy lips the rare, scholastic lore
Fell on the soul that all but deified thee,
  While at each pause, I, childlike, pray'd for more.

How had I watch'd the shadow of each feeling
  That moved thy soul glance o'er that radiant face,
"Taming my wild heart" to that dear revealing,
  And glorying in thy genius and thy grace!

Then hadst thou loved me with a love abiding,
  And I had now been less unworthy thee,
For I was generous, guileless, and confiding,
  A frank enthusiast—buoyant, fresh, and free.

But *now,*—my loftiest aspirations perish'd,
  My holiest hopes a jest for lips profane,

The tenderest yearnings of my soul uncherish'd,
    A soul-worn slave in Custom's iron chain,—

Check'd by those ties that make my lightest sigh,
    My faintest blush, at thought of thee, a crime—
How must I still my heart, and school my eyes,
    And count in vain the slow dull steps of Time.

Wilt thou come back? Ah! what avails to ask thee,
    Since honour, faith, forbid thee to return?
Yet to forgetfulness I dare not task thee,
    Lest thou too soon that *easy lesson* learn!

NEW ENGLAND'S MOUNTAIN-CHILD

Where foams the fall—a tameless storm—
    Through Nature's wild and rich arcade,
Which forest-trees entwining form,
    There trips the Mountain-maid!

She binds not her luxuriant hair
    With dazzling gem or costly plume,
But gayly wreathes a rose-bud there,
    To match her maiden-bloom.

She clasps no golden zone of pride
    Her fair and simple robe around;
By flowing riband, lightly tied,
    Its graceful folds are bound.

And thus attired,—a sportive thing,
    Pure, loving, guileless, bright, and wild,—
    Proud Fashion! match me, in your ring,
New England's Mountain-child!

Frances Sargent Osgood

She scorns to sell her rich, warm heart,
  For paltry gold, or haughty rank;
But gives her love, untaught by art,
  Confiding, free, and frank!

And once bestow'd, no fortune-change
  That high and generous faith can alter;
Through grief and pain—too pure to range—
  She will not fly or falter.

Her foot will bound as light and free
  In lowly hut as palace-hall;
Her sunny smile as warm will be,—
  For Love to her is all!

Hast seen where in our woodland-gloom
  The rich magnolia proudly smiled?—
So brightly doth she bud and bloom,
  New England's Mountain-child!

THE EXILE'S LAMENT

I am not happy here, mother!
  I pine to go to you;
I weary for your voice and smile,
  Your love—the fond and true!

My English home is cold, mother,
  And dark and lonely too!
I never shall be happy here,—
  I pine to go to you!

Frances Sargent Osgood

Full many a simple melody
  I make of home and you;
But no one loves and sings the song
  As Lizzie used to do!

I've friends, who kindly welcome give,
  And whom I'll ne'er forget;
But they love others more than me,
  And I am not their pet!

In at my lattice laughs the sun,
  And plays about my feet;
I'd welcome it if you were here
  Its summer warmth to greet!

The sky ne'er seems so blue, mother,—
  So balmy soft the air!
And oh! the flowers are not so pure
  As those I used to wear!

My baby Ellen gayly plays,
  But none are here to note,
With partial praise, her winning ways,
  Or catch the gems that float—

The gems of thought that sparkle o'er
  Her mind's untroubled sea;
Then vanish in its depths before
  We well know what they be!

How oft, when lovelier than their wont
  Her cheeks' pure roses glow,
And fairer 'neath the sunlit hair
  Her veined temples show,

I want it watch'd by other eye,
    That face—so bright to me;
And sigh, "If mother now were by!—
    If Lizzie could but see!"

Oh! my English home is cold, mother,
    And dark and lonely too;
I never shall be happy here,—
    I pine to go to you!

I will not call it "home," mother,
    From those I love so far!—
That only can be home to me,
    Where you and Lizzie are.

ELLEN LEARNING TO WALK

My beautiful trembler! how wildly she shrinks!
    And how wistful she looks while she lingers!
Papa is extremely uncivil, she thinks,—
    She but pleaded for one of his fingers!

What eloquent pleading! the hand reaching out,
    As if doubting so strange a refusal;
While her blue eyes say plainly, "What is he about
    That he does not assist me as usual?"

Come on, my pet Ellen! we won't let you slip,—
    Unclasp those soft arms from his knee, love;
I see a faint smile round that exquisite lip,
    A smile half reproach and half glee, love.

So! that's my brave baby! one foot falters forward,
   Half doubtful the other steals by it!
What, shrinking again! why, you shy little coward!
   'Twon't kill you to walk a bit!—try it!

There! steady, my darling! huzza! I have caught her!
   I clasp her, caress'd and caressing!
And she hides her bright face, as if what we had taught her
   Were something to blush for—the blessing!

Now back again! Bravo! that shout of delight,
   How it thrills to the hearts that adore her!
Joy, joy for her mother! and blest be the night
   When her little light feet first upbore her!

THE CHILD PLAYING WITH A WATCH

Art thou playing with Time in thy sweet baby-glee?
Will he pause on his pinions to frolic with thee?
Oh, show him those shadowless, innocent eyes,
That smile of bewildered and beaming surprise;
Let him look on that cheek where thy rich hair reposes,
Where dimples are playing "bopeep" with the roses:
His wrinkled brow press with light kisses and warm,
And clasp his rough neck with thy soft wreathing arm.
Perhaps thy bewitching and infantine sweetness
May win him, for once, to delay in his fleetness—
To pause, ere he rifle, relentless in flight,
A blossom so glowing of bloom and of light:
Then, then would I keep thee, my beautiful child,
With thy blue eyes unshadowed, thy blush undefiled—

With thy innocence only to guard thee from ill,
In life's sunny dawning, a lily-bud still!
Laugh on, my own Ellen! that voice, which to me
Gives a warning so solemn, makes music for thee
And while I at those sounds feel the idler's annoy
Thou hear'st but the tick of the pretty gold toy;
Thou seest but a smile on the brow of the churl—
May his frown never awe thee, my own baby-girl.
And oh, may his step, as he wanders with thee,
Light and soft as thine own little fairy tread be!
While still in all seasons, in storms and fair weather
May Time and my Ellen be playmates together

CAPRICE

Reprove me not that still I change
   With every changing hour,
For glorious Nature gives me leave
   In wave, and cloud, and flower.

And you and all the world would do—
   If all but dared—the same;
True to myself—if false to you,
   Why should I reck your blame?

Then cease your carping, cousin mine—
   Your vain reproaches cease;
I revel in my right divine—
   I glory in caprice!

You soft, light cloud, at morning hour
   Look'd dark and full of tears:

Frances Sargent Osgood

At noon it seem'd a rosy flower—
    Now, gorgeous gold appears.

So yield I to the deepening light
    That dawns around my way:
Because you linger with the night,
    Shall I my noon delay?

No! cease your carping, cousin mine—
    Your cold reproaches cease;
The chariot of the cloud be mine—
    Take thou the reins, Caprice!

'Tis true you play'd on Feeling's lyre
    A pleasant tune or two,
And oft beneath your minstrel fire
    The hours in music flew;

But when a hand more skill'd to sweep
    The harp, its soul allures,
Shall it in sullen silence sleep
    Because not touch'd by yours!

Oh, there are rapturous tones in mine
    That mutely pray release;
They wait the master-hand divine—
    So tune the chords, Caprice!

Go—strive the sea-wave to control;
    Or, wouldst thou keep me thine,
Be thou all being to my soul,
    And fill each want divine:

Play every string in Love's sweet lyre—
    Set all its music flowing;

Be air, and dew, and light, and fire,
    To keep the soul-flower growing;

Be less—thou art no love of mine,
    So leave my love in peace;
'Tis helpless woman's right divine—
    Her only right—caprice!

And I will mount her opal car,
    And draw the rainbow reins,
And gayly go from star to star,
    Till not a ray remains;

And we will find all fairy flowers
    That are to mortals given,
And wreathe the radiant, changing hours,
    With those "sweet hints" of heaven.

Her humming-birds are harness'd there—
    Oh! leave their wings in peace;
Like "flying gems" they glance in air—
    We'll chase the light, Caprice!

I TURNED FROM THE MONITOR

I turn'd from the monitor, smiled at the warning
    That whisper'd of doubt, of desertion to me;
I heard of thy falsehood; the dark rumour scorning,
    I gave up the soul of my soul unto thee.

Too wildly! I worshipp'd thy mind-illumed beauty;
    Too fondly I cherish'd my dream of thy truth;
Forgetting, in thee, both my pride and my duty,
    I made thee the god of my passionate youth.

And dearly and deeply I rue that devotion;
    Thou hast broken the heart that beat only for thee;
Not even thy voice can now wake an emotion;
    I am calm as thyself while I bid thee "Be free!"

THE DAISY'S MISTAKE

A sunbeam and zephyr were playing about,
    One spring, ere a blossom had peep'd from the stem,
When they heard, underground, a faint, fairy-like shout;
    'Twas the voice of a field-daisy calling to them.

"Oh! tell me, my friend, has the winter gone by?
    Is it time to come up? Is the Crocus there yet?
I know you are sporting above, and I sigh
    To be with you and kiss you;—'tis long since we met!

"I've been ready this great while,—all dress'd for the show;
    I've a gem on my bosom that's pure as a star;
And the frill of my robe is as white as the snow;
    And I mean to be brighter than Crocuses are."

Now the zephyr and sunbeam were wild with delight!
    It seem'd a whole age since they'd play'd with a flower;
So they told a great fib to the poor little sprite,
    That was languishing down in her underground bower.

"Come out! little darling! as quick as you can!
    The Crocus, the Cowslip, and Buttercup too,
Have been up here this fortnight, we're having grand times,
    And all of them hourly asking for you!

"The Cowslip is crown'd with a topaz tiara!
    The Crocus is flaunting in golden attire;

But you, little pet! are a thousand times fairer;
    To see you but once, is to love and admire!

"The skies smile benignantly all the day long;
    The bee drinks your health in the purest of dew,
The lark has been waiting to sing you a song,
    Which he practised in Cloudland on purpose for you!

"Come, come! you are either too bashful or lazy!
    Lady Spring made this season an early entrée;
And she wonder'd what could have become of her Daisy;
    We'll call you coquettish, if still you delay!"

Then a still, small voice, in the heart of the flower,
    It was Instinct, whisper'd her, "Do not go!
You had better be quiet, and wait your hour;
    It isn't too late even yet for snow!"

But the little field-blossom was foolish and vain,
    And she said to herself, "What a belle I shall be!"
So she sprang to the light, as she broke from her chain,
    And gayly she cried, "I am free! I am free!"

A shy little thing is the Daisy, you know;
    And she was half frighten'd to death, when she found
Not a blossom had even begun to blow:
    How she wish'd herself back again under the ground!

The tear in her timid and sorrowful eye
    Might well put the zephyr and beam to the blush;
But the saucy light laugh'd, and said, "Pray don't cry!"
    And the gay zephyr sang to her, "Hush, sweet, hush!"

They kiss'd her and petted her fondly at first;
    But a storm arose, and the false light fled;

And the zephyr changed into angry breeze,
   That scolded her till she was almost dead!

The gem on her bosom was stain'd and dark,
   The snow of her robe had lost its light,
And tears of sorrow had dimm'd the spark
   Of beauty and youth, that made her bright!

And so she lay with her fair head low,
   And mournfully sigh'd in her dying hour,
"Ah! had I courageously answer'd 'No!'
   I had now been safe in my native bower!"

A MOTHER'S PRAYER IN ILLNESS

Yes, take them first, my Father! Let my doves
Fold their white wings in heaven, safe on thy breast,
Ere I am call'd away: I dare not leave
Their young hearts here, their innocent, thoughtless hearts!
Ah! how the shadowy train of future ills
Comes sweeping down life's vista as I gaze!
   My May! my careless, ardent-temper'd May—
My frank and frolic child, in whose blue eyes
Wild joy and passionate wo alternate rise;
Whose cheek the morning in her soul illumes;
Whose little, loving heart a word, a glance,
Can sway to grief or glee; who leaves her play,
And puts up her sweet mouth and dimpled arms
Each moment for a kiss, and softly asks,
With her clear, flutelike voice, "Do you love me?"
Ah, let me stay! ah, let me still be by,
To answer her and meet her warm caress!

For I away, how oft in this rough world
That earnest question will be asked in vain!
How oft that eager, passionate, petted heart,
Will shrink abashed and chilled, to learn at length
The hateful, withering lesson of distrust!
Ah! let her nestle still upon this breast,
In which each shade that dims her darling face
Is felt and answered, as the lake reflects
The clouds that cross yon smiling heaven! and thou,
My modest Ellen—tender, thoughtful, true;
Thy soul attuned to all sweet harmonies:
My pure, proud, noble Ellen! with thy gifts
Of genius, grace, and loveliness, half hidden
'Neath the soft veil of innate modesty,
How will the world's wild discord reach thy heart
To startle and appal! Thy generous scorn
Of all things base and mean—thy quick, keen taste,
Dainty and delicate—thy instinctive fear
Of those unworthy of a soul so pure,
Thy rare, unchildlike dignity of mien,
All—they will all bring pain to thee, my child!
And oh, if even their grace and goodness meet
Cold looks and careless greetings, how will all
The latent evil yet undisciplined
In their young, timid souls, forgiveness find?
Forgiveness, and forbearance, and soft chidings,
Which I, their mother, learn'd of Love to give!
Ah, let me stay!—albeit my heart is weary,
Weary and worn, tired of its own sad beat,
That finds no echo in this busy world
Which cannot pause to answer—tired alike
Of joy and sorrow, of the day and night:
Ah, take them first, my Father, and then me!
And for their sakes, for their sweet sakes, my Father,
Let me find rest beside them, at thy feet!

Frances Sargent Osgood

THE HAND THAT SWEPT THE SOUNDING LYRE

The hand that swept the sounding lyre
    With more than mortal skill,
The lightning eye, the heart of fire,
    The fervent lip are still!
No more, in rapture or in wo,
    With melody to thrill,
        Ah! nevermore!

Oh! bring the flowers he cherish'd so,
    With eager childlike care;
For o'er his grave they'll love to grow,
    And sigh their sorrow there:
Ah me! no more their balmy glow
    May soothe his heart's despair,
        No! nevermore!

But angel hands shall bring him balm
    For every grief he knew,
And Heaven's soft harps his soul shall calm
    With music sweet and true,
And teach to him the holy charm
    Of Israfel [1] anew,
        For evermore!

Love's silver lyre he play'd so well
    Lies shatter'd on his tomb;
But still in air its music-spell
    Floats on through light and gloom,

---

1. Israfel, the Muslim angel of music, is also the subject of a poem of the same name by Poe.

And in the hearts where soft they fell,
His words of beauty bloom
For evermore!

YES, LOWER TO THE LEVEL

Yes, "lower to the level"
    Of those who laud thee now!
Go, join the joyous revel,
    And pledge the heartless vow!
Go, dim the soul-born beauty
    That lights that lofty brow!
Fill, fill the bowl! let burning wine
Drown, in thy soul, Love's dream divine!

Yet when the laugh is lightest,
    When wildest goes the jest,
When gleams the goblet brightest,
    And proudest heaves thy breast.
And thou art madly pledging
    Each gay and jovial guest,—
A ghost shall glide amid the flowers—
The shade of Love's departed hours!

And thou shalt shrink in sadness
    From all the splendour there,
And curse the revel's gladness,
    And hate the banquet's glare;
And pine, mid Passion's madness,
    For true Love's purer air,
And feel thou'dst give their wildest glee
For one unsullied sigh from me!

Yet deem not this my prayer, love,
  Ah! no, if I could keep
Thy alter'd heart from care, love,
  And charm its griefs to sleep,
Mine only should despair, love,
  I—I alone would weep!
I—I alone would mourn the flowers
That fade in Love's deserted bowers!

AH! WOMAN STILL

Ah! woman still
  Must veil the shrine,
Where feeling feeds the fire divine,
  Nor sing at will,
  Untaught by art,
The music prison'd in her heart!
  Still gay the note,
  And light the lay,
The woodbird warbles on the spray,
  Afar to float;
  But homeward flown,
Within his nest, how changed the tone!

Oh! none can know,
  Who have not heard
The music-soul that thrills the bird,
  The carol low
  As coo of dove

The author made this note to the title: "A reply to one who said, 'Write from your heart.'"

He warbles to his woodland-love!
    The world would say
    'Twas vain and wild,
The impassion'd lay of Nature's child;
    And Feeling so
    Should veil the shrine
Where softly glow her fires divine!

ANNE LYNCH BOTTA

(1815–1891)

꙳꙳꙳꙳꙳

BETTER REMEMBERED as a skillful hostess and author of a popular college textbook than as a poet, Anne Lynch Botta nevertheless deserves inclusion here because she and her work vividly illustrate certain patterns of nineteenth-century poetic production. Lynch was well educated at the Albany Female Seminary, moved to New York, entertained many notables including William Cullen Bryant and Edgar Allan Poe in her well-known salon, and taught school. She was self-sufficient and extremely independent, successfully petitioning Congress to be granted the unpaid portion of her grandfather's military salary. She even worked briefly as Henry Clay's private secretary before leaving Washington to return once again to her beloved New York.

Like Rose Terry, Lynch was middle-aged before she married. Vincenzo Botta was a Dante scholar from Italy who became a professor of Italian at New York University. Five years later the poet gave symbolic form to this cross-cultural marriage by publishing the *Handbook of Universal Literature* (1860), an anthology frequently used in nineteenth-century college classes on world classics. Botta was always interested in being au courant with the latest ideas and, in addition to her dedication to history and literature, she attended sermons and lectures by individuals of many different persuasions.

Before marrying Botta, Lynch had published her first book of poems and made herself a name by contributing poems, letters, and criticism to the major magazines. Her book went through three editions, and at mid-century her poetry was praised by Poe for its energy and vigor. In 1881 a new collection of her poetry was published under the name of Anne C. L. Botta. It contained a sonnet, unusually ardent for her, entitled "Love"; indeed, the new book gave more prominence to the heart than her earlier one.

Though Poe and Griswold preferred her Romantic ethereal poems such as "The Ideal" and "The Ideal Found," contemporary readers may find more interesting her humorous "To an Astronomer" or her "Lines (To One Who Wished to Read a Poem I Had Written)" where a younger Lynch insisted that her poetry did *not* represent her. Other poems of comparative interest are "Tarpeia"—a quite different treatment of this classical figure than Louise Imogen Guiney's—and the tributes to Milton and Elizabeth Barrett Browning. The least accessible aspect of her poetry, from a modern standpoint, is its sometimes intrusive moralizing.

Anne Lynch Botta maintained an active interest in women's advancement and education but did not support women's suffrage. In this she disagreed with her close friend and equally energetic society woman, Julia Ward Howe.

Selected Works: "Leaves from the Diary of a Recluse" in *The Gift* (1843); *Poems* (1849); *Poems* (1881); *Memoirs of Anne C. Lynch Botta Written by Her Friends with Selections from Her Correspondence and from Her Writings* (1893).

Selected Criticism: Botta, V., ed. *Memoirs of Anne C. L. Botta.* 1893; Dolan, A. M. "The Literary Salon in New York: 1830–1860," Ph.D. diss. Columbia (1957).

LINES

To One Who Wished To Read a Poem I Had Written

Nay, read it not, thou wouldst not know
    What lives within my heart,
For from that fount it does not flow;
    'Tis but the voice of Art.

Anne Lynch Botta

I could not bid my proud heart speak,
   Before the idle throng;
Rather in silence would it break
   With its full tide of Song.

Yes, rather would it break, than bare,
   To cold and careless eyes,
The hallowed dreams that linger there,
   The tears and agonies.

My lyre is skillful to repress
   Each deep, impassioned tone;
Its gushing springs of tenderness
   Would flow for one alone.

The rock, that to the parching sand
   Would yield no dewy drop,
Struck by the pilgrim prophet's wand,
   Gave all its treasures up.

My heart then, is my only lyre;
   The prophet hath not spoken,
Nor kindled its celestial fire;
   So, let its chords be broken.

I would not thou shouldst hear those lays,
   Though harsh they might not be;
Though thou, perchance, might'st hear and praise,
   Thy would not speak of me.

Anne Lynch Botta

THE IDEAL

"La vie est un sommeil, l'amour en est le rêve."[1]

A sad, sweet dream! It fell upon my soul
   When song and thought first woke their echoes there,
Swaying my spirit to its wild control,
   And with the shadow of a fond despair,
Darkening the fountain of my young life's stream.
It haunts me still, and yet I know 'tis but a dream.

Whence art thou, shadowy presence, that canst hide
   From my charmed sight the glorious things of earth?
A mirage o'er life's desert dost thou glide?
   Or with those glimmerings of a former birth,
A "trailing cloud of glory," hast thou come
From some bright world afar, our unremembered home?

I know thou dwell'st not in this dull, cold Real,
   I know thy home is in some brighter sphere;
I know I shall not meet thee, my Ideal,
   In the dark wanderings that await me here:
Why comes thy gentle image then, to me,
Wasting my night of life in one long dream of thee?

The city's peopled solitude, the glare
   Of festal halls, moonlight, and music's tone,
All breathe the sad refrain—thou are not there!
   And even with Nature I am still alone:
With joy I see her summer bloom depart;
I love drear winter's reign—'t is winter in my heart.

---

1. Fr., life is sleep, love is the dream of it.

And if I sigh upon my brow to see
   The deep'ning shadow of Time's restless wing,
'T is for the youth I might not give to thee,
   The vanished brightness of my first sweet spring;
That I might give thee not the joyous form
Unworn by tears and cares, unblighted by the storm.

And when the hearts I should be proud to win,
   Breathe, in those tones that woman holds so dear,
Words of impassioned homage unto mine,
   Coldly and harsh they fall upon my ear;
And as I listen to the fervent vow,
My weary heart replies, "Alas! it is not thou."

And when the thoughts within my spirit glow,
   That would outpour themselves in words of fire,
If some kind influence bade the music flow,
   Like that which woke the notes of Memnon's lyre,[2]
Thou, sunlight of my life, wak'st not the lay,
And song within my heart, unuttered, dies away.

Depart, oh shadow! fatal dream, depart!
   Go! I conjure thee leave me this poor life,
And I will meet with firm, heroic heart,
   Its threat'ning storms and its tumultuous strife,
And with the poet-seer will see thee stand
To welcome my approach to thine own spirit-land.

---

2. See the note below to Maria White Lowell's "Africa."

Anne Lynch Botta

THE IDEAL FOUND

I've met thee, whom I dared not hope to meet,
  Save in th' enchanted land of my day dreams:
Yes, in this common world, this waking state,
  Thy living presence on my vision beams—
Life's dream embodied in reality!
And in thine eyes I read indifference to me!

Yes, in those star-like eyes I read my fate,
  My horoscope is written in their gaze:
My "house of life" henceforth is desolate:
  But the dark aspect my firm heart surveys,
Nor faints nor falters even for thy sake:
'T is calm and nerved and strong: no, no, it shall not break!

For I am of that mood that will defy—
  That does not cower before the gathering storm;
That face to face will meet its destiny,
  And undismayed confront its darkest form.
Wild energies awaken in this strife,
This conflict of the soul with the grim phantom Life.

But ah! if thou hadst loved me—had I been
  All to thy dreams that to mine own thou art—
Had those dark eyes beamed eloquent on mine,
  Pressed for one moment to that noble heart
In the full consciousness of faith unspoken,
Life could have given no more—then had my proud heart broken!

The Alpine glacier from its height may mock
  The clouds and lightnings of the winter sky,
And from the tempest and the thunder's shock
  Gather new strength to lift its summit high;

But kissed by sunbeams of the summer day,
It bows its icy crest and weeps itself away.

Thou know'st the fable of the Grecian maid[1]
   Wooed by the veiled immortal from the skies,
How in his full perfections, once she prayed,
   That he would stand before her longing eyes,
And how that brightness, too intense to bless,
Consumed her o'erwrought heart with its divine excess.

To me there is a meaning in the tale.
   I have not prayed to meet thee: I can brook
That thou shouldst wear to me that icy veil;
   I can give back thy cold and careless look:
Yet shrined within my heart, still thou shalt seem
What there thou ever wert, a beautiful, bright dream!

TARPEIA

"Give me the bracelets that your warriors wear,"
   The Roman traitress to the Sabine cried,
   "Give me the toys, and I will be your guide,
And to your host the city's gates unbar."
Then to the walls each eager warrior rushed,
   And on the base Tarpeia as he passed,
   Each from his arm the massive circlet cast,

---

1. For the story of Semele and Zeus, alluded to here, see the note to Rose Terry Cooke's poem "Semele."

According to legend, Tarpeia was a vestal virgin whose father was the Roman gatekeeper. Her story is recounted again by Louise Guiney.

Till her slight form beneath the weight was crushed.
Thus are our idle wishes. Thus we sigh
   For some imagined good yet unattained;—
   For wealth, or fame, or love, and which once gained
May like a curse o'er all our future lie.
Thus in our blindness do we ask of fate,
The gifts that once bestowed may crush us with their weight.

TO AN ASTRONOMER

Upon the Professor we'll waste not a glance,
   Since he has no eyes for us poor terrestrials;
With his heart can we have any possible chance,
   When he gives us for rivals a host of celestials?
What cares he for eyes, whether hazel or blue,
   Or for any slight charms such as we share between us,—
When, his glass in his hand, he can sit the night through,
   And ogle at leisure Diana and Venus.

LINES

On an Incident Observed from the Deck of a Steamboat on the Mississippi River

Where the dark primeval forests
   Rise against the western sky,
And "the Father of the Waters"
   In his strength goes rushing by:

There an eagle, flying earthward
   From his eyrie far above,

Anne Lynch Botta

With a serpent of the forest
    In a fierce encounter strove.

Now he gains and now he loses,
    Now he frees his ruffled wings;
And now high in air he rises;
    But the serpent round him clings.

In that death embrace entwining,
    Now they sink and now they rise;
But the serpent wins the battle
    With the monarch of the skies.

Yet his wings still struggle upward,
    Though that crushing weight they bear;
But more feebly those broad pinions
    Srike the waves of upper air.

Down to earth he sinks a captive
    In that writhing, living chain;
Never o'er the blue horizon
    Will his proud form sweep again.

Never more in lightning flashes
    Will his eye of terror gleam
Round the high and rocky eyrie,
    Where his lonely eaglets scream.

Oh majestic, royal eagle,
    Soaring sunward from thy birth,
Thou hast lost the realm of heaven
    For one moment on the earth!

Anne Lynch Botta

THE WOUNDED VULTURE

A kingly vulture sat alone,
　　Lord of the ruin round,
Where Egypt's ancient monuments
　　Upon the desert frowned.

A hunter's eager eye had marked
　　The form of that proud bird,
And through the voiceless solitude
　　His ringing shot was heard.

It rent that vulture's pluméd breast,
　　Aimed with unerring hand,
And his life-blood gushed warm and red
　　Upon the yellow sand.

No struggle marked the deadly wound,
　　He gave no piercing cry,
But calmly spread his giant wings,
　　And sought the upper sky.

In vain with swift pursuing shot
　　The hunter seeks his prey,
Circling and circling upward still
　　On his majestic way.

Up to the blue empyrean
　　He wings his steady flight,
Till his receding form is lost
　　In the full flood of light.

Oh wounded heart! oh suffering soul!
　　Sit not with folded wing,

Where broken dreams and ruined hopes
   Their mournful shadows fling.

Outspread thy pinions like that bird,
   Take thou the path sublime,
Beyond the flying shafts of Fate,
   Beyond the wounds of Time.

Mount upward! brave the clouds and storms!
   Above life's desert plain
There is a calmer, purer air,
   A heaven thou, too, may'st gain.

And as that dim, ascending form
   Was lost in day's broad light,
So shall thine earthly sorrows fade,
   Lost in the Infinite.

LOVE

As some dark stream within a cavern's breast,
   Flows murmuring, moaning for the distant sun,
So ere I met thee, murmuring its unrest,
   Did my life's current coldly, darkly run.
And as that stream, beneath the sun's full gaze,
   Its separate course and life no more maintains,
   But now absorbed, transfused, far o'er the plains,
It floats, etherealized in those warm rays;
   So in the sunlight of thy fervid love,
My heart, so long to earth's dark channels given,
   Now soars, all pain, all doubt, all ill above,
And breathes the ether of the upper heaven:
   So thy high spirit holds and governs mine;
   So is my life, my being, lost in thine.

Anne Lynch Botta

MILTON

Oh bard! what though upon thy mortal eyes
    There fell no glimmering ray of earthly light,
   And the deep shadow of eternal night
Shut from thy gaze our lovely earth and skies,
Yet was it to thy spirit's vision given
   To gaze upon the splendors of that shore
   Eye had not seen, nor heart conceived before.
Then didst thou, Poet Laureate of Heaven,
   Sing of those courts and of that angel host,
Of that majestic Spirit who in vain
Dared, warred, and fell, never to rise again,
   And of that Paradise so early lost,
In strains "posterity shall not let die,"
In "thoughts that wander through eternity."

TO ELIZABETH BARRETT BROWNING

I have not met thee in this outward world,
Bounded by time and space; but in that realm
O'er which imagination holds her reign,—
There have I seen thy spirit face to face,
Majestic, and yet lovely. There have I
Sat at thy feet to listen to thy voice,
And as the symphony sublimely rose,
Reverence and awe had held me spell-bound there,
But that there fell upon my listening ear
Low breathing sighs, the sound of falling tears,
The under-tone of human love and woe,
That touched the trembling chords of sympathy,
And drew me near to thy great woman's heart.

Anne Lynch Botta

Thou crownéd queen of Song! from this free land
That owns allegiance only unto God.
And Genius, his anointed, o'er the sea
I send my vows of homage, and my heart
Sends love and blessings unto thee and thine.

JULIA WARD HOWE

(1819–1910)

☙☙☙☙☙☙

HOWE IS ONE of the few popular women poets of the nineteenth century whose name is familiar to modern readers, but such readers usually know only the "Battle-Hymn of the Republic." When this poem first appeared in 1862 in the *Atlantic Monthly,* Howe was already established as a poet. Her *Passion Flowers* (1854) was a popular volume, and she often declaimed her poetry before large crowds, though her later verse was not as popular.

Her career is similar in many respects to that of Elizabeth Oakes-Smith. She married Samuel Gridley Howe (known as Chev) in 1843 after a pampered childhood and much private tutoring. She was especially attracted to German literature and philosophy. After marrying Howe, who directed the Perkins Institute for the Blind in New York City, she discovered that her husband (twenty years her senior) expected her to give up her intellectual pursuits and attend to household duties. She calls him a man "of iron will" in her "Rough Sketch." In the next sixteen years, Howe had six children, but she still managed to find time to write and persevered in her intention to publish, despite her husband's opposition. Julia and Chev at one time considered a separation but they were passionately involved with one another and were eventually reconciled. Indeed, Julia Ward Howe opposed divorce. She pursued several careers as writer, lecturer, preacher, and female activist. In 1868 she helped to found the American Women's Suffrage Association and the first women's club of the Northeast. Howe also became very much involved with the world peace movement, traveling to Europe to meet with like-minded leaders and intellectuals.

A great many of Howe's writings were never printed though her publications themselves are numerous and include plays, essays, biographies, sermons, and travel books. Many later expository works concern feminist issues such as equal access for women to higher education and the professions, and a more equitable distribution of power between men and women in the home. Like most of her contemporaries, Julia Ward Howe felt that the home was sacred and that women should build upon that foundation rather than threaten the basis of society by rejecting domesticity altogether.

Howe is best remembered for her patriotic works such as the "Battle-Hymn" but many of her lesser-known poems are equally stirring. In the early years she wrote about silent suffering and frustration as did her peers but some of her *Later Lyrics* (1866) such as "The Wedding" and "The Soul-Hunter" are more deeply haunting. *From Sunset Ridge* (1898) brings together early and later poems, many of which—"The Telegrams" and "A New Sculptor," for example—deserve to be better known.

Selected Works: *Words for the Hour.* 1857; *Sex and Education,* 1874; *Margaret Fuller, Marchessa Ossoli.* 1883; *Reminiscences 1819–1899.* 1899.

Selected Criticism: Clifford, Deborah P. *Mine Eyes Have Seen the Glory.* Boston: Little, 1979; Richards, Laura, and Maud Howe Elliott. *Julia Ward Howe 1819–1910.* Boston: Houghton, 1915; Tharp, Louise. *Three Saints and a Sinner.* Boston: Little, 1956.

BATTLE-HYMN OF THE REPUBLIC

Mine eyes have seen the glory of the coming of the Lord:
He is trampling out the vintage where the grapes of wrath are stored;
He hath loosed the fateful lightning of his terrible swift sword:
    His truth is marching on.

I have seen Him in the watch-fires of a hundred circling camps;
They have builded Him an altar in the evening dews and damps;
I can read His righteous sentence by the dim and flaring lamps.
    His day is marching on.

I have read a fiery gospel, writ in burnished rows of steel:
"As ye deal with my contemners, so with you my grace shall deal;
Let the Hero, born of woman, crush the serpent with his heel,
    Since God is marching on."

He has sounded forth the trumpet that shall never call retreat;
He is sifting out the hearts of men before his judgment-seat:
Oh! be swift, my soul, to answer Him! be jubilant, my feet!
    Our God is marching on.

In the beauty of the lilies Christ was born across the sea,
With a glory in his bosom that transfigures you and me:
As he died to make men holy, let us die to make men free,
    While God is marching on.

THE WEDDING

        In her satin gown so fine
        Trips the bride within the shrine.
        Waits the street to see her pass,
        Like a vision in a glass.
        Roses crown her peerless head:
        Keep your lilies for the dead!

        Something of the light without
        Enters with her, veiled about;

Julia Ward Howe

Sunbeams, hiding in her hair,
Please themselves with silken wear;
Shadows point to what shall be
In the dim futurity.

Wreathe with flowers the weighty yoke
Might of mortal never broke.
From the altar of her vows
To the grave's unsightly house
Measured is the path, and made:
All the work is planned and paid.

As a girl, with ready smile,
Where shall rise some ponderous pile,
On the chosen, festal day,
Turns the initial sod away,
So the bride with fingers frail
Founds a temple or a jail,—

Or a palace, it may be,
Flooded full with luxury,
Open yet to deadliest things,
And the Midnight Angel's wings.
Keep its chambers purged with prayer:
Faith can guard it, Love is rare.

Organ, sound thy wedding-tunes!
Priest, recite the sacred runes!
Hast no ghostly help nor art
Can enrich a selfish heart,
Blessing bind 'twixt greed and gold,
Joy with bloom for bargain sold?

Hail, the wedded task of life!
Mending husband, moulding wife.

Julia Ward Howe

Hope brings labor, labor peace;
Wisdom ripens, goods increase;
Triumph crowns the sainted head,
And our lilies wait the dead.

THE SOUL-HUNTER

Who hunts so late 'neath evening skies,
A smouldering love-brand in his eyes?
His locks outshame the black of night,
Its stars are duller than his sight
        Who hunts so late, so dark.

A drooping mantle shrouds his form,
To shield him from the winter's storm?
Or is there something at his side,
That, with himself, he strives to hide,
        Who hunts so late, so dark?

He hath such promise, silver sweet,
Such silken hands, such fiery feet,
That, where his look has charmed the prey,
His swift-winged passion forces way,
        Who hunts so late, so dark.

Sure no one underneath the moon
Can whisper to so soft a tune:
The hours would flit from dusk to dawn
Lighter than dews upon the lawn
        With him, so late, so dark.

But, should there break a day of need,
Those hands will try no valorous deed:
No help is in that sable crest,
Nor manhood is that hollow breast
  That sighed so late, so dark.

O maiden! of the salt waves make
Thy sinless shroud, for God's dear sake;
Or to the flame commit thy bloom;
Or lock thee, living, in the tomb
  So desolate and dark,—

Before thou list one stolen word
Of him who lures thee like a bird.
He wanders with the Devil's bait,
For human souls he lies in wait,
  Who hunts so late, so dark.

KOSMOS

Of dust the primal Adam came
In wondrous sequency evolved,
With speech that gave creation name,
Of art and artist never solved.

With something of a mother-pang
The Sun conceived the starry spheres
That from her burning bosom sprang,—
Immortal children of her tears.

From height of heat, and stress of span,
The measured Earth took poise and hold;

And beasts, the prophecy of man,
And man, were latent in her mould.

And hid in man a world intense,
The centre point of things that be,
With soul that conquers out of sense
Its incomplete divinity.

Around one infinite intent
All power and inspiration move,
Thrilling with light the firmament,
Lifting the heart of man with love.

A WILD NIGHT

The storm is sweeping o'er the land,
    And raging o'er the sea:
It urgeth sharp and dismal sounds,
    The Psalm of Misery.

The straining of the cordage now,
    The creaking of a spar,
The deep dumb shock the vessel feels
    When billows strike and jar,

It breathes of distant seamen's hearts
    That think upon their wives;
Of wretches clinging to the mast,
    And wrestling for their lives.

The clouds are flying through the sky
    Like spectres of affright:
Yon pale witch moon doth blast them all
    With bleared and ghastly light.

Julia Ward Howe

Great Demons flutter through the dark
   Flame touched, with dusky wing;
And Passion crouches out of sight
   Like a forbidden thing.

The blast doth scourge the forest through,
   Great oaks, and bushes small;
And God, the fable of the fools,
   Looks silently on all.

Oh! if He watches, as I know,
   Safe let Him keep our rest,
And give my little ones and me
   The shelter of His breast.

No harm shall come on earth, we trust;
   But, if mischance must be,
Most let Him help those weary souls
   That struggle with the sea!

THE TELEGRAMS

Bring the hearse to the station,
   When one shall demand it, late;
For that dark consummation
   The traveler must not wait.
Men say not by what connivance
   He slid from his weight of woe,
Whether sickness or weak contrivance,
   But we know him glad to go.
      On and on and ever on!
      What next?

Nor let the priest be wanting
  With his hollow eyes of prayer,
While the sexton wrenches, panting,
  The stone from the dismal stair.
But call not the friends who left him
  When fortune and pleasure fled:
Mortality hath not bereft him,
    That they should confront him, dead.
        On and on and ever on!
          What next?

Bid my mother be ready:
  We are coming home to-night:
Let my chamber be still and shady
  With the softened nuptial light.
We have traveled so gayly, madly,
  No shadow hath crossed our way;
Yet we come back like children, gladly,
  Joy-spent with our holiday.
        On and on and ever on!
          What next?

Stop the train at the landing,
  And search every carriage through;
Let no one escape your handing,
  None shiver, or shrink from view.
Three blood-stained guests expect him;
  Three murders oppress his soul;
Be strained every nerve to detect him
  Who feasted, and killed, and stole.
        On and on and ever on!
          What next?

Be rid of the notes they scattered;
  The great house is down at last;

The image of gold is shattered,
    And never can be recast.
The bankrupts show leaden features,
    And weary, distracted looks,
While harpy-eyed, wolf-souled creatures
    Pry through their dishonored books.
        On and on and ever on!
        What next?

Let him hasten, lest worse befall him,
    To look on me, ere I die:
I will whisper one curse to appall him,
    Ere the black flood carry me by.
His bridal? The friends forbid it;
    I have shown them his proofs of guilt;
Let him hear, with my laugh, who did it;
    Then hurry, Death, as thou wilt!
        On and on and ever on!
        What next?

Thus the living and dying daily
    Flash forward their wants and words,
While still on Thought's slender railway
    Sit scathless the little birds:
They heed not the sentence dire
    By magical hands exprest,
And only the sun's warm fire
    Stirs softly their happy breast.
        On and on and ever on!
        God next!

Julia Ward Howe

THE ROUGH SKETCH

S. G. H.[1]

A great grieved heart, an iron will,
As fearless blood as ever ran;
A form elate with nervous strength
And fibrous vigor,—all a man.

A gallant rein, a restless spur,
The hand to wield a biting scourge;
Small patience for the tasks of time,
Unmeasured power to speed and urge.

He rides the errand of the hour,
But sends no herald on his ways;
The world would thank the service done,
He cannot stay for gold or praise.

Not lavishly he casts abroad
The glances of an eye intense,
And, did he smile but once a year,
It were a Christmas recompense.

I thank a poet for his name,
The "Down of Darkness" this should be;
A child, who knows no risk it runs,
Might stroke its roughness harmlessly.

One helpful gift the gods forgot,
Due to the man of lion mood;
A woman's soul to match with his
In high resolve and hardihood.

---

1. S. G. H. is Samuel Gridley Howe, the poet's husband.

Julia Ward Howe

A NEW SCULPTOR

Once to my Fancy's hall a stranger came,
    Of mien unwonted;
And its pale shapes of glory without shame
    Or speech confronted.

Fair was my hall,—a gallery of gods
    Smoothly appointed,
With nymphs and satyrs from the dewy sods
    Freshly anointed.

Great Jove sat throned in state, with Hermes near,
    And fiery Bacchus,
Pallas and Pluto, and those Powers of fear
    Whose visions rack us.

Artemis wore her crescent free of stars,
    The hunt just scented;
Glad Aphrodite met the warrior Mars,
    The myriad-tented.

Rude was my visitant, of sturdy form,
    Draped in such clothing
As the world's great, whom luxury makes warm,
    Look on with loathing.

And yet methought his service-badge of soil
    With honor wearing,
And in his dexter hand, embossed with toil,
    A hammer bearing.

But while I waited till his eye should sink,
    O'ercome with beauty,

Julia Ward Howe

With heart-impatience brimming to the brink
    Of courteous duty,

He smote my marbles many a murderous blow,
    His weapon poising;
I, in my wrath and wonderment of woe,
    No comment voicing.

"Come, sweep this rubbish from the workman's way,
    Wreck of past ages!
Afford me here a lump of harmless clay,
    Ye grooms and pages!"

Then from that voidness of our mother-earth
    A frame he builded,
Of a new feature, with the power of birth
    Fashioned and welded.

It had a might mine eyes had never seen,—
    A mien, a stature,
As if the centuries that rolled between
    Had greatened Nature.

It breathed, it moved; above Jove's classic sway
    A place was won it:
The rustic sculptor motioned, then "To-day"
    He wrote upon it.

"What man art thou?" I cried, "and what this wrong
    That thou hast wrought me?
My marbles lived on symmetry and song:
    Why hast thou brought me

A form of all necessities, that asks
    Nurture and feeding?

Not this the burthen of my maidhood's tasks,
    Nor my high breeding."

"Behold," he said, "Life's great impersonate,
    Nourished by labor!
Thy gods are gone with old-time faith and fate;
    Here is thy Neighbor."

THE TEA-PARTY

I am not with you, sisters, in your talk;
I sit not in your fancied judgment-seat:
Not thus the sages in their council walk,
Not in this wise the calm great spirits meet.

My life has striven for broader scope than yours;
The daring of its failure and its fact
Have taught how deadly difficult it is
To suit the high endeavor with the act.

I do not reel my satire by the yard,
To flout the fronts of honorable men;
Nor, with poor cunning, underprize the heart
Whose impulse is not open to my ken.

Ah! sisters, but your forward speech comes well
To help the woman's standard, new-unfurled:
In carpet council ye may win the day;
But keep your limits,—do not rule the world.

What strife should come, what discord rule the times,
Could but your pettish will assert its way!

No lengthened wars of reason, but a rage,
Shown and repented twenty times a day.

Ye're all my betters,—one in beauty more,
And one in sharpness of the wit and tongue,
And one in trim, decorous piety,
And one with arts and graces ever young.

But well I thank my father's sober house
Where shallow judgment had no leave to be,
And hurrying years, that, stripping much beside,
Turned as they fled, and left me charity.

SPRING-BLOSSOMS

The little daisies, two by two,
The lilies wet with frosted dew,
The sweet procession of the Spring
Carries my baby's offering.

I leave the thoughts that take his place,
Imaginations winged in space,
And fold his shadow to my breast,
With the dear lips that mine have prest.

Ever my introverted eyes
Recover that past paradise;
Not without hell pain shuddered through
Where life declined, to rise anew.

Oh! to my darling carry this,
The old-time phrase, the frequent kiss;

Remind him how, in his decay,
My life's enamel melts away.

Tell him my time must also come
To enter his restricted home,
Where my soul furniture shall be
His lovely immortality.

"SAVE THE OLD SOUTH!"

Two hands the God of Nature gave,
One swift to smite, one fond to save,
Betwixt the cradle and the grave.

Where Strength hews out his stony stent,[1]
Where woods are felled and metals blent,
The right hand measures his content.

Where Skill sits tireless at her loom,
Where beauty wafts her transient bloom,
The tender saving hand has room.

And Fate, as in a tourney fine,
The differing powers does match and join,
That each may wear the crown divine.

The title refers to a cry representing the conservative feelings of Southerners after the Civil War. In this poem Howe juxtaposes a male insistence upon re- tributive justice with a female emphasis upon mercy and healing.

1. A stent in mining is a joining of two passageways created by excavation.

But manhood in its zeal and haste
Leaves cruel overthrow and waste
Upon its pathway, roughly traced.

Then woman comes with patient hand,
With loving heart of high command,
To save the councils of the land.

Round this old church so poor to see,
Record of years that swiftly flee,
She draws the chain of sympathy.

The men who make their gold their weal,
Who guard with powder and with steel,
Have not a weapon she can feel.

Before the venerable pile,
Armed with a reason and a smile,
She stations with benignant wile.

Like Barbara Frietchie[2] in her day,
She has a royal will to say:
"You shall not tear one stone away."

You disavow the spirit need
That avarice may build with heed
The gilded monuments of greed.

---

2. The poem "Barbara Frietchie" (1863) by Whittier dramatizes a fictional encounter between Stonewall Jackson's Southern troops and ninety-six-year-old Frietchie who displays a Union flag. Frietchie utters the famous lines: "Shoot, if you must, this old gray head, / But spare your country's flag." Jackson out of gallantry forbids his men to harm her. Howe points here to woman's nonviolent power to resist.

Julia Ward Howe

What hope, what help can patriots know?
Only this counter mandate slow,
"The mothers will not have it so."

Mothers! the wrongs of ages wait!
Amend them, ministers of fate!
Redeem the church, reform the state!

A THOUGHT FOR WASHING DAY

The clothes-line is a Rosary
    Of household help and care;
Each little saint the Mother loves
    is represented there.

And when across her garden plot
    She walks, with thoughtful heed,
I should not wonder if she told
    Each garment for a bead.

For Celia's scarlet stockings hang
    Beside Amelia's skirt,
And Bilbo's breeches, which of late
    Were sadly smeared with dirt.

Yon kerchief small wiped bitter tears
    For ill-success at school;
This pinafore was torn in strife
    'Twixt Fred and little Jule.

And that device of finer web,
    And over-costly lace,

Adorned our Eldest when she danced
    At some gay fashion place.

A stranger passing, I salute
    The Household in its wear,
And smile to think how near of kin
    Are love and toil and prayer.

MIDDLE AGE

Left alone with the cows to-day,
The younger members all gone away;
The trees would go, but their roots are set,
Their patent of freedom not made out yet.
So here I sit, in state serene,
Every one's servant and no one's queen,
Watching the butterflies bright and brown,
That float like leaves from God's autumn crown.

My children are chasing the swift delight
Oft neared, but ne'er o'ertaken quite:
The sweet cup fails from the lips too soon,
The harmony waits for its perfect tune;
In bluest ether some scutcheon dark
Heralds the storm-fiend to the bark;
God's monitors set, if the sense should pall,
To whisper the spirit: "This is not all."

The grave of the Past in my garden lies
For daily and hourly sacrifice.
The Christ life blesses my daily care,

For his is the lesson and his the prayer.
But the endless Future touches me too
In the unseen Babe that, old and new,
Is carried along in the household ways
With its waiting mother, too dear for praise.

I look at the ancient blue on high
That saw the first Parents live and die,
By this very sun which, burning still,
Mirrors God's patient and constant will.
And I look below at the ancient green
Where the life of the aeons has garnered been;
There, standing where others stand between,
I study the lesson of human fate
On the wondrous page, at my narrow date.

And this later freedom, this thoughtful calm
That sobers the strophe and quickens the psalm,
That gathers the blessing and loses the pain,
And counts nought for lost in the final gain,
And the children, born without pangs of mine,
And the dreams that in young eyes dazzle and shine,
And the faith that follows the prophet's soul
Where truth unseen has its distant goal.
Let me end the song ere I turn the page,—
All this is the burthen of middle age.

ALICE CARY

(1820–1871)

꘎꘎꘎꘎꘎

ALICE WAS THE OLDER of the two widely known Cary sisters and was remembered as the more serious and practical one. Both she and Phoebe were born on what was then considered the Western frontier, in the area around Cincinnati, Ohio. She and her sister had little education but took an early interest in literature. After their mother's death, they were forced to nurture their ambitions as best they could, since their stern stepmother was unsympathetic to their literary interests.

In her teens Alice began sending poems to periodicals. When she was thirty, she moved to New York City, having decided to pursue a literary life. Her career was aided by Rufus Griswold who admired the work of both Cary sisters. Phoebe joined her in New York a year later. By the mid-1850s the two women were well established in their careers, several times printing books of poetry jointly. Alice drew the admiration of both Poe and Whittier, who composed a tribute to her called "The Singer."

In addition to poetry, Alice Cary published novels and sketches on many subjects. She and her sister were ardent Universalists, as well as being feminists in the style of their day, actively engaged with women's clubs and the work of Susan B. Anthony and Elizabeth Cady Stanton. The sisters were apparently very well satisfied with their lives as single women though they preserved a strong belief in marriage as an ideal.

Alice Cary's poetry and prose are memorable for their realism. *Clovernook,* an extremely successful prose picture of life on the frontier, gave rise to several sequels and was pirated in five English editions. Far from idealizing life in the West, Cary shows how difficult an existence without culture, adequate medical care, or physical security can be. Still, she remains true to her roots, and some of her most notable poems—such as "The Washerwoman," "Growing Rich," and the tribute to Abraham Lincoln—reveal her love for common people and her democratic instincts. She was already in sympathy with many of the basic ideas of Realism, at a time when Romanticism was still the primary literary influence. Her ending to "Contradiction" suggests a critique of popular notions of individualism: "I think you will own it is custom or fate / That has made you the creature you are, not your will." Alice Cary's poetry sometimes conveys a sense of sadness and frustration common to other women's poems of this period, but in such works as "To Solitude" her skill with language and her ability to construct powerful endings illustrate her unusual gifts.

Selected Works: Poems of Alice and Phoebe Cary. 1850; Clovernook; or, Recollections of Our Neighborhood in the West. 1852; Poems. 1855; Married, Not Mated; or, How They Lived at Woodside and Throckmorton Hall. 1856; Ballads, Lyrics, and Hymns. 1866.

Selected Criticism: Ames, Mary Clemmer. A Memorial of Alice and Phoebe Cary, with Some of Their Later Poems. 1873; Fetterley, Judith. Intro. to Alice Cary, Clovernook Sketches and Other Stories. New Brunswick: Rutgers UP, 1988; Fetterley, Judith, and Marjorie Pryse. "Profile of Alice Cary." Legacy 1:1 (1984); Greeley, Horace. "Alice and Phoebe Cary." Eminent Women of the Age. Hartford: Betts, 1868; Kolodny, Annette. The Land before Her. Chapel Hill: U of North Carolina P, 1984; Pulsifer, Janice G. "Alice and Phoebe Cary, Whittier's Sweet Singers of the West." Essex Institute Historical Collections, 109 (1973).

THE WASHERWOMAN

At the north end of our village stands,
With gable black and high,

Alice Cary

A weather-beaten house,—I've stopt
   Often as I went by,

To see the strip of bleaching grass
   Slipped brightly in between
The long straight rows of hollyhocks,
   And currant-bushes green;

The clumsy bench beside the door,
   And oaken washing-tub,
Where poor old Rachel used to stand,
   And rub, and rub, and rub!

Her blue-checked apron speckled with
   The suds, so snowy white;
From morning when I went to school
   Till I went home at night,

She never took her sunburnt arms
   Out of the steaming tub:
We used to say 't was weary work
   Only to hear her rub.

With sleeves stretched straight upon the grass
   The washed shirts used to lie;
By dozens, I have counted them
   Some days, as I went by.

The burly blacksmith, battering at
   His red-hot iron bands,
Would make a joke of wishing that
   He had old Rachel's hands!

And when the sharp and ringing strokes
   Had doubled up his shoe,

As crooked as old Rachel's back,
　　He used to say 't would do.

And every village housewife, with
　　A conscience clear and light,
Would send for her to come and wash
　　An hour or two at night!

Her hair beneath her cotton cap
　　Grew silver white and thin;
And the deep furrows in her face
　　Ploughed all the roses in.

Yet patiently she kept at work,—
　　We school-girls used to say
The smile about her sunken mouth
　　Would quite go out some day.

Nobody ever thought the spark
　　That in her sad eyes shone,
Burned outward from a living soul
　　Immortal as their own.

And though a tender flush sometimes
　　Into her cheek would start,
Nobody dreamed old Rachel had
　　A woman's loving heart!

At last she left her heaps of clothes
　　One quiet autumn day,
And stript from off her sunburnt arms
　　The weary suds away;

That night within her moonlit door
　　She sat alone,—her chin

Sunk in her hand,—her eyes shut up,
  As if to look within.

Her face uplifted to the star
  That stood so sweet and low
Against old crazy Peter's house—
  (He loved her long ago!)

Her heart had worn her body to
  A handful of poor dust,—
Her soul was gone to be arrayed
  In marriage-robes, I trust.

GROWING RICH

And why are you pale, my Nora?
  And why do you sigh and fret?
The black ewe had twin lambs to-day,
  And we shall be rich folk yet.

Do you mind the clover-ridge, Nora,
  That slopes to the crooked stream?
The brown cow pastured there this week,
  And her milk is sweet as cream.

The old gray mare that last year fell
  As thin as any ghost,
Is getting a new white coat, and looks
  As young as her colt, almost.

And if the corn-land should do well,
  And so, please God, it may,

I'll buy the white-faced bull a bell,
　　To make the meadows gay.

I know we are growing rich, Johnny,
　　And that is why I fret,
For my little brother Phil is down
　　In the dismal coal-pit yet.

And when the sunshine sets in th' corn,
　　The tassels green and gay,
It will not touch my father's eyes,
　　That are going blind, they say.

But if I were not sad for him,
　　Nor yet for little Phil,
Why, darling, Molly's hand, last year,
　　Was cut off in the mill.

And so, nor mare nor brown milch-cow.
　　Nor lambs can joy impart,
For the blind old man and th' mill and mine
　　Are all upon my heart.

HOW AND WHERE

　How are we living?
Like herbs in a garden that stand in a row,
And have nothing to do but to stand there and grow?
　　Our powers of perceiving
　　So dull and so dead,
They simply extend to the objects about us,—
The moth, having all his dark pleasure without us,—
　　The worm in his bed!

If thus we are living,
And fading and falling, and rotting, alas!—
Like the grass, or the flowers that grow in the grass,—
    Is life worth our having?
    The insect a-humming—
The wild bird is better, that sings as it flies,—
The ox, that turns up his great face to the skies,
    When the thunder is coming.

    Where are we living?
In passion, and pain, and remorse do we dwell,—
Creating, yet terribly hating, our hell?
    No triumph achieving?
    No grossness refining?
The wild tree does more; for his coat of rough barks
He trims with green mosses, and checks with the marks
    Of the long summer shining.

    We're dying, not living:
Our senses shut up, and our hearts faint and cold;
Upholding old things just because they are old;
    Our good spirits grieving,
    We suffer our springs
Of promise to pass without sowing the land,
And hungry and sad in the harvest-time stand,
    Expecting good things!

TO SOLITUDE

    I am weary of the working.
        Weary of the long day's heat;

Alice Cary

To thy comfortable bosom,
 Wilt thou take me, spirit sweet?

Weary of the long, blind struggle
 For a pathway bright and high,—
Weary of the dimly dying
 Hopes that never quite all die.

Weary searching a bad cipher
 For a good that must be meant;
Discontent with being weary,—
 Weary with my discontent.

I am weary of the trusting
 Where my trusts but torments prove:
Wilt thou keep faith with me? wilt thou
Be my true and tender love?

I am weary drifting, driving
 Like a helmless bark at sea;
Kindly, comfortable spirit,
 Wilt thou give thyself to me?

Give thy birds to sing me sonnets?
 Give thy winds my cheeks to kiss?
And thy mossy rocks to stand for
 The memorials of our bliss?

I in reverence will hold thee,
 Never vexed with jealous ills,
Though thy wild and wimpling waters
Wind about a thousand hills.

Alice Cary

MY CREED

I hold that Christian grace abounds
    Where charity is seen; that when
We climb to Heaven, 't is on the rounds
    Of love to men.

I hold all else, named piety,
    A selfish scheme, a vain pretense;
Where centre is not—can there be
    Circumference?

This I moreover hold, and dare
    Affirm where'er my rhyme may go,—
Whatever things be sweet or fair,
    Love makes them so.

Whether it be the lullabies
    That charm to rest the nursling bird,
Or that sweet confidence of sighs
    And blushes, made without a word.

Whether the dazzling and the flush
    Of softly sumptuous garden bowers,
Or by some cabin door, a bush
    Of ragged flowers.

'T is not the wide phylactery,
    Nor stubborn fast, nor stated prayers,
That make us saints: we judge the tree
    By what it bears.

And when a man can live apart
    From works, on theologic trust,
I know the blood about his heart
    Is dry as dust.

PICTURES OF MEMORY

Among the beautiful pictures
    That hang on Memory's wall,
Is one of a dim old forest,
    That seemeth best of all:
Not for its gnarled oaks olden,
    Dark with the mistletoe;
Nor for the violets golden
    That sprinkle the vale below;
Nor for the milk-white lilies,
    That lead from the fragrant hedge,
Coquetting all day with the sunbeams,
    And stealing their golden edge;
Not for the vines on the upland
    Where the bright red berries rest,
Nor the pinks, nor the pale, sweet cowslip,
    It seemeth to me the best.
I once had a little brother,
    With eyes that were dark and deep—
In the lap of that old dim forest
    He lieth in peace asleep:
Light as the down of the thistle,
    Free as the winds that blow,
We roved there the beautiful summers,
    The summers of long ago;

But his feet on the hills grew weary,
    And, one of the autumn eves,
I made for my little brother
    A bed of the yellow leaves.
Sweetly his pale arms folded
    My neck in a meek embrace,
As the light of immortal beauty
    Silently covered his face:
And when the arrows of sunset
    Lodged in the tree-tops bright,
He fell, in his saint-like beauty,
    Asleep by the gates of light.
Therefore, of all the pictures
    That hang on Memory's wall,
The one of the dim old forest
    Seemeth the best of all.

FAME

Fame guards the wreath we call a crown
    With other wreaths of fire,
And dragging this or that man down
    Will not raise you the higher!
Fear not too much the open seas,
    Nor yet yourself misdoubt;
Clear the bright wake of geniuses,
    Then steadily steer out.
That wicked men in league should be
    To push your craft aside,
Is not the hint of modesty,
    But the poor conceit of pride.

Alice Cary

LIFE

Solitude—Life is inviolate solitude—
    Never was truth so apart from the dreaming
    As lieth the selfhood inside of the seeming,
Guarded with triple shield out of all quest,
    So that the sisterhood nearest and sweetest,
    So that the brotherhood kindest, completest,
Is but an exchanging of signals at best.

Desolate—Life is so dreary and desolate—
    Women and men in the crowd meet and mingle,
    Yet with itself every soul standeth single,
Deep out of sympathy moaning its moan—
    Holding and having its brief exultation—
    Making its lonesome and low lamentation—
Fighting its terrible conflicts alone.

Separate—Life is so sad and so separate—
    Under love's ceiling with roses for lining,
    Heart mates with heart in a tender entwining.
Yet never the sweet cup of love filleth full—
    Eye looks in eye with a questioning wonder,
    Why are we thus in our meeting asunder?
Why are our pulses so slow and so dull?

Fruitless, fruitionless—Life is fruitionless—
    Never the heaped up and generous measure—
    Never the substance of satisfied pleasure—
Never the moment with rapture elate—
    But draining the chalice, we long for the chalice,
    And live as an alien inside of our palace,
Bereft of our title and deeds of estate.

Alice Cary

Pitiful—Life is so poor and so pitiful—
    Cometh the cloud on the goldenest weather—
    Briefly the man and his youth stay together—
Falleth the frost ere the harvest is in,
    And conscience descends from the open aggression
    To timid and troubled and tearful concession,
And downward and down into parley with sin.

Purposeless—Life is so wayward and purposeless—
    Always before us the object is shifting.
    Always the means and the method are drifting,
We rue what is done—what is undone deplore—
    More striving for high things than things that are holy.
    And so we go down to the valley so lowly
Wherein there is work, and device never more.

Vanity, vanity—all would be vanity,
    Whether in seeking or getting our pleasures—
    Whether in spending or hoarding our treasures—
Whether in indolence, whether in strife—
    Whether in feasting and whether in fasting,
    But for our faith in the Love ever-lasting—
But for the life that is better than life.

ABRAHAM LINCOLN

Foully Assassinated, April 1865—Inscribed to Punch[1]

No glittering chaplet brought from other lands!
    As in his life, this man, in death, is ours;

---

1. *Punch* is a British political journal; thus, the extended references to royalty.

Alice Cary

His own loved prairies o'er his "gaunt gnarled hands"
  Have fitly drawn their sheet of summer flowers!

What need hath he now of a tardy crown,
  His name from mocking jest and sneer to save?
When every ploughman turns his furrow down
  As soft as though it fell upon his grave.

He was a man whose like the world again
  Shall never see, to vex with blame or praise;
The landmarks that attest his bright, brief reign
  Are battles, not the pomps of gala days!

The grandest leader of the grandest war
  That ever time in history gave a place;
What were the tinsel flattery of a star
  To such a breast! or what a ribbon's grace!

'T is to th' *man,* and th' man's honest worth,
  The nation's loyalty in tears upsprings;
Through him the soil of labor shines henceforth
  High o'er the silken broideries of kings.

The mechanism of external forms—
  The shrifts that couriers put their bodies through,
Were alien ways to him—his brawny arms
  Had other work than posturing to do!

Born of the people, well he knew to grasp
  The wants and wishes of the weak and small;
Therefore we hold him with no shadowy clasp—
  Therefore his name is household to us all.

Therefore we love him with a love apart
  From any fawning love of pedigree—

His was the royal soul and mind and heart—
    Not the poor outward shows of royalty.

Forgive us then, O friends, if we are slow
    To meet your recognition of his worth—
We're jealous of the very tears that flow
    From eyes that never loved a humble hearth.

THE WEST COUNTRY

Have you been in our wild west country? then
    You have often had to pass
Its cabins lying like birds' nests in
    The wild green prairie grass.

Have you seen the women forget their wheels
    As they sat at the door to spin—
Have you seen the darning fall away
    From their fingers worn and thin,

As they asked you news of the villages
    Where they were used to be,
Gay girls at work in the factories
    With their lovers gone to sea!

Ah, have you thought of the bravery
    That no loud praise provokes—
Of the tragedies acted in the lives
    Or poor, hard-working folks!

Of the little more, and the little more
    Of hardship which they press

Upon their own tired hands to make
    The toil for the children less:

And not in vain; for many a lad
    Born to rough work and ways,
Strips off his ragged coat, and makes
    Men clothe him with their praise.

CONTRADICTION

I love the deep quiet—all buried in leaves,
    To sit the day long just as idle as air,
Till the spider grows tame at my elbow, and weaves,
    And toadstools come up in a row round my chair.

I love the new furrows—the cones of the pine,
    The grasshopper's chirp, and the hum of the mote;
And short pasture-grass where the clover-blooms shine
    Like red buttons set on a holiday coat.

Flocks packed in the hollows—the droning of bees,
    The stubble so brittle—the damp and flat fen;
Old homesteads I love, in their clusters of trees,
    And children and books, but not women nor men.

Yet, strange contradiction! I live in the sound
    Of a sea-girdled city—'t is thus that it fell,
And years, oh, how many! have gone since I bound
    A sheaf for the harvest, or drank at a well.

And if, kindly reader, one moment you wait
    To measure the poor little niche that you fill,
I think you will own it is custom or fate
    That has made you the creature you are, not your will.

Alice Cary

THE BRIDAL VEIL

We're married, they say, and you think you have won me,—
Well, take this white veil from my head, and look on me;
Here's matter to vex you, and matter to grieve you,
Here's doubt to distrust you, and faith to believe you,—
I am all as you see, common earth, common dew;
Be wary, and mould me to roses, not rue!

Ah! shake out the filmy thing, fold after fold,
And see if you have me to keep and to hold,—
Look close on my heart—see the worst of its sinning,—
It is not yours to-day for the yesterday's winning—
The past is not mine—I am too proud to borrow—
You must grow to new heights if I love you to-morrow.

I have wings flattened down and hid under my veil:
They are subtle as light—you can never undo them,
And swift in their flight—you can never pursue them,
And spite of all clasping, and spite of all bands,
I can slip like a shadow, a dream, from your hands.

Nay, call me not cruel, and fear not to take me,
I am yours for my life-time, to be what you make me,—
To wear my white veil for a sign, or a cover,
As you shall be proven my lord, or my lover;
A cover for peace that is dead, or a token
Of bliss that can never be written or spoken.

Alice Cary

LIFE'S MYSTERY

Life's sadly solemn mystery
   Hangs o'er me like a weight;
The glorious longing to be free,
   The gloomy bars of fate.

Alternately the good and ill,
   The light and dark, are strung;
Fountains of love within my heart,
   And hate upon my tongue.

Beneath my feet the unstable ground,
   Above my head the skies;
Immortal longings in my soul,
   And death before my eyes.

No purely pure, and perfect good,
   No high, unhindered power;
A beauteous promise in the bud,
   And mildew on the flower.

The glad, green brightness of the spring;
   The summer, soft and warm;
The faded autumn's fluttering gold,
   The whirlwind and the storm.

To find some sure interpreter
   My spirit vainly tries;
I only know that God is love,
   And know that love is wise.

MARIA WHITE LOWELL

(1821–1853)

✖✖✖✖✖✖

MARIA WHITE LOWELL probably would have disappeared from view had not Thomas Wentworth Higginson advised Emily Dickinson to read her poems. Only sixteen of them appeared in print during her life, and her most popular works, "The Alpine Sheep" and "The Morning-Glory," seem sentimental today. In 1855, two years after his wife's death, James Russell Lowell had 50 copies of her selected poems privately printed; these he distributed to friends. Maria White Lowell's reputation would probably have died there, were it not for Amy Lowell and Dickinson's 1870 letter to Higginson: "You told me of Mrs. Lowell's Poems. Would you tell me where I could find them or are they not for sight?" (#332).

In 1907 Houghton Mifflin published 330 copies of the 1855 *Poems.* Then Amy Lowell discovered the first wife of her elder cousin and helped to interest others in her work. In 1936 Brown University Press published *The Poems of Maria Lowell,* which included previously unpublished letters and a biography. S. Foster Damon, who was professor of English at Brown and a close friend of Amy Lowell until her death in 1925, wrote an introduction.

Maria White was born into an intellectual middle-class family and educated under strict, ascetic discipline at an Ursuline covent; it was burned by a Know-Nothing mob in 1834. She was brought up as a Unitarian but had a strong Puritan streak that predisposed her toward spiritual contemplation and social reform. Between 1839 and 1844 she participated in Margaret Fuller's "Conversations." Maria, like many of the other participants, was an ardent supporter of temperance and abolition. She soon became part of a young people's group called The Band in which she met James Russell Lowell. He was impressed by her great memory for poetry and attracted by her ethereal beauty. Together they read Goethe, and his instinctively conservative nature seemed to soften under her influence.

In 1843 Maria began to publish her poetry. In 1844 she married James. The couple had four children; the first three died in infancy. When Walter, born in 1851, appeared to be more healthy, the Lowells traveled to Rome, hoping to explore European culture. In 1852 Walter died also, however, followed by Maria the next year. James Russell Lowell was heartbroken. His letters about his wife, both during her short life and afterward, are unusually fond, if paternalistic by our standards. According to Hope Vernon, he confessed to a friend: "She is quite cutting me out as a poet—though she laughs when I tell her so, God bless her!"

Maria White Lowell's poems are in many ways similar to those written by other women of her time, but "Africa," "An Opium Fantasy," and "The Sick-Room" have impressed readers with their original imagery and fervency. The ending of "An Opium Fantasy" is particularly striking. One can only wonder how Lowell would have developed as a poet had she lived longer.

Selected Criticism: Damon, S. Foster. *The Poems of Maria Lowell* (Providence: Brown UP, 1936); Vernon.

THE MORNING-GLORY

We wreathed about our darling's head the morning-glory bright;
Her little face looked out beneath, so full of life and light,
So lit as with a sunrise, that we could only say
She is the morning-glory bright, and her poor types are they.

So always from that happy time we called her by that name,
And very fitting did it seem, for sure as morning came,

Maria White Lowell

Behind her cradle-bars she'd smile to catch the first faint ray,
As from the trellis smiles the flower, and opens to the day.

But not so beautiful they rear their airy cups of blue,
As turned her sweet eyes to the light, brimmed with sleep's tender dew;
And not so close their tendrils fine round their supports are thrown,
As those dear arms, whose outstretched plea called all hearts to her own.

We used to think how she had come, even as comes the flower,
The last and perfect added gift, to crown Love's morning hour;
And how in her was imaged forth the love we could not say,
As on the little dew-drops round shines back the heart of day.

We never could have thought, O God! that she would wither up
Almost before the day was done, like the morning-glory's cup;
We never could have thought that she would bow her noble head,
Till she lay stretched before our sight, withered, and cold, and dead.

The morning-glory's blossoming will soon be coming round,
We see their rows of heart-shaped leaves upspringing from the ground,
The tender things the winter killed, renew again their birth,
But the glory of our morning has passed away from earth.

In vain, O Earth! our aching eyes stretch over thy green plain,
Too harsh thy dews, too cold thine air, her spirit to detain;
But in the groves of Paradise, full surely we shall see
Our morning-glory beautiful twine round our dear Lord's knee.

AFRICA

She sat where the level sands
Sent back the sky's fierce glare;

Maria White Lowell

She folded her mighty hands,
And waited with calm despair,
While the red sun dropped down the streaming air.

Her throne was broad and low,
Builded of cinnamon;—
Huge ivory, row on row,
Varying its columns dun,
Barred with the copper of the setting sun.

Up from the river came
The low and sullen roar
Of lions, with eyes of flame,
That haunted its reedy shore,
And the neigh of the hippopotamus trampling the watery floor.

Her great dusk face no light
From the sunset-glow could take;
Dark as the primal night
Ere over the earth God spake:
It seemed for her a dawn could never break.

She opened her massy lips,
And sighed with a dreary sound,
As when by the sand's eclipse
Bewildered men are bound,
And like a train of mourners the columned winds sweep round.

She said: "My torch at fount of day
I lit, now smouldering in decay;
Through futures vast I grope my way.

"I was sole Queen the broad earth through:
My children round my knees upgrew,
And from my breast sucked Wisdom's dew.

"Day after day to them I hymned;
  Fresh knowledge still my song o'erbrimmed,
  Fresh knowledge, which no time had dimmed.

"I sang of Numbers; soon they knew
  The spell they wrought, and on the blue
  Foretold the stars in order due;—

"Of Music; and they fain would rear,
  Something to tell its influence clear;
  Uprose my Memnon,[1] with nice ear,

"To wait upon the morning air,
  Until the sun rose from his lair
  Swifter, at greet of lutings rare.

"I sang of Forces whose great bands
  Could knit together feeble hands
  To uprear Thought's supreme commands;

"Then, like broad tents, beside the Nile
  They pitched the Pyramids' great pile;
  Where light and shade divided smile;

"And on white walls, in stately show,
  Did Painting with fair movement go,
  Leading the long processions slow.

"All laws that wondrous Nature taught,
  To serve my children's skill I brought,
  And still for fresh devices sought.

---

1. See note to Lydia Sigourney's poem "Christian Settlements in Africa." The statue of Memnon was said to produce a sound like the snapping of a cord when first struck by dawn's rays. Memnon is referred to also in Anne Lynch Botta's poem "The Ideal."

Maria White Lowell

"What need to tell? they lapsed away,
  Their great light quenched in twilight gray,
  Within their winding tombs they lay,

"And centuries went slowly by,
  And looked into my sleepless eye,
  Which only turned to see them die.

"The winds like mighty spirits came,
  Alive and pure and strong as flame,
  At last to lift me from my shame;

"For oft I heard them onward go,
  Felt in the air their great wings row,
  As down they dipped in journeying slow.

"Their course they steered above my head,
  One strong voice to another said,—
  'Why sits she here so drear and dead?

"Her kingdom stretches far away;
  Beyond the utmost verge of day,
  Her myriad children dance and play.'

"Then throbbed my mother's heart again,
  Then knew my pulse's finer pain,
  Which wrought like fire within my brain.

"I sought my young barbarians, where
  A mellower light broods on the air,
  And heavier blooms swing incense rare.

"Swart-skinned, crisp-haired, they did not shun
  The burning arrows of the sun;
  Erect as palms stood every one.

"I said,—These shall live out their day
  In song and dance and endless play;
  The children of the world are they.

"Nor need they delve with heavy spade;
  Their bread, on emerald dishes laid,
  Sets forth a banquet in each shade.

"Only the thoughtful bees shall store
  Their honey for them evermore;
  They shall not learn such toilsome lore;

"Their finest skill shall be to snare
  The birds that flaunt along the air,
  And deck them in their feathers rare.

"So centuries went on their way,
  And brought fresh generations gay
  On my savannahs green to play.

"There came a change. They took my free,
  My careless ones, and the great sea
  Blew back their endless sighs to me:

"With earthquake shudderings oft the mould
  Would gape; I saw keen spears of gold
  Thrusting red hearts down, not yet cold,

"But throbbing wildly; dreadful groans
  Stole upward through Earth's ribbed stones,
  And crept along through all my zones.

"I sought again my desert bare,
  But still they followed on the air,
  And still I hear them everywhere.

"So sit I dreary, desolate,
Till the slow-moving hand of Fate
Shall lift me from my sunken state."

Her great lips closed upon her moan;
Silently sate she on her throne,
Rigid and black, as carved in stone.

THE SLAVE-MOTHER

Her new-born child she holdeth, but feels within her heart
It is not hers, but his who can out-bid her in the mart;
And through the gloomy midnight her prayer goes up on high,
"God grant my little helpless one in helplessness may die!"

"If she must live to womanhood, oh may she never know,
Uncheered by mother's happiness, the mother's depth of wo!
And may I lie within my grave before that day I see,
When she sits, as I am sitting, with a slave-child on her knee!"

The little arms steal upward, and then upon her breast
She feels the brown and velvet hands that never are at rest;

No sense of joy they waken, but thrills of bitter pain,—
She thinks of him who counteth o'er the gold those hands shall gain.

Then on her face she looketh, but not as mother proud,
And seeth how her features, as from out a dusky cloud,
Are tenderly unfolding, far softer than her own,
And how upon the rounded cheek a fairer light is thrown;

And she trembles in her agony, and on her prophet heart
There drops a gloomy shadow down, that never can depart,—
She cannot look upon that face, where, in the child's pure bloom,
Is writ with such dread certainty the woman's loathsome doom.

She cannot bear to know her child must be as she hath been,
Yet she sees but one deliverance from infamy and sin,—
And so she cries at midnight, with exceeding bitter cry,
"God grant my little helpless one in helplessness may die!"

ROUEN, PLACE DE LA PUCELLE

Here blooms the legend, fed by Time and Chance,
    Fresh as the morning, though with centuries old,
The whitest lily on the shield of France,
    With heart of virgin gold.

Along the square she moved, sweet Joan of Arc,
    With face more pallid than a daylit star,
Half-seen, half-doubted, while before her dark
    Stretched the array of war.

Swift passed the battle-smoke of lying breath
    From off her path, as if a wind had blown,
Showing no faithless King, but righteous Death,
    On the low wooden throne.

Place de la Pucelle means The Maid's Square—a reference to Joan of Arc, who was imprisoned, tried, and burned at the stake in Rouen. The very small square is near the place of her execution.

He would reward her: she who meekly wore
  Alike the gilded mail and peasant gown,
As meekly now received one honor more,
    The formless, fiery crown.

A white dove trembled up the heated air,
  And in the opening zenith found its goal;
Soft as a downward feather, dropped a prayer
    For each repentant soul.

THE SICK-ROOM

A spirit is treading the earth,
  As wind treads the vibrating string;
I know thy feet so beautiful,
    Thy punctual feet, O Spring!

They slide from far-off mountains,
  As slides the untouched snow;
They move over deepening meadows,
    As vague cloud-shadows blow.

Thou wilt not enter the chamber,
  The door stands open in vain;
Thou art pluming the wands of cherry
    To lattice the window pane.

Thou flushest the sunken orchard
  With the lift of thy rosy wing;
The peach will not part with her sunrise
    Though great noon-bells should ring.

O life, and light, and gladness,
    Tumultuous everywhere!
O pain and benumbing sadness,
    That brood in the heavy air!

Here the fire alone is busy,
    And wastes, like the fever's heat,
The wood that enshrined past summers,
    Past summers, as bounteous as fleet.

The beautiful hanging gardens
    That rocked in the morning wind,
And sheltered a dream of Faëry,
    And life so timid and kind,

The shady choir of the bobolink,
    The race-course of squirrels gay,—
They are changed into trembling smoke-wreaths,
    And a heap of ashes gray.

AN OPIUM FANTASY

Soft hangs the opiate in the brain,
And lulling soothes the edge of pain,
Till harshest sound, far off or near,
Sings floating in its mellow sphere.

What wakes me from my heavy dream?
    Or am I still asleep?
Those long and soft vibrations seem
    A slumberous charm to keep.

The graceful play, a moment stopped,
    Distance again unrolls,
Like silver balls, that, softly dropped,
    Ring into golden bowls.

I question of the poppies red,
    The fairy flaunting band,
While I weed, with drooping head,
    Within their phalanx stand.

"Some airy one, with scarlet cap,
    The name unfold to me
Of this new minstrel, who can lap
    Sleep in his melody?"

Bright grew their scarlet-kerchiefed heads,
    As freshening winds had blown,
And from their gently swaying beds
    They sang in undertone,

"Oh, he is but a little owl,
    The smallest of his kin,
Who sits beneath the midnight's cowl,
    And makes this airy din."

"Deceitful tongues, of fiery tints,
    Far more than this you know,—
That he is your enchanted prince,
    Doomed as an owl to go;

"Nor his fond play for years hath stopped,
    But nightly he unrolls
His silver balls, that, softly dropped,
    Ring into golden bowls."

PHOEBE CARY

(1824–1871)

♯♯♯♯♯♯

LIKE HER SISTER ALICE, Phoebe grew up on the Ohio frontier and watched her mother and two sisters die of tuberculosis in the 1830s. Phoebe published her first poem at the age of fourteen, and after her father's remarriage, she and Alice began to dream of leaving the homestead for a more fulfilling life devoted to literature.

Phoebe moved to New York City the year after Alice did. Their poems had already appeared in Griswold's *Female Poets of America* and in a separate edition of their own, *Poems of Alice and Phoebe Cary,* in 1850. After six years of magazine and book publishing, Alice and Phoebe had earned enough money to buy their own home on 20th Street in New York where they lived for the rest of their lives, organizing popular Sunday "evenings" for their friends.

Phoebe was known to have rejected several marriage proposals in order to remain with her sister to whom she was completely devoted. Mary Clemmer Ames's memoir claims that Phoebe was the more emotional of the two women, often playing Sensibility to Alice's Sense. She was addicted to stylish clothes and jewels but very shy in public. In fact, though often involved in reform activities, both women were extremely diffident. Phoebe's brief stint on the staff of Susan B. Anthony's journal *Revolution* made her wary of all subsequent attempts to enlist her in activities that might require her to go before the public.

Nevertheless, the voice in Phoebe's poetry is often quite spirited. Like Alice, she experimented with dialects and developed portraits of simple folk, often written in dialogue. Phoebe was the lighter of the two spirits, however, and more given to parody, as her poems "Was He Henpecked?" and "Dorothy's Dower" illustrate. Both poets give lively expression to their feminist views, especially on the subject of inequalities between men and women in the sexual and domestic spheres, but neither is uncritical of the foibles of the female sex. Phoebe's "Advice Gratis to a Certain Woman" gives a clear sense that Alice and Phoebe's feminism did not assume that all women were saintly.

Of the two sisters Alice was probably the more talented. Phoebe published much less, confining herself to poetry rather than branching out into prose. Though several of Phoebe's poems are charming upon first reading, they are not so rewarding in rereading as are Alice's best ones.

In February 1871 Alice succumbed to tuberculosis. Five months later, in Newport where she had gone to recover from Alice's death, Phoebe died of hepatitis. In her 1873 memorial Ames claims: "It is impossible to estimate either sister without any reference to the other—as impossible as to tell what a husband and wife would have been, had they never lived together." Sisterhood is nowhere better represented than in their alliance.

Selected Works: Poems and Parodies. 1854; Poems of Faith, Hope, and Love. 1868; Poetical Works of Alice and Phoebe Cary. Ed. M. C. Ames. 1876; Poetical Works. 1880.

Selected Criticism: Ames, Mary Clemmer. A Memorial to Alice and Phoebe Cary, with Some of Their Later Poems. 1873; Greeley, Horace. "Alice and Phoebe Cary." Eminent Women of the Age. Hartford: Betts, 1868; Pulsifer, Janice G. "Alice and Phoebe Cary, Whittier's Sweet Singers of the West." Essex Institute Historical Collections, 109 (1973).

WAS HE HENPECKED?

"I'll tell you what it is, my dear,"
    Said Mrs. Dorking, proudly,
"I do not like that chanticleer
    Who crows o'er us so loudly.

Phoebe Cary

"And since I must his laws obey,
    And have him walk before me,
I'd rather like to have my say
    Of who should lord it o'er me."

"*You'd like to vote?*" he answered slow,
    "Why, treasure of my treasures,
What can you, or what should you know
    Of public men, or measures?

"Of course, you have ability,
    Of nothing am I surer;
You're quite as wise, perhaps, as I;
    You're better, too, and purer.

"I'd have you just for mine alone;
    Nay, so do I adore you,
I'd put you queen upon a throne,
    And bow myself before you."

"*You'd put me! you?* now that is what
    I do not want, precisely;
I want myself to choose the spot
    That I can fill most wisely."

"My dear, you're talking like a goose—
    Unhenly, and improper"—
But here again her words broke loose,
    In vain he tried to stop her:

"I tell you, though she never spoke
    So you could understand her,
A goose knows when she wears a yoke,
    As quickly as a gander."

Phoebe Cary

"Why, bless my soul! what would you do?
    Write out a diagnosis?
Speak equal rights? join with their crew
    And dine with the Sorosis?

"And shall I live to see it, then—
    My wife a public teacher?
And would you be a crowing hen—
    That dreadful unsexed creature?"

"Why, as to that, I do not know;
    Nor see why you should fear it;
If I can crow, why let me crow,
    If I can't, then you won't hear it!"

"Now, why," he said, "can't such as you
    Accept what we assign them?
You have your rights, 't is very true,
    But then, we should define them!

"We would not peck you cruelly,
    We would not buy and sell you;
And you, *in turn,* should think, and be,
    And do, just what we tell you!

"I do not want you made, my dear,
    The subject of rude men's jest;
I like you in your proper sphere,
    The circle of a hen's nest!

"I'd keep you in the chicken-yard,
    Safe, honored, and respected;
From all that makes us rough and hard,
    Your sex should be protected."

"Pray, did it ever make you sick?
    Have I gone to the dickens?
Because you let me scratch and pick
    Both for myself and chickens?"

"Oh, that's a different thing, you know,
    Such duties are parental;
But for some work to do, you'd grow
    Quite weak and sentimental."

"Ah! yes, it's well for you to talk
    About a parent's duty!
Who keeps your chickens from the hawk?
    Who stays in nights, my beauty?"

"But, madam, you may go each hour,
    Lord bless your pretty faces!
We'll give you anything, but power
    And honor, trust and places.

"We'd keep it hidden from your sight
    How public scenes are carried;
Why, men are coarse, and swear, and fight"—
    "I know it, dear; I'm married!"

"Why, now you gabble like a fool;
    But what's the use of talking?:
'T is yours to serve, and mine to rule,
    I tell you, Mrs. Dorking!"

"Oh, yes," she said, "you've all the sense;
    Your sex are very knowing;
Yet some of you are on the fence,
    And only good at crowing."

"Ah! preciousest of precious souls,
　　Your words with sorrow fill me;
To see you voting at the polls
　　I really think would kill me.

"To mourn my home's lost sanctity;
　　To feel you did not love me;
And worse, to see you fly so high,
　　And have you roost above me!"

"Now, what you fear in equal rights
　　I think you've told precisely;
That's just about the 'place it lights,'"[1]
　　Said Mrs. Dorking wisely.

DOROTHY'S DOWER

In Three Parts

PART I

"My sweetest Dorothy," said John,
　　Of course before the wedding,
As metaphorically he stood,
　　His gold upon her shedding,
"Whatever thing you wish or want
　　Shall be hereafter granted,
For all my worldly goods are yours."
　　The fellow was enchanted!

---

1. This expression means, what it comes down to.

Phoebe Cary

"About that little dower you have,
　　You thought might yet come handy,
Throw it away, do what you please,
　　Spend it on sugar-candy!
I like your sweet, dependent ways,
　　I love you when you tease me;
The more you ask, the more you spend,
　　The better you will please me."

PART II

"Confound it, Dorothy!" said John,
　　"I have n't got it by me.
You have n't, have you, spent that sum,
　　The dower from Aunt Jemima?
No; well that's sensible for you;
　　This fix is most unpleasant;
But money's tight, so just take yours
　　And use it for the present.
Now I must go——to——meet a man!
　　By George! I'll have to borrow!
Lend me a twenty——that's all right!
　　I'll pay you back to-morrow."

PART III

"Madam," says John to Dorothy,
　　And past her rudely pushes,
"You think a man is made of gold,
　　And money grows on bushes!
Tom's shoes! your doctor! Can't you now
　　Get up some new disaster?

You and your children are enough
    To break John Jacob Astor.
Where's what you had yourself, when I
    Was fool enough to court you?
That little sum, till you got me,
    'T was what had to support you!"
"It's lent and gone, not very far;
    Pray don't be apprehensive."
"*Lent!* I've had use enough for it:
    My family is expensive.
I did n't, as a woman would,
    Spend it on sugar-candy!"
"No, John, I think the most of it
    Went for cigars and brandy!"

THE OLD MAN'S DARLING

So I'm "crazy," in loving a man of three-score;
Why, I never had come to my senses before,
But I'm doubtful of yours, if you're thinking to prove
My insanity, just by the fact of my love.

You would like to know what are his wonderful wiles?
Only delicate praises, and flattering smiles!
'T is no spell of enchantment, no magical art,
But the way he says "darling," that goes to my heart.

Yes, he's "sixty," I cannot dispute with you there,
But you'd make him a hundred, I think, if you dare;
And I'm glad all his folly of first love is past,
Since I'm sure, of the two, it is best to be last.

"His hair is as white as the snowdrift," you say;
Then I never shall see it change slowly to gray;
But I almost could wish, for his dear sake alone,
That my tresses were nearer the hue of his own.

"He can't see;" then I'll help him to see and to hear,
If it's needful, you know, I can sit very near;
And he's young enough yet to interpret the tone
Of a heart that is beating up close to his own.

I "must aid him;" ah! that is my pleasure and pride,
I should love him for this if for nothing beside;
And though I've more reasons than I can recall,
Yet the one that "he needs me" is strongest of all.

So, if I'm insane, you will own, I am sure,
That the case is so hopeless it's past any cure;
And, besides, it is acting no very wise part,
To be treating the head for disease of the heart.

And if anything could make a woman believe
That no dream can delude, and no fancy deceive;
That she never knew lover's enchantment before,
It's being the darling of one of three-score!"

PEACE

O Land, of every land the best—
    O Land, whose glory shall increase;
Now in your whitest raiment drest
    For the great festival of peace:

Phoebe Cary

Take from your flag its fold of gloom,
  And let it float undimmed above,
Till over all our vales shall bloom
  The sacred colors that we love.

On mountain high, in valley low,
  Set Freedom's living fires to burn;
Until the midnight sky shall show
  A redder pathway than the morn.

Welcome, with shouts of joy and pride,
  Your veterans from the war-path's track;
You gave your boys, untrained, untried;
  You bring them men and heroes back!

And shed no tear, though think you must
  With sorrow of the martyred band;
Not even for him whose hallowed dust
  Has made our prairies holy land.

Though by the places where they fell,
  The places that are sacred ground,
Death, like a sullen sentinel,
  Paces his everlasting round.

Yet when they set their country free
  And gave her traitors fitting doom,
They left their last great enemy,
  Baffled, beside an empty tomb.

Not there, but risen, redeemed, they go
  Where all the paths are sweet with flowers;
They fought to give us peace, and lo!
  They gained a better peace than ours.

Phoebe Cary

THE SPIRITUAL BODY

I have a heavenly home,
  To which my soul may come,
And where forever safe it may abide;
  Firmly and sure it stands,
  That house not made with hands,
And garnished as a chamber for a bride!

'T is such as angels use,
  Such as good men would choose;
It hath all fair and pleasant things in sight:
  Its walls as white and fine
  As polished ivory shine,
And through its windows comes celestial light.

'T is builded fair and good,
  In the similitude
Of the most royal palace of a king;
  And sorrow may not come
  Into that heavenly home,
Nor pain, nor death, nor any evil thing.

Near it that stream doth pass
  Whose waters, clear as glass,
Make glad the city of our God with song;
  Whose banks are fair as those
  Whereon stray milk-white does,
Feeding among the lilies all day long.

And friends who once were here
  Abide in dwellings near;
They went up thither on a heavenly road;
  While I, though warned to go,
  Yet linger here below,
Clinging to a most miserable abode.

The evil blasts drive in
Through chinks, which time and sin
Have battered in my wretched house of clay;
Yet in so vile a place,
Poor, unadorned with grace
I choose to live, or rather choose to stay.

And here I make my moan
About the days now gone,
About the souls passed on to their reward;
The souls that now have come
Into a better home,
And sit in heavenly places with their Lord.

'T is strange that I should cling
To this despisèd thing,
To this poor dwelling crumbling round my head;
Making myself content
In a low tenement
After my joys and friends alike are fled!

Yet I shall not, I know,
Be ready hence to go,
And dwell in my good palace, fair and whole,
Till unrelenting Death
Blows with his icy breath
Upon my naked and unsheltered soul!

DRAWING WATER

He had drunk from founts of pleasure,
And his thirst returned again;
He had hewn out broken cisterns,
And behold! his work was vain.

Phoebe Cary

And he said, "Life is a desert,
    Hot, and measureless, and dry;
And God will not give me water,
    Though I strive, and faint, and die."

Then he heard a voice make answer,
    "Rise and roll the stone away;
Sweet and precious springs lie hidden
    In thy pathway every day."

And he said, his heart was sinful,
    Very sinful was his speech:
"All the cooling wells I thirst for
    Are too deep for me to reach."

But the voice cried, "Hope and labor;
    Doubt and idleness is death;
Shape a clear and goodly vessel,
    With the patient hands of faith."

So he wrought and shaped the vessel,
    Looked, and lo! a well was there;
And he drew up living water,
    With a golden chain of prayer.

JOHN GREENLEAF WHITTIER

Great master of the poet's art!
    Surely the sources of thy powers
Lie in that true and tender heart.
    Whose every utterance touches ours.

Phoebe Cary

For, better than thy words, that glow
  With sunset dyes or noontide heat,
That count the treasures of the snow,
  Or paint the blossoms at our feet,

Are those that teach the sorrowing how
  To lay aside their fear and doubt,
And in submissive love to bow
  To love that passeth finding out.

And thou for such hast come to be
  In every home an honored guest—
Even from the cities by the sea
  To the broad prairies of the West.

Thy lays have cheered the humble home
  Where men who prayed for freedom knelt;
And women, in their anguish dumb,
  Have heard thee utter what they felt.

And thou hast battled for the right
  With many a brave and trenchant word.
And shown us how the pen may fight
  A mightier battle than the sword.

And therefore men in coming years
  Shall chant thy praises loud and long;
And woman name thee through their tears
  A poet greater than his song.

But not thy strains, with courage rife,
  Nor holiest hymns, shall rank above
The rhythmic beauty of thy life,
  Itself a canticle of love!

Phoebe Cary

OUR GOOD PRESIDENT

Our sun hath gone down at the noonday,
    The heavens are black;
And over the morning, the shadows
    Of night-time are back.

Stop the proud boasting mouth of the cannon;
    Hush the mirth and the shout;—
God is God! and the ways of Jehovah
    Are past finding out.

Lo! the beautiful feet on the mountains,
    That yesterday stood,
The white feet that came with glad tidings
    Are dabbled in blood.

The Nation that firmly was settling
    The crown on her head,
Sits like Rizpah,[1] in sackcloth and ashes,
    And watches her dead.

Who is dead? who, unmoved by our wailing,
    Is lying so low?
O my Land, stricken dumb in your anguish,
    Do you feel, do you know,

That the hand which reached out of the darkness
    Hath taken the whole;

---

1. The story of Rizpah is recounted in 2 Sam. 3.7 ff. see especially 2 Sam. 21.10. She was one of Saul's concubines. To appease the Gibeonites whom he had offended, David gave them Rizpah's two sons. They were hanged, but Rizpah sat by their bodies wearing sackcloth for many days until David took pity on her and had them buried in the family tomb.

Phoebe Cary

Yea, the arm and the head of a people,—
    The heart and the soul?

And that heart, o'er whose dread awful silence
    A nation has wept;
Was the truest, and gentlest, and sweetest,
    A man ever kept.

Why, he heard from the dungeons, the rice-fields,
    The dark holds of ships
Every faint, feeble cry which oppression
    Smothered down on men's lips.

In her furnace, the centuries had welded
    Their fetter and chain;
And like withes, in the hands of his purpose,
    He snapped them in twain.

Who can be what he was to the people,—
    What he was to the state?
Shall the ages bring to us another
    As good and as great?

Our hearts with their anguish are broken,
    Our wet eyes are dim;
For us is the loss and the sorrow,
    The triumph for him!

For, ere this, face to face with his Father
    Our martyr hath stood;
Giving into his hand a white record,
    With its great seal of blood!

Phoebe Cary

DO YOU BLAME HER?

Ne'er lover spake in tenderer words,
    While mine were calm, unbroken;
Though I suffered all the pain I gave
    In the No, so firmly spoken.

I marvel what he would think of me,
    Who called it a cruel sentence,
If he knew I had almost learned to day
    What it is to feel repentance.

For it seems like a strange perversity,
    And blind beyond excusing,
To lose the thing we could have kept,
    And after, mourn the losing.

And this, the prize I might have won,
    Was worth a queen's obtaining;
And one, if far beyond my reach,
    I had sighed, perchance, for gaining.

And I know—ah! no one knows so well
    Though my heart is far from breaking—
'T was a loving heart, and an honest hand,
    I might have had for the taking.

And yet, though never one beside
    Has place in my thought above him,
I only like him when he is by,
    'T is when he is gone I love him.

Sadly of absence poets sing,
    And timid lovers fear it;

But an idol has been worshiped less
    Sometimes when we came too near it.

And for him my fancy throws to-day
    A thousand graces o'er him;
For he seems a god when he stands afar
    And I kneel in my thought before him.

But if he were here, and knelt to me
    With a lover's fond persistence,
Would the halo brighten to my eyes
    That crows him now in the distance?

Could I change the words I have said, and say
    Till one of us two shall perish,
Forsaking others, I take this man
    Alone, to love and to cherish?

Alas! whatever beside to-day
    I might dream like a fond romancer,
I know my heart so well that I know
    I should give him the self-same answer.

LUCY LARCOM

(1824–1893)

꧁꧂꧁꧂꧁꧂

LUCY LARCOM received only slight notice in the anthologies compiled by Griswold and Stedman, but her poems, issued in a "Household Edition" in 1884, had broad appeal. Her talent was in many ways similar to that of Alice and Phoebe Cary. She maintained sympathy with the working class and was a skillful writer of monologues.

Lucy grew up in Beverly, Massachusetts, her father a retired shipmaster. In *A New England Girlhood* (1889), Larcom recalls her early childhood there in a rural society about to disappear. Her rather idyllic existence, allowing her freedom to wander and explore, was suddenly disrupted when her father died. Her mother moved her many children to Lowell, where she ran a boardinghouse, and Lucy and her sisters worked in the Lowell Mills.

Considered enlightened in their day, the Lowell Mills employed girls from New England farm families. (See Alice Cary's poem "The West Country.") To supplement the long hours of work, Lowell offered unusual educational activities. Lucy, who worked in various capacities from the time she was eleven, read poetry, learned German, and contributed poems to the twin publications that eventually merged as the well-known *Lowell Offering* in 1842. While at Lowell, Larcom enjoyed her friendships with girls from many backgrounds and was excited by the hustle and bustle of the mill.

In 1846 she moved with her sister's family to Illinois where she attended the Monticello Female Seminary. She then returned to Massachusetts, teaching at Wheaton College from 1854 to 1862. During this period she also published poetry in a variety of literary journals, and in 1868 her first book of poems came out. After 1862 she was the editor of a children's magazine called *Our Young Folks,* which published work by many eminent American writers of both sexes, and in the 1870s she collaborated with Whittier on several projects.

An ardent reader of Wordsworth, Larcom wrote many poems about nature. In 1879 she published *Landscape in American Poetry,* a volume of critical essays. Even *An Idyl of Work* (1875) dedicated "To Working Women by One of Their Sisterhood," seems almost preindustrial compared to Rebecca Harding Davis's *Life in the Iron Mills.* Larcom believed that "any needed industry, thoughtfully pursued, brings the laborer into harmony with the unceasing activities of the universe." She did not despise her mill work which at that time was less arduous than some industrial jobs.

Still, Lucy Larcom did not have an easy life. She was both poor and torn by emotional conflicts. There are really three Lucy Larcoms: the rebellious feminist of the popular "A Loyal Woman's No," the yearning intellectual of "The Rose Enthroned," and the moral naturalist of "November." Though she never fully united her warring spirits, Larcom's religion and strong beliefs in hard work and moral effort gave her life both purpose and meaning.

Selected Works: Poems. 1868; *Wild Roses of Cape Ann, and Other Poems.* 1881; *At the Beautiful Gate, and Other Songs of Faith.* 1892.

Selected Criticism: Addison, Daniel Dulany, ed. *Lucy Larcom: Life, Letters, and Diary.* Boston: Houghton, 1894; Eisler, B. *The Lowell Offering.* New York: Lippincott, 1977; Cott, Nancy. Foreword to *A New England Girlhood.* Boston: Northeastern, 1986; Marchalonis, Shirley. "Profile of Lucy Larcom." *Legacy* 5:1 (1988); Marchalonis, Shirley. *The Worlds of Lucy Larcom.* Athens: U of Georgia P, 1989.

GETTING ALONG

We trudge on together, my good man and I,
Our steps growing slow as the years hasten by;

Lucy Larcom

Our children are healthy, our neighbors are kind,
And with the world round us we've no fault to find.

'T is true that he sometimes will choose the worst way
For sore feet to walk in, a weary hot day;
But then my wise husband can scarcely go wrong,
And, somehow or other, we're getting along.

There are soft summer shadows beneath our home trees:
How handsome he looks, sitting there at his ease!
We watch the flocks coming while sunset grows dim,
His thoughts on the cattle, and mine upon him.

The blackbirds and thrushes come chattering near;
I love the thieves' music, but listen with fear:
He shoots the gay rogues I would pay for their song;—
We're different, sure; still, we're getting along.

He seems not to know what I eat, drink, or wear;
He's trim and he's hearty, so why should I care?
No harsh word from him my poor heart ever shocks:
I would n't mind scolding,—so seldom he talks.

Ah, well! 't is too much that we women expect:
He only has promised to love and protect.
See, I lean on my husband, so silent and strong;
I'm sure there's no trouble;—we're getting along.

Life is n't so bright as it was long ago,
When he visited me amid tempest and snow,
And would bring me a ribbon or jewel to wear,
And sometimes a rosebud to twist in my hair:

But when we are girls, we can all laugh and sing;
Of course, growing old, life's a different thing!

Lucy Larcom

My good man and I have forgot our May song,
But still we are quietly getting along.

It is true I was rich; I had treasures and land;
But all that he asked was my heart and my hand:
Though people do say it, 't is what they can't prove,—
"He married for money; she,—poor thing! for love."

My fortune is his, and he saves me its care;
To make his home cheerful's enough for my share.
He seems always happy our broad fields among;
And so I'm contented:—we're getting along.

With stocks to look after, investments to find,
It's not very strange that I'm seldom in mind:
He can't stop to see how my time's dragging on,—
And oh! *would* he miss me, if I should be gone?

Should he be called first, I must follow him fast,
For all that's worth living for then will be past.
But I'll not think of losing him: fretting is wrong,
While we are so pleasantly getting along.

UNWEDDED

Behold her there in the evening sun,
    That kindles the Indian Summer trees
To a separate burning bush, one by one,
    Wherein the Glory Divine she sees!

Mate and nestlings she never had:
    Kith and kindred have passed away;

Yet the sunset is not more gently glad,
    That follows her shadow, and fain would stay.

For out of her life goes a breath of bliss,
    And a sunlike charm from her cheerful eye,
That the cloud and the loitering breeze would miss;
    A balm that refreshes the passer-by.

"Did she choose it, this single life?"—
    Gossip, she saith not, and who can tell?
But many a mother, and many a wife,
    Draws a lot more lonely, we all know well.

Doubtless she had her romantic dream,
    Like other maidens, in May-time sweet,
That flushes the air with a lingering gleam,
    And goldens the grass beneath her feet:—

A dream unmoulded to visible form,
    That keeps the world rosy with mists of youth,
And holds her in loyalty close and warm,
    To her grand ideal of manly truth.

"But is she happy, a woman, alone?"—
    Gossip, alone in this crowded earth,
With a voice to quiet its hourly moan,
    And a smile to heighten its rarer mirth?

There are ends more worthy than happiness:
    Who seeks it, is digging joy's grave, we know.
The blessed are they who but live to bless;
    She found out that mystery, long ago.

To her motherly, sheltering atmosphere,
    The children hasten from icy homes;

The outcast is welcome to share her cheer;
   And the saint with a fervent benison comes.

For the heart of woman is large as man's;
   God gave her His orphaned world to hold,
And whispered through her His deeper plans
   To save it alive from the outer cold.

And here is a woman who understood
   Herself, her work, and God's will with her,
To gather and scatter His sheaves of good,
   And was meekly thankful, though men demur.

Would she have walked more nobly, think,
   With a man beside her, to point the way,
Hand joining hand in the marriage-link?
   Possibly, Yes: it is likelier, Nay.

For all men have not wisdom and might:
   Love's eyes are tender, and blur the map;
And a wife will follow by faith, not sight,
   In the chosen footprint, at any hap.

Having the whole, she covets no part:
   Hers is the bliss of all blessed things.
The tears that unto her eyelids start,
   Are those which a generous pity brings;

Or the sympathy of heroic faith
   With a holy purpose, achieved or lost.
To stifle the truth is to stop her breath,
   For she rates a lie at its deadly cost.

Her friends are good women and faithful men,
   Who seek for the True, and uphold the Right;

And who shall proclaim her the weaker, when
    Her very presence puts sin to flight?

"And dreads she never the coming years?"—
    Gossip, what are the years to her?
All winds are fair, and the harbor nears,
    And every breeze a delight will stir.

Transfigured under the sunset trees,
    That wreathe her with shadowy gold and red,
She looks away to the purple seas,
    Whereon her shallop will soon be sped.

She reads the hereafter by the here:
    A beautiful Now, and a better To Be:
In life is all sweetness, in death no fear:—
    You waste your pity on such as she.

THE ROSE ENTHRONED

It melts and seethes, the chaos that shall grow
    To adamant beneath the house of life;
In hissing hatred atoms clash, and go
    To meet intenser strife.

And ere that fever leaves the granite veins,
    Down thunders over them a torrid sea:
Now Flood, now Fire, alternate despot reigns,
    Immortal foes to be.

Built by the warring elements they rise,
    The massive earth-foundations, tier on tier,

Lucy Larcom

Where slimy monsters with unhuman eyes
        Their hideous heads uprear.

The building of the world is not for you,
    That glare upon each other, and devour!
Race floating after race fades out of view,
        Til beauty springs from power.

Meanwhile from crumbling rocks and shoals of death
    Shoots up rank verdure to the hidden sun;
The gulfs are eddying to the vague, sweet breath
        Of richer life begun;

Richer and sweeter far than aught before,
    Though rooted in the grave of what has been:
Unnumbered burials yet must heap Earth's floor
        Ere she her heir shall win;

And ever nobler lives and deaths more grand,
    For nourishment of that which is to come;
While mid the ruins of the work she planned,
        Sits Nature, blind and dumb.

For whom or what she plans, she knows no more
    Than any mother of her unborn child:
Yet beautiful forewarnings murmur o'er
        Her desolations wild.

Slowly, the clamor and the clash subside;
    Earth's restlessness her patient hopes subdue;
Mild oceans shoreward heave a pulse-like tide;
        The skies are veined with blue.

And life works through the growing quietness,
    To bring some darling mystery into form:

Beauty her fairest Possible would dress
        In colors pure and warm.

Within the depths of palpitating seas,
    A tender tint, anon a line of grace,
Some lovely thought from its dull atom frees,
        The coming joy to trace:—

A penciled moss on tablets of the sand,
    Such as shall veil the unbudded maiden-blush
Of beauty yet to gladden the green land;—
        A breathing, through the hush,

Of some sealed perfume longing to burst out,
    And give its prisoned rapture to the air;—
A brooding hope, a promise through a doubt,
        Is whispered everywhere.

And, every dawn a shade more clear, the skies
    A flush as from the heart of heaven disclose:
Through earth and sea and air a message flies,
        Prophetic of the Rose.

At last a morning comes, of sunshine still,
    When not a dewdrop trembles on the grass,
When all winds sleep, and every pool and rill
        Is like a burnished glass,

Where a long looked-for guest might lean to gaze;
    When Day on Earth rests royally—a crown
Of molten glory, flashing diamond rays,
        From heaven let lightly down.

In golden silence, breathless, all things stand;
    What answer waits this questioning repose?

Lucy Larcom

A sudden gush of light and odors bland,
    And, lo,—the Rose! the Rose!

The birds break into canticles around;
    The winds lift Jubilate to the skies;
For, twin-born with the rose on Eden-ground,
    Love blooms in human eyes.

Life's marvelous queen-flower blossoms only so,
    In dust of low ideals rooted fast:
Ever the Beautiful is moulded slow
    From truth in errors past.

What fiery fields of Chaos must be won,
    What battling Titans rear themselves a tomb,
What births and resurrections greet the sun
    Before the Rose can bloom!

And of some wonder-blossom yet we dream
    Whereof the time that is enfolds the seed;
Some flower of light, to which the Rose shall seem
    A fair and fragile weed.

A LOYAL WOMAN'S NO

No! is my answer from this cold, bleak ridge,
    Down to your valley: you may rest you there:
The gulf is wide, and none can build a bridge
    That your gross weight would safely hither bear.

Lucy Larcom

Pity me, if you will. I look at you
    With something that is kinder far than scorn,
And think, "Ah, well! I might have grovelled, too;
    I might have walked there, fettered and forsworn."

I am of nature weak as others are;
    I might have chosen comfortable ways;
Once from these heights I shrank, beheld afar,
    In the soft lap of quiet, easy days.

I might,—I will not hide it,—once I might
    Have lost, in the warm whirlpools of your voice,
The sense of Evil, the stern cry of Right;
    But Truth has steered me free, and I rejoice.

Not with the triumph that looks back to jeer
    At the poor herd that call their misery bliss;
But as a mortal speaks when God is near,
    I drop you down my answer: it is this:

I am not yours, because you prize in me
    What is the lowest in my own esteem:
Only my flowery levels can you see,
    Nor of my heaven-smit summits do you dream.

I am not yours, because you love yourself:
    Your heart has scarcely room for me beside.
I will not be shut in with name and pelf;
    I spurn the shelter of your narrow pride!

Not yours,—because you are not man enough
    To grasp your country's measure of a man.
If such as you, when Freedom's ways are rough,
    Cannot walk in them, learn that women can!

Lucy Larcom

Not yours,—because, in this the nation's need,[1]
   You stoop to bend her losses to your gain,
And do not feel the meanness of your deed:
   I touch no palm defiled with such a stain!

Whether man's thought can find too lofty steeps
   For woman's scaling, care not I to know;
But when he falters by her side, or creeps,
   She must not clog her soul with him to go.

Who weds me, must at least with equal pace
   Sometimes move with me at my being's height:
To follow him to his superior place,
   His rarer atmosphere, were keen delight.

You lure me to the valley: men should call
   Up to the mountains, where the air is clear.
Win me and help me climbing, if at all!
   Beyond these peaks great harmonies I hear:—

The morning chant of Liberty and Law!
   The dawn pours in, to wash out Slavery's blot;
Fairer than aught the bright sun ever saw,
   Rises a Nation without stain or spot!

The men and women mated for that time
   Tread not the soothing mosses of the plain;
Their hands are joined in sacrifice sublime;
   Their feet firm set in upward paths of pain.

Sleep your thick sleep, and go your drowsy way!
   You cannot hear the voices in the air!

---

1. The "nation's need" refers to the Civil War.

Lucy Larcom

Ignoble souls will shrivel in that day;
   The brightness of its coming can you bear?

For me, I do not walk these hills alone:
   Heroes who poured their blood out for the truth,
Women whose hearts bled, martyrs all unknown,
   Here catch the sunrise of immortal youth

On their pale cheeks and consecrated brows:—
   It charms me not, your call to rest below.
I press their hands, my lips pronounce their vows:
   Take my life's silence for your answer: No!

WEAVING

All day she stands before her loom;
   The flying shuttles come and go;
By grassy fields, and trees in bloom,
   She sees the winding river flow:
And fancy's shuttle flieth wide,
And faster than the waters glide.

Is she entangled in her dreams.
   Like that fair weaver of Shalott.[1]
Who left her mystic mirror's gleams,
   To gaze on light Sir Lancelot?
Her heart, a mirror sadly true,
Brings gloomier visions into view.

---

1. The fair weaver of Shalott is Elaine, the maid of Shalott, and subject of a long poem by Tennyson, "The Lady of Shalott."

Lucy Larcom

"I weave, and weave, the livelong day:
  The woof is strong, the warp is good:
I weave, to be my mother's stay;
  I weave, to win my daily food:
But ever as I weave," saith she,
  "The world of women haunteth me.

"The river glides along, one thread
  In nature's mesh, so beautiful!
The stars are woven in; the red
  Of sunrise; and the rain-cloud dull.
Each seems a separate wonder wrought;
Each blends with some more wondrous thought.

"So, at the loom of life, we weave
  Our separate shreds, that varying fall,
Some stained, some fair; and, passing, leave
  To God the gathering up of all,
In that full pattern, wherein man
Works blindly out the eternal plan.

"In his vast work, for good, or ill,
  The undone and the done he blends:
With whatsoever woof we fill,
  To our weak hands His might He lends,
And gives the threads beneath His eye
The texture of eternity.

"Wind on, by willow and by pine,
  Thou blue, untroubled Merrimack!
Afar, by sunnier streams than thine,
  My sisters toil, with foreheads black;
And water with their blood this root,
Whereof we gather bounteous fruit.

Lucy Larcom

"I think of women sad and poor;
  Women who walk in garments soiled:
Their shame, their sorrow, I endure;
  By their defect my hope is foiled:
The blot they bear is on my name;
Who sins, and I am not to blame?

"And how much of your wrong is mine,
  Dark women slaving at the South?
Of your stolen grapes I quaff the wine;
  The bread you starve for fills my mouth:
The beam unwinds, but every thread
With blood of strangled souls is red.

"If this be so, we win and wear
  A Nessus-robe[2] of poisoned cloth;
Or weave them shrouds they may not wear,—
  Fathers and brothers falling both
On ghastly, death-sown fields, that lie
Beneath the tearless Southern sky.

"Alas! the weft has lost its white.
  It grows a hideous tapestry,
That pictures war's abhorrent sight:
  Unroll not, web of destiny!
Be the dark volume left unread,
The tale untold, the curse unsaid!"

So up and down before her loom
  She paces on, and to and fro,
Till sunset fills the dusty room,
  And makes the water redly glow,

---

2. In Greek mythology this robe is given to Heracles by his wife after he has betrayed her. The robe envelops him in poisonous fire.

As if the Merrimack's calm flood
Were changed into a stream of blood.

Too soon fulfilled, and all too true
   The words she murmured as she wrought:
But, weary weaver, not to you
   Alone was war's stern message brought:
"Woman!" it knelled from heart to heart,
"Thy sister's keeper know thou art!"

FERN-LIFE

Yes, life! though it seems half a death,
   When the flowers of the glen
Bend over, with color and breath,
   Till we tremble again;

Till we shudder with exquisite pain
   Their beauty to see,
While our dumb hope, through fibre and vein,
   Climbs up to be free.

No blossom—scarce leaf—on the ground,
   Vague fruitage we bear,—
Point upward, reach fingers around,
   In a tender despair.

And we pencil rare patterns of grace
   Men's footsteps about:
A charm in our wilderness-place
   They find us, no doubt.

Yet why must this possible more
    Forever be less?
The unattained flower in the spore
    Hints a human distress.

We fern-folk with grave whispers crowd
    The solemn wood-gloom,
Or weave over clods our green cloud
    Of nebulous bloom.

To fashion our life as a flower,
    In weird curves we reach,—
O man, with your beautiful power
    Of presence and speech!

Yet the heart of the human must grope
    Through its nobler despair;
For it can but look upward, and hope
    All perfection to share.

And to dream of the sweetness we miss
    Is not wholly in vain;
For the soul can be glad in a bliss
    It may never attain.

THE TRUE WITNESS

Dear friend, I heard thee say to me,
    "Christ is a dream:
The fiction of thy heart is He,
    Its self-lit gleam."

In vain I tried to think the thought:
    Life so bereft,
So empty, fancy pictured not;
    Nothing was left;

Scarcely the earth whereon I stood;
    A star grown dim:
Earth, its Creator made so good,
    So full of Him!

For all truth in humanity
    With Him is one;
Through His dear children God I see,
    Father through Son.

Thine own pure life—thought, word, and deed,
    A holy flame—
In lines of light that all may read,
    Writes out His name.

No loving voice, however weak,
    But echoes His;
Dear friend, because I hear thee speak,
    I know He is!

THEY SAID

They said of her, "She never can have felt
    The sorrows that our deeper natures feel:"
They said, "Her placid lips have never spelt
    Hard lessons taught by Pain; her eyes reveal
    No passionate yearning, no perplexed appeal

To other eyes. Life and her heart have dealt
With her but lightly."—When the Pilgrims dwelt
　　First on these shores, lest savage hands should steal
To precious graves with desecrating tread,
　　The burial-field was with the ploughshare crossed,
　　And there the maize her silken tresses tossed.
With thanks those Pilgrims ate their bitter bread,
　　While peaceful harvests hid what they had lost.
　　What if her smiles concealed from you her dead?

NOVEMBER

Who said November's face was grim?
　　Who said her voice was harsh and sad?
I heard her sing in wood-paths dim.
　　I met her on the shore, so glad,
So smiling. I could kiss her feet!
There never was a month so sweet.

October's splendid robes, that hid
　　The beauty of the white-limbed trees,
Have dropped in tatters; yet amid
　　Those perfect forms the gazer sees
A proud wood-monarch here and there,
Garments of wine-dipped crimson wear.

In precious flakes the autumnal gold
　　Is clinging to the forest's fringe:
Yon bare twig to the sun will hold
　　Each separate leaf, to show the tinge
Of glorious rose-light reddening through
Its jewels, beautiful as few.

Lucy Larcom

Where short-lived wild-flowers bloomed and died
    The slanting sunbeams fall across
Vine-broideries, woven from side to side
    Above mosaics of tinted moss.
So does the Eternal Artist's skill
Hide beauty under beauty still.

And if no note of bee or bird
    Through the rapt stillness of the woods
Or the sea's murmurous trance be heard,
    A Presence in these solitudes
Upon the spirit seems to press
The dew of God's dear silences.

And if, out of some inner heaven,
    With soft relenting comes a day
Whereto the heart of June is given,
    All subtle scents and spicery
Through forest crypts and arches steal,
With power unnumbered hurts to heal.

Through yonder rended veil of green,
    That used to shut the sky from me,
New glimpses of vast blue are seen;
    I never guessed that so much sea
Bordered my little plot of ground,
And held me clasped so close around.

This is the month of sunrise skies
    Intense with molten mist and flame;
Out of the purple deeps arise
    Colors no painter yet could name:
Gold-lilies and the cardinal-flower
Were pale against this gorgeous hour.

Still lovelier when athwart the east
   The level beam of sunset falls:
The tints of wild-flowers long deceased
   Glow then upon the horizon walls;
Shades of the rose and violet
Close to their dear world lingering yet.

What idleness, to moan and fret
   For any season fair, gone by!
Life's secret is not guesed at yet;
   Veil under veil its wonders lie.
Through grief and loss made glorious
The soul of past joy lives in us.

More welcome than voluptuous gales
   This keen, crisp air, as conscience clear:
November breathes no flattering tales;
   The plain truth-teller of the year,
Who wins her heart, and he alone,
Knows she has sweetness all her own.

R. W. E.

May 25, 1880

Doors hast thou opened for us, thinker, seer!
   Bars let down into pastures measureless;
The air we breathe to-day, through thee, is freer
   Than, buoyant with its freshness, we can guess.

The initials of the title are those of Ralph Waldo Emerson (25 May 1803 – 27 Apr. 1882).

Lucy Larcom

Thy forehead toward the unrisen morning set,
    Nature and life faced with their own calm gaze,
No human thought inhospitably met,
    Thou beckonest onward, as in earlier days:

A voice that wandered towards us, like a breeze,
    From great expanses beyond time and space,
With hints of unexplored eternities
    Stirring the sluggish soul new paths to trace;

A word that gave us lightness, as of wings;
    Home, welcome, freedom in the Everywhere!
The mention of thy name, like Nature's, brings
    A sense of widening worlds and ampler air.

FRANCES HARPER

(1825–1911)

THOUGH MATERIAL about her life is scanty, Frances Harper has long been recognized as an important figure in African-American cultural history. Her novel *Iola Leroy; or, Shadows Uplifted* (1892) has been the focus of much recent critical attention, and her reputation as a poet, earlier in decline, is now also on the rise, inspiring several new studies.

Frances Ellen Watkins was born to free parents but orphaned at an early age and raised by an uncle, whose Baltimore school for free blacks Frances attended until, at fourteen, she went to work in the home of a white bookseller. Her early writings have not survived but apparently they drew her to the attention of influential abolitionists with whom her aunt and uncle worked in the antislavery movement. Though Frances earned money at a variety of jobs including sewing, taking care of children, and teaching, she soon gave these up to become one of the most successful lyceum lecturers on the American circuit. According to William Still, she even lectured in the South, always addressing subjects related to the improvement of life for black people. Her oratorical style was both dignified and dramatic; sometimes she lectured every night of the week. *Forest Leaves,* her first book (c. 1845), went relatively unnoticed; on the other hand, her second offering— *Poems on Miscellaneous Subjects* (1854)—proved an extremely popular work, selling as many as 10,000 copies in a single year and 50,000 copies in two decades.

Frances married M. Fenton Harper in 1860, but very little is known of the marriage, except that she became the mother of a daughter, Mary, who died at an early age. Still states that, once married, Frances felt the need to retire from public life. Her husband died four years later, however, and Harper returned to her career as a writer and lecturer, advocating racial uplift, temperance, and support for women's issues. In 1896 she was active in founding the National Association of Colored Women.

Harper's poetry is ardent and incantatory. Early on she addressed issues of race when other black women poets like Mary Tucker Lambert were hesitant to undertake them. Such poems as "Vashti" and "Bury Me in a Free Land" have become classics and have spawned many imitations. At a recent meeting of the Modern Language Association, many contemporary black women spoke of the importance of Frances Harper's poetry to their own work and to black cultural pride. In addition to the more conventional lyrics included here, Frances Harper wrote several persona poems in the voice of a woman named Chloe. *Moses,* a long biblical allegory in blank verse, was her most ambitious project.

Selected Works: Moses: A Story of the Nile. 1869; *Sketches of Southern Life.* 1872; *The Martyr of Alabama and Other Poems.* 1894.

Selected Criticism: Ammons, Elizabeth. "Profile of Frances Harper." *Legacy* 2:2 (1985); Brown, Hallie Q. *Homespun Heroines and Other Women of Distinction.* 1926—rpt. Arno 1971; Giddings, Paula. *When and Where I Enter.* New York: Bantam, 1984; Graham, Maryemma. Intro. to *Complete Poems of Frances Ellen Watkins Harper.* New York: Oxford UP, 1988; Robinson, W. H. *Early Black American Poets.* Dubuque, IA: Brown, 1969; Sherman; Stetson, Erlene. *Black Sister.* Bloomington: Indiana UP, 1981; Sterling, Dorothy, ed. *We Are Your Sisters.* New York: Norton, 1984; Still, William. *The Underground Rail Road.* Philadelphia: Porter and Coates. 1872—rpt. Arno, 1968.

DELIVERANCE

Rise up! rise up! Oh Israel,
    Let a spotless lamb be slain;
The angel of death will o'er you bend
    And rend your galling chain.

Sprinkle its blood upon the posts
    And lintels of your door;
When the angel sees the crimson spots
    Unharmed he will pass you o'er.

Gather your flocks and herds to-night,
    Your children by your side;
A leader from Arabia comes
    To be your friend and your guide.

With girded loins and sandled feet
    Await the hour of dread,
When Mizraim[1] shall wildly mourn
    Her first-born and her dead.

The sons of Abraham no more
    Shall crouch 'neath Pharaoh's hand,
Trembling with agony and dread.
    He'll thrust you from the land.

And ye shall hold in unborn years
    A feast to mark this day,
When joyfully the fathers rose
    And cast their chains away.

When crimson tints of morning flush
    The golden gates of day,
Or gorgeous hue of even melt
    In sombre shades away,

---

1. Egypt is given this name in Gen. 10. The story of Exodus was often used to give courage to the slaves, foretelling their own deliverance. Harper metaphorically superimposes the two instances of a need for liberation.

Then ye shall to your children teach
  The meaning of this feast,
How from the proud oppressor's hand
  Their fathers were released.

And ye shall hold through distant years
  This feast with glad accord,
And children's children yet shall learn
  To love and trust the Lord.

Ages have passed since Israel trod
  In triumph through the sea,
And yet they hold in memory's urn
  Their first great jubilee.

THE REVEL

"He knoweth not that the dead are there."

In yonder halls reclining
  Are forms surpassing fair,
And brilliant lights are shining,
  But, oh! the dead are there!

There's music, song and dance,
  There's banishment of care,
And mirth in every glance,
  But, oh! the dead are there!

Frances Harper

The wine cup's sparkling glow
    Blends with the viands rare,
There's revelry and show,
    But still, the dead are there!

'Neath that flow of song and mirth
    Runs the current of despair,
But the simple sons of earth
    Know not the dead are there!

They'll shudder start and tremble,
    They'll weep in wild despair
When the solemn truth breaks on them,
    That the dead, the dead are there!

THE RAGGED STOCKING

Do you see this ragged stocking,
    Here a rent and there a hole?
Each thread of this little stocking
    Is woven around my soul.

Do you wish to hear my story?
    Excuse me, the tears will start,
For the sight of this ragged stocking
    Stirs the fountains of my heart.

You say that my home is happy;
    To me 'tis earth's fairest place,
But its sunshine, peace and gladness
    Back to this stocking I trace.

Frances Harper

I was once a wretched drunkard;
    Ah! you start and say not so;
But the dreadful depths I've sounded,
    And I speak of what I know.

I was wild and very reckless
    When I stood on manhood's brink,
And joining with pleasure-seekers
    Learned to revel and drink.

Strong drink is a raging demon,
    In his hands are shame and woe,
He mocketh the strength of the mighty
    And bringeth the strong man low.

The light of my home was darkened
    By the shadow of my sin;
And want and woe unbarr'd the door,
    And suffering entered in.

The streets were full one Christmas eve,
    And alive with girls and boys,
Merrily looking through window-panes
    At bright and beautiful toys.

And throngs of parents came to buy
    The gifts that children prize,
And homeward trudged with happy hearts,
    The love-light in their eyes.

I thought of my little Charley
    At home in his lowly bed,
With the shadows around his life,
    And in shame I bowed my head.

Frances Harper

I entered my home a sober man,
　My heart by remorse was wrung,
And there in the chimney corner,
　This little stocking was hung.

Faded and worn as you see it;
　To me 'tis a precious thing,
And I never gaze upon it
　But unbidden tears will spring.

I began to search my pockets,
　But scarcely a dime was there;
But scanty as was the pittance,
　This stocking received its share.

For a longing seized upon me
　To gladden the heart of my boy,
And I brought him some cakes and candy,
　And added a simple toy.

Then I knelt by this little stocking
　And sobbed out an earnest prayer,
And arose with strength to wrestle
　And break from the tempter's snare.

And this faded, worn-out stocking,
　So pitiful once to see,
Became the wedge that broke my chain.
　And a blessing brought to me.

Do you marvel then I prize it?
　When each darn and seam and hole
Is linked with my soul's deliverance
　From the bondage of the bowl?

And to-night my wife will tell you,
   Though I've houses, gold and land,
He holds no treasure more precious
   Than this stocking in my hand.

LET THE LIGHT ENTER!

The Dying Words of Goethe

"Light! more light! the shadows deepen,
   And my life is ebbing low,
Throw the windows widely open;
   Light! more light! before I go.

"Softly let the balmy sunshine
   Play around my dying bed,
O'er the dimly lighted valley
   I with lonely feet must tread.

"Light! more light! for Death is weaving
   Shadows 'round my waning sight,
And I fain would gaze upon him
   Through a stream of earthly light."

Not for greater gifts of genius;
   Not for thoughts more grandly bright.
All the dying poet whispers
   Is a prayer for light, more light.

Heeds he not the gathered laurels,
   Fading slowly from his sight;

Frances Harper

All the poet's aspirations
        Centre in that prayer for light.

Gracious Saviour, when life's day-dreams
        Melt and vanish from the sight,
May our dim and longing vision
        Then be blessed with light, more light.

BURY ME IN A FREE LAND

Make me a grave where'er you will,
In a lowly plain, or a lofty hill,
Make it among earth's humblest graves,
But not in a land where men are slaves.

I could not rest if around my grave
I heard the steps of a trembling slave:
His shadows above my silent tomb
Would make it a place of fearful gloom.

I could not rest if I heard the tread
Of a coffle gang to the shambles led,
And the mother's shriek of wild despair
Rise like a curse on the trembling air.

I could not sleep if I saw the lash
Drinking her blood at each fearful gash,
And I saw her babes torn from her breast,
Like trembling doves from their parent nest.

I'd shudder and start if I heard the bay
Of blood-hounds seizing their human prey.

Frances Harper

And I heard the captive plead in vain
As they bound afresh his galling chain.

If I saw young girls from their mother's arms
Bartered and sold for their youthful charms,
My eye would flash with a mournful flame,
My death-paled cheek grow red with shame.

I would sleep, dear friends, where bloated might
Can rob no man of his dearest right;
My rest shall be calm in any grave
Where none can call his brother a slave.

I ask no monument, proud and high
To arrest the gaze of the passers-by;
All that my yearning spirit craves,
Is bury me not in a land of slaves.

VASHTI

She leaned her head upon her hand
    And heard the King's decree—
"My lords are feasting in my halls;
    Bid Vashti come to me.

"I've shown the treasures of my house,
    My costly jewels rare,
But with the glory of her eyes
    No rubies can compare.

Vashti was an Old Testament queen, wife of King Ahasuerus. When she refused
to be displayed to the king's men, he divorced her (Esth. 1.10–19).

"Adorn'd and crown'd I'd have her come,
  With all her queenly grace,
And, 'mid my lords and mighty men,
  Unveil her lovely face.

"Each gem that sparkles in my crown,
  Or glitters on my throne,
Grows poor and pale when she appears,
  My beautiful, my own!"

All waiting stood the chamberlains
  To hear the Queen's reply.
They saw her cheek grow deathly pale,
  But light flash'd to her eye:

"Go, tell the King," she proudly said,
  "That I am Persia's Queen,
And by his crowds of merry men
  I never will be seen.

"I'll take the crown from off my head
  And tread it 'neath my feet,
Before their rude and careless gaze
  My shrinking eyes shall meet.

"A queen unveil'd before the crowd!—
  Upon each lip my name!—
Why, Persia's women all would blush
  And weep for Vashti's shame!

"Go back!" she cried, and waved her hand,
  And grief was in her eye:
"Go, tell the King," she sadly said,
  "That I would rather die."

Frances Harper

They brought her message to the King;
    Dark flash'd his angry eye;
'Twas as the lightning ere the storm
    Hath swept in fury by.

Then bitterly outspoke the King,
    Through purple lips of wrath—
"What shall be done to her who dares
    To cross your monarch's path?"

Then spoke his wily counsellors—
    "O King of this fair land!
From distant Ind to Ethiop,
    All bow to thy command.

"But if, before thy servant's eyes,
    This thing they plainly see,
That Vashti doth not heed thy will
    Nor yield herself to thee,

"The women, restive 'neath our rule,
    Would learn to scorn our name,
And from her deed to us would come
    Reproach and burning shame.

"Then, gracious King, sign with thy hand
    This stern but just decree,
That Vashti lay aside her crown,
    Thy Queen no more to be."

She heard again the King's command,
    And left her high estate;
Strong in her earnest womanhood,
    She calmly met her fate.

And left the palace of the King,
    Proud of her spotless name—
A woman who could bend to grief,
    But would not bow to shame.

PRESIDENT LINCOLN'S PROCLAMATION OF FREEDOM

It shall flash through the coming ages;
    It shall light the distant years;
And eyes now dim with sorrow
    Shall be clearer through their tears.

It shall flush the mountain ranges;
    And the valleys shall grow bright;
It shall bathe the hills in radiance,
    And crown their brows with light.

It shall flood with golden splendor
    And the huts of Caroline,
And the sun-kissed brow of labor
    With lustre new shall shine.

It shall gild the gloomy prison,
    Darken'd by the nation's crime,
Where the dumb and patient millions
    Wait the better coming time.

By the light that gilds their prison,
    They shall seize its mould'ring key,
And the bolts and bars shall vibrate
    With the triumphs of the free.

Like the dim and ancient chaos,
    Shrinking from the dawn of light,
Oppression, grim and hoary,
    Shall cower at the sight.

And her spawn of lies and malice
    Shall grovel in the dust,
While joy shall thrill the bosoms
    Of the merciful and just.

Though the morning seemed to linger
    O'er the hill-tops far away,
Now the shadows bear the promise
    Of the quickly coming day.

Soon the mists and murky shadows
    Shall be fringed with crimson light,
And the glorious dawn of freedom
    Break refulgent on the sight.

THE ARTIST

He stood before his finished work;
    His heart beat warm and high;
But they who gazed upon the youth
    Knew well that he must die.

For many days a fever fierce
    Had burned into his life;
But full of high impassioned art,
    He bore the fearful strife.

And wrought in extacy and hope
    The image of his brain;
He felt the death throes at his heart,
    But labored through the pain.

The statue seemed to glow with life—
    A costly work of art;
For it he paid the fervent blood
    From his own eager heart.

With kindling eye and flushing cheek
    But slowly laboring breath,
He gazed upon his finished work,
    Then sought his couch of death.

And when the plaudits of the crowd
    Came like the south wind's breath.
The dreamy, gifted child of art
    Had closed his eyes in death.

AUNT CHLOE'S POLITICS

Of course, I don't know very much
    About these politics,
But I think that some who run 'em,
    Do mighty ugly tricks.

I've seen 'em honey-fugle round,
    And talk so awful sweet,
That you'd think them full of kindness
    As an egg is full of meat.

Frances Harper

Now I don't believe in looking
    Honest people in the face,
And saying when you're doing wrong,
    That 'I haven't sold my race.'

When we want to school our children,
    If the money isn't there,
Whether black or white have took it,
    The loss we all must share.

And this buying up each other
    Is something worse than mean,
Though I thinks a heap of voting,
    I go for voting clean.

A DOUBLE STANDARD

Do you blame me that I loved him?
    If when standing all alone
I cried for bread a careless world
    Pressed to my lips a stone.

Do you blame me that I loved him.
    That my heart beat glad and free,
When he told me in the sweetest tones
    He loved but only me?

Can you blame me that I did not see
    Beneath his burning kiss
The serpent's wiles, nor even hear
    The deadly adder hiss?

Frances Harper

Can you blame me that my heart grew cold
   That the tempted, tempter turned;
When he was feted and caressed
   And I was coldly spurned?

Would you blame him, when you draw from me
   Your dainty robes aside.
If he with gilded baits should claim
   Your fairest as his bride?

Would you blame the world if it should press
   On him a civic crown;
And see me struggling in the depth
   Then harshly press me down?

Crime has no sex and yet to-day
   I wear the brand of shame;
Whilst he amid the gay and proud
   Still bears an honored name.

Can you blame me if I've learned to think
   Your hate of vice a sham,
When you so coldly crushed me down
   And then excused the man?

Would you blame me if to-morrow
   The coroner should say,
A wretched girl, outcast, forlorn,
   Has thrown her life away?

Yes, blame me for my downward course,
   But oh! remember well,
Within your homes you press the hand
   That led me down to hell.

Frances Harper

AN APPEAL TO MY COUNTRY WOMEN

You can sigh o'er the sad-eyed Armenian
    Who weeps in her desolate home.
You can mourn o'er the exile of Russia
    From kindred and friends doomed to roam.

You can pity the men who have woven
    From passion and appetite chains
To coil with a terrible tension
    Around their heartstrings and brains.

You can sorrow o'er little children
    Disinherited from their birth,
The wee waifs and toddlers neglected,
    Robbed of sunshine, music and mirth.

For beasts you have gentle compassion;
    Your mercy and pity they share.
For the wretched, outcast and fallen
    You have tenderness, love and care.

But hark! from our Southland are floating
    Sobs of anguish, murmurs of pain,
And women heart-stricken are weeping
    Over their tortured and their slain.

On their brows the sun has left traces;
    Shrink not from their sorrows in scorn.
When they entered the threshold of being
    The children of a King were born.

Frances Harper

Each comes as a guest to the table
    The hands of our God has outspread,
To fountains that ever leap upward,
    To share in the soil we all tread.

When we plead for the wrecked and fallen,
    The exile from far-distant shores,
Remember that men are still wasting
    Life's crimson around our own doors.

Have ye not, oh, my favored sisters,
    Just a plea, a prayer, or a tear,
For mothers who dwell 'neath the shadows
    Of agony, hatred and fear?

Men may tread down the poor and lowly,
    May crush them in anger and hate,
But surely the mills of God's justice
    Will grind out the grist of their fate.

Oh, people sin-laden and guilty,
    So lusty and proud in your prime,
The sharp sickles of God's retribution
    Will gather your harvest of crime.

Weep not, oh my well-sheltered sisters,
    Weep not for the Negro alone,
But weep for your sons who must gather
    The crops which their fathers have sown.

Go read on the tombstones of nations
    Of chieftains who masterful trod,
The sentence which time has engraven,
    That they had forgotten their God.

Frances Harper

'Tis the judgment of God that men reap
  The tares which in madness they sow,
Sorrow follows the footsteps of crime,
  And Sin is the consort of Woe.

ROSE TERRY COOKE

(1827–1892)

ROSE TERRY COOKE has been admired mainly as the writer of local color short stories about New England. Often compared to Sarah Orne Jewett and Mary E. Wilkins Freeman, she has usually been denigrated as a poet. Among her conventional verses, however, are many poems that stand out as strikingly different from those written by other women of her time. "Fantasia," for instance, is a haunting and troubling lyric that toys—as do many of her poems—with the sensuality of violence.

Rose Terry grew up in the Hartford area in a privileged family, the daughter of parents who both came from old, well-established Puritan stock. She was a sickly child, but her father doted on her and spent long hours with her out of doors. Her mother insisted that she memorize a page of the dictionary every day and keep a daily record. Rose responded to this early training by becoming literary, writing poems and plays from childhood onward. She was also well educated, graduating from the Hartford Female Seminary at the age of sixteen, after which she began several years of teaching.

That same year (1843) she joined the Congregational Church, and for the rest of her life her devotion to and pungent criticism of Puritanism were essential ingredients of her poems and stories. Cooke records a struggle with doubt in "The Iconoclast," suggesting that she, like Alice Cary, was not immune to the depredations of spiritual despair.

In 1848 an inheritance from a great uncle gave her the freedom to quit teaching and devote herself to writing. The 1850s were a time of significant literary production of both short stories and the poems that she published first in magazines and then in book form in 1861. Throughout the 1860s, however, Rose Terry was ill and unhappy, spending much time with her sister's family in the frustrating role of the old-maid aunt.

In 1873, at the age of forty-six, she married Rollin Cooke, a widower with two children sixteen years younger than she was. The rest of her life was a struggle with financial difficulties brought on by her husband's inability to turn a profit in business. Cooke found herself pressured by the need to sell her literary productions. Her stories were the most profitable and some of the best, including "How Celia Changed Her Mind" and "Freedom Wheeler's Controversy with Providence," were published in book form.

Though her prose is realistic, Cooke was unquestionably a powerful Romantic poet. "Blue-Beard's Closet" and her tribute to John Brown are two vivid examples. Cooke's sensuality and her various challenges to bourgeois cultural codes demonstrate her originality; her best work is often startling to contemplate in the context of poems by her contemporaries.

Selected Works: Poems. 1861; *Somebody's Neighbours.* 1881; *The Deacon's Week, and What Deacon Baxter Said.* 1887; *Poems.* 1888; *Huckleberries Gathered from New England Hills.* 1891; *Matred and Tamar, A Drama,* in *Resources for American Literary Study* 14:1–2 (1984); "The Memorial of A. B., or Matilda Muffin" (excerpt) in *Legacy* 2:2 (1985); *How Celia Changed Her Mind and Selected Stories,* ed. Elizabeth Ammons. New Brunswick: Rutgers UP, 1986.

Selected Criticism: Ammons, Elizabeth. Intro. to *How Celia Changed Her Mind;* Brooks, Van Wyck. *New England: Indian Summer.* New York: Dutton, 1940; Downey, Jean. "A Biographical and Critical Study of Rose Terry Cooke." Diss. U of Ottawa, 1956; Spofford, Harriet. *A Little Book of Friends.* Boston: Little, 1916; Toth, Susan Allen. "Rose Terry Cooke." *American Literary Realism* 42 (Spring 1971): 170–76; Westbrook, Perry. *Acres of Flint.* Metuchen, NJ: Scarecrow, 1951—rev. ed. 1981.

Rose Terry Cooke

A STORY

In a gleam of sunshine a gentian stood,
    Dreaming her life away,
While the leaves danced merrily through the wood,
    And rode on the wind for play.

She stood in the light and looked at the sky,
    Till her leaves were as fair a blue;
But she shut her heart from the butterfly
    And the coaxing drops of dew.

Dreaming and sunning that autumn noon,
    She stayed the idlest bee
That ever lingered to hear the tune
    Of the wind in a rustling tree.

He had a golden cuirass on,
    And a surcoat black as night,
And he wandered ever from shade to sun,
    Seeking his own delight.

Now were the blossoms of Summer fled,
    And the bumble-bee felt the frost;
He knew that the asters all lay dead,
    And the honey-vine cups were lost.

So he poised and fluttered above the flower,
    And tried his tenderest arts,
With whispers and kisses, a weary hour,
    Till he opened its heart of hearts.

Not for love of the gentian blue,
    But for his own wild will;

All he wanted was honey-dew,
   And there he drank his fill.

No more dreaming in sun or shade!
   It never could close again!
The gentian withered, alone, dismayed;
   The bee flew over the plain.

"NON FIT"

The poet's thoughts are full of might,
Elate with glory and delight;
New tints are in his heavens spread;
On odors keen his sense is fed,
And strains accordant angels sing;
Through all his sleep their echoes ring.

The poet has a lonely soul;
He hears the seas in thunder roll,
Perceives the rapture of the rose,
And every tone of Nature knows;
But cannot speak the tongue of men,
Or give their greetings back again.

His eyes alight with love intense,
His face all calm with innocence;
The green leaves kiss his waving hair,

The Latin title can be translated as either "it isn't done" or "it doesn't happen." Here it seems to stand simply as a negation. The poet refuses to follow the path of convention.

The wild-birds sing him carols rare,
Intent to celebrate and bless;
His Eden fills the wilderness.

But all his songs are minor-keyed;
His prayers are less to praise than plead,
His smiles are full of grief asleep,
His heart like ocean's bitter deep;
For tears and laughter, hand in hand,
About his vibrant nature stand.

At this the world admiring gaze,
And think they feed his soul with praise;
But whisper in a loud aside,
"Is this your poet's vaunted pride?
Why, better be the common clay
Than thus 'twixt heaven and hell astray."

But he, respiring sudden fire,
Hears and replies in righteous ire,
"Better to sound the depths of hell,
If thence to heaven our praises swell;
Nobler than life, or love, to die
Transfixed with immortality!"

FANTASIA

When I am a sea-flower
Under the cool green tide,
Where the sunshine slants and quivers,
And the quaint, gray fishes glide,
I'll shut and sleep at noonday,

At night on the waves I'll ride,
And see the surf in moonshine
Rush on the black rocks' side.

When I am a sea-bird,
Under the clouds I'll fly,
And 'light on a rocking billow
Tossing low and high.
Safe from the lee-shore's thunder,
Mocking the mariner's cry,
Drifting away on the tempest,
A speck on the sullen sky!

When I am a sea-wind,
I'll watch for a ship I know,
Through the sails and rigging
Merrily I will blow.
The crew shall be like dead men
White with horror and woe;
Then I'll sing like a spirit,
And let the good ship go.

MONOTROPA

Loves serene, uncarnate Graces!
Born of pure dreams in lonely places,
Where the black untrodden earth
Rejects the dancing sunshine's mirth,

The Greek word of the title means living alone or solitary. The monotropa is a forest flower also known as Indian pipe.

And slow leaves, dropping through the wood,
Stir to sound the solitude.
Through what tranquil, odorous airs,
Undisturbed by sighs or prayers,
Paler than pale alabaster
Wrought to life by some old master,
Did ye into vision rise,
And nocturnal moths surprise?

Clustered in undraperied whiteness,
Pierced by stars to lucent brightness,
Cooler than a baby's lips,
Pure as dew that nightly drips,
Utterly intact and calm,
Cold to summer's rapturous balm,
So divine that in ye lingers
A shuddering dread of mortal fingers,
Though their tips be pink and fine,
Under the caress ye pine,
Blackened with the passion-fever
That your cool bells shun forever.

Sweetest souls of beauty-lovers,
Above your cups the gold bee hovers,
In sequestered maze and awe,
Repelled by instinct's sacred law;
Knowing well no sweetness lies
In your frosted chalices.
Never bird, nor bee, nor moth,
Inebriate with sunny sloth,
Dare intrude on hallowed ground,
Cease thyself, vain rhythmic sound!

Rose Terry Cooke

LA COQUETTE

You look at me with tender eyes,
That, had you worn a month ago,
Had slain me with divine surprise:—
But now I do not see them glow.

I laugh to hear your laughter take
A softer thrill, a doubtful tone,—
I know you do it for my sake.
You rob the nest whose bird is flown.

Not twice a fool, if twice a child!
I know you now, and care no more
For any lie you may have smiled,
Than that starved beggar at your door.

He has the remnants of your feast;
You offer me your wasted heart!
He may enact the welcome guest;
I shake the dust off and depart.

If you had known a woman's grace
And pitied me who died for you,
I could not look you in the face,
When now you tell me you are "true."

True!—If the fallen seraphs wear
A lovelier face of false surprise
Than you at my unmoving air,
There is no truth this side the skies.

But this *is* true, that once I loved.—
You scorned and laughed to see me die;

Rose Terry Cooke

And now you think the heart so proved
Beneath your feet again shall lie!

I had the pain when you had power;
Now mine the power, who reaps the pain?
You sowed the wind in that black hour;
Receive the whirlwind for your gain!

SEMELE

"For there bee none of those pagan fables in whiche there lyeth not a more subtle
  meanynge than the extern expression thereof should att once signifye."—
Marriages of ye Deade.

Spirit of light divine!
  Quick breath of power,
Breathe on these lips of mine,
  Persuade the bud to flower;
Cleave thy dull swathe of cloud! no longer waits the hour.

Exulting, rapturous flame,
  Dispel the night!
I dare not breathe thy name,
  I tremble at thy light,
Yet come! in fatal strength,—come, in all matchless might.

Burn, as the leaping fire
  A martyr's shroud;

In Greek mythology Semele is the mother of Dionysus. Zeus, the father, ap-
peared to Semele during her pregnancy, but his appearance as lightning immo-
lated her. The child was saved in Zeus's thigh.

Burn, like an Indian pyre,
   With music fierce and loud.
Come Power! Love calls thee,—come, with all the god endowed!

Immortal life in death,
   On these rapt eyes,
On this quick, failing breath,
   In dread and glory rise.
The altar waits thy torch,—come, touch the sacrifice!

Come! not with gifts of life,
   Not for my good;
My soul hath kept her strife
   In fear and solitude;
More blest the inverted torch,[1] the horror-curdled blood.

Better in light to die
   Than silent live;
Rend from these lips one cry,
   One death-born utterance give,
Then, clay, in fire depart! then, soul, in heaven survive!

BLUE-BEARD'S CLOSET

Fasten the chamber!
Hide the red key;
Cover the portal,
That eyes may not see.
Get thee to market,

---

1. The inverted torch is a signal in Classical iconography of a doomed marriage. Edith Thomas used this image for a book title.

To wedding and prayer;
Labor or revel,
The chamber is there!

In comes a stranger—
"Thy pictures how fine,
Titian or Guido,
Whose is the sign?"
Looks he behind them?
Ah! have a care!
"Here is a finer."
The chamber is there!

Fair spreads the banquet,
Rich the array;
See the bright torches
Mimicking day;
When harp and viol
Thrill the soft air,
Comes a light whisper:
The chamber is there!

Marble and painting,
Jasper and gold,
Purple from Tyrus,
Fold upon fold,
Blossoms and jewels,
Thy palace prepare:
Pale grows the monarch;
The chamber is there!

Once it was open
As shore to the sea;
White were the turrets,
Goodly to see;
All through the casements

Flowed the sweet air;
Now it is darkness;
The chamber is there!

Silence and horror
Brood on the walls;
Through every crevice
A little voice calls:
"Quicken, mad footsteps,
On pavement and stair;
Look not behind thee,
The chamber is there!"

Out of the gateway,
Through the wide world,
Into the tempest
Beaten and hurled,
Vain is thy wandering,
Sure thy despair,
Flying or staying,
The chamber is there!

SAMSON AGONISTES

December 2, 1859

You bound and made your sport of him, Philistia![1]
You set your sons at him to flout and jeer;

John Brown was hanged for the raid on Harper's Ferry on 2 December 1859. Samson, a figure of strength in the Bible, is chained between two pillars by the Philistines. Judges 16.25–30 recounts that he leans against the restraints until he brings the entire house down. Cooke alludes here also to Milton's tragedy *Samson Agonistes*. Agon means struggle.

1. Philistia is the country of the Philistines in which the blinded Samson is held

You loaded down his limbs with heavy fetters;
	Your mildest mercy was a smiling sneer.

One man amidst a thousand who defied him—
	One man from whom his awful strength had fled,—
You brought him out to lash him with your vengeance,
	Ten thousand curses on one hoary head!

You think his eyes are closed and blind forever,
	Because you seared them to this mortal day;
You draw a longer breath of exultation,
	Because your conqueror's power has passed away.

Oh, fools! his arms are round your temple-pillars;
	Oh, blind! his strength divine begins to wake;—
Hark! the great roof-tree trembles from its centre,
	Hark! how the rafters bend and swerve and shake!

THE ICONOCLAST

A thousand years shall come and go,
	A thousand years of night and day,
And man, through all their changing show,
	His tragic drama still shall play.

Ruled by some fond ideal's power,
	Cheated by passion or despair,
Still shall he waste life's trembling hour,
	In worship vain, and useless prayer.

---

captive. America, Cooke suggests, might also be seen here as a world of "philis-
tines," or unenlightened individuals.

Ah! where are they who rose in might,
    Who fired the temple and the shrine,
And hurled, through earth's chaotic night,
    The helpless gods it deemed divine?

Cease, longing soul, thy vain desire!
    What idol, in its stainless prime,
But falls, untouched of axe or fire,
    Before the steady eyes of Time.

He looks, and lo! our altars fall,
    The shrine reveals its gilded clay,
With decent hands we spread the pall,
    And, cold with wisdom, glide away.

Oh! where were courage, faith, and truth,
    If man went wandering all his day
In golden clouds of love and youth,
    Nor knew that both his steps betray?

Come, Time, while here we sit and wait,
    Be faithful, spoiler, to thy trust!
No death can further desolate
    The soul that knows its god was dust.

CAPTIVE

The Summer comes, the Summer dies,
    Red leaves whirl idly from the tree,
But no more cleaving of the skies,
    No southward sunshine waits for me!

You shut me in a gilded cage,
  You deck the bars with tropic flowers,
Nor know that freedom's living rage
  Defies you through the listless hours.

What passion fierce, what service true,
  Could ever such a wrong requite?
What gift, or clasp, or kiss from you
  Were worth an hour of soaring flight?

I beat my wings against the wire,
  I pant my trammelled heart away;
The fever of one mad desire
  Burns and consumes me all the day.

What care I for your tedious love,
  For tender word or fond caress?
I die for one free flight above,
  One rapture of the wilderness!

AFTER THE CAMANCHES

Saddle, saddle, saddle!
  Mount and gallop away!
Over the dim green prairie,
  Straight on the track of day.
Spare not spur for mercy,
  Hurry with shout and thong,
Fiery and tough is the mustang,
  The prairie is wide and long.

272

Saddle, saddle, saddle!
  Leap from the broken door
Where the brute Camanche entered
  And the white-foot treads no more.
The hut is burned to ashes,
  There are dead men stark outside,
But only a long dark ringlet
  Left of the stolen bride.

Go, like the east-wind's howling!
  Ride with death behind.
Stay not for food or slumber,
  Till the thieving wolves ye find!
They came before the wedding,
  Swifter than prayer or priest;
The bridemen danced to bullets,
  The wild dogs ate the feast.

Look to rifle and powder!
  Fasten the knife-belt sure;
Loose the coil of the lasso,
  Make the loop secure;
Fold the flask in the poncho,
  Fill the pouch with maize,
And ride as if to-morrow
  Were the last of living days!

Saddle, saddle, saddle!
  Redden spur and thong;
Ride like the mad tornado,
  The track is lonely and long.
Spare not horse nor rider;
  Fly for the stolen bride;
Bring her home on the crupper,
  A scalp on either side!

Rose Terry Cooke

THE SQUIRE'S BOAR HUNT

Come, gallop my masters! Come gallop my men!
There's roaring and routing in Enderby Fen,
Hark! hear the hounds' music! the boar is at bay.
There'll be fun in the Fen before curfew to-day.

A squeal? there's the brood with the sow at their head.
Hola! through the osiers how fleet they have fled!
But the lord of the lair is not trotting beside.—
Ride faster! spur deeper! the boar will abide.

Whoop! down in yon sallets his holt is. I see
The glint of his eye past that pollarded tree.
Now Ripper! Now Bolder! down! down from the bank!
Now Brave, to his ear, sir! Now Stark to his flank!

Spur John o' the Garner. Rush on with your spear!
The dogs will hold firm. Holy saints! he is clear!
He has ripped up old Bolder from muzzle to stern,
And Brave lies behind him; and Stark has his turn.

Loose Vixen and Badger! a sanglier[1] is he
Set the hounds on at force; send the relays to me!
Am I hunting the boar like a damsel at play?
Gogs ounds![2] shall he daunt me and 'scape me to-day?

Ho! Vixen hath seized him. Pst! to him, my lass!
Here comes the fresh relay. Now guard the morass!
Will he fight? will he flee? Holy Hubert! look here,
He's routing! he's charging! he's snapped my good spear!

---

1. A full-grown wild boar separated from the herd.
2. This expression is a corruption of the expletive "God's Wounds."

Well done! John o' Garner. I pattered a prayer,
Sure thought I he had me; and but you were there
I too had been slashed with the rip of his tusk.
Bless the rood! it is over. We're home-set by dusk.

Ha! here's my young master. Yes, look you, that boar
Had nigh served your Dad that you had me no more.
But John o' the Garner like fire-flaught came on,
Upright in the stirrup, his spear-point borne down;

His good charger volted; his stout arm made thrust;
Pricked right twixt the shoulders my lord tasted dust!
Look ye there, at those tushes! that wicked red eye!
That ear that Brave tore, when he tossed him to die!

A sanglier of hundreds! have off with his head!
Full nobly and bravely our hunting hath sped.
Come! Up from the Fen, and away o'er the moor!
We'll end with high revel this hunt of the boar.

IN THE HAMMOCK

How the stars shine out at sea!
Swing me, Tita! Faster, girl!
I'm a hang-bird in her nest,
All with scarlet blossoms drest,
Swinging where the winds blow free.

Ah! how white the moonlight falls.
Catch my slipper! there it goes,
Where that single fire-fly shines,
Tangled in the heavy vines,
Creeping by the convent walls.

Ay de mi! to be a nun!
Juana takes the veil to-day,
She hears mass behind a grate,
While for me ten lovers wait
At the door till mass is done.

Swing me, Tita! Seven are tall.
Two are crooked, rich, and old,
But the other—he's too small;
Did you hear a pebble fall?
And his blue eyes are too cold.

If I were a little nun,
When I heard that voice below,
I should scale the convent wall;
I should follow at his call,
Shuddering through the dreadful snow.

Tita! Tita! hold me still!
Now the vesper bell is ringing,
Bring me quick my beads and veil.
Yes, I know my cheek is pale
And my eyes shine—I've been swinging.

AN END

I have had all: over and in that all,
Like the soul's speck of fire in a man's eye,
One little mote did crawl
And spread and fly, till wide eternity
Straightened itself to measure out a pall
        Where I might lie.

Rose Terry Cooke

Life tempted me, as the great hungry sea
Calls with inevitable voice to youth:
Why should I turn and flee?
Nor fear, nor ruth, nor the still voice of truth
Kept the red wine or bitter lees from me:
      I lived, forsooth!

All things of earth in sequence of their birth
Sprang to my fevered lips and met disdain,
Mad in its angry mirth.
Love's honeyed gain was the bee's patient pain,
Wrought for no worth.
I have had all. I had it all in vain!

As in the cup where the brown night-moths sup,
Under the honey, under the perfume,
One little spot looks up,
And through that bloom foretells the seed-time's gloom,
So my unsated thirst in each drained cup
      Found lurking room.

Yet I know God hung over me this rod
That I should follow where two bleeding feet
Before this track have trod:
And, as earth's sweet is finite, incomplete,
He satisfies me whose infinite, complete,
      Fills star and sod.

HELEN HUNT JACKSON

(1830–1885)

THE POETRY OF JACKSON has only recently been the focus of serious modern scrutiny, due to her relationship to Emily Dickinson, but her prose, especially her romantic novel about Native Americans (*Ramona*), has kept her reputation alive. Jackson's life was full of adventure. She grew up as the privileged daughter of an Amherst College classics professor and his wife. Her parents, who were dogmatic Puritans and against whose beliefs Helen rebelled, died when the poet was in her teens. She married Edward Hunt in 1852, but her husband—a military officer—was killed in 1863 in the Brooklyn Navy Yard as he was testing a new torpedo he had invented. Neither of the poet's two sons lived to adulthood.

Severely depressed, Helen turned to publishing poetry. Typical of the early work of many women poets, her first published book was a "Persian tale." Helen Hunt's poems and essays attracted unusual attention, however, including that of Emerson who in the 1870s thought her the best of contemporary women poets.

Having become self-supporting, Jackson resisted the idea of remarrying, but in 1873 she met a Quaker banker, William S. Jackson of Colorado. A man of great wealth and distinction, he agreed not to interfere with her writing. The couple was married in 1875. Around 1879 she became deeply angered at the plight of the Indians and this led to the publication of *A Century of Dishonor* (1881) and *Ramona* (1884), about which Jackson said: "I did not write *Ramona;* it was written through me. My life-blood went into it" (*NAW* 261).

During this time she also began corresponding with Emily Dickinson, strongly encouraging her to publish. Jackson was a great facilitator, and championed the work not only of Dickinson but also of younger women such as Edith M. Thomas.

Except for *Verses* (1870), the best books of Jackson's poetry appeared posthumously. Jackson published much of her work anonymously (for instance, in the "No Name Series" where Emily Dickinson's poems also appeared). During her life Jackson used the initials H. H. and pseudonyms such as Marah, Rip Van Winkle, and Saxe Holm. The later publications appeared under her own name, however, which, after *Ramona*'s popularity, added to their appeal.

In *Sonnets and Lyrics* (1886) and *Poems* (1891), one can see that Jackson was ahead of her time in choosing a style based on simple declarative statement, natural diction, and the technique of verbal surprise. "The Prince is Dead" and "Her Eyes" epitomize the simple style, and "Covert" and "Danger" exemplify Jackson's talent for effective conclusions. Her most popular poems, however, were "Coronation" and "Acquainted with Grief." Jackson was also admired by Stedman and Higginson, who in 1899 called her, not Emily Dickinson, the premier woman poet of the age.

Selected Works: Saxe Holm's Stories. 1874; *The Story of Boon.* 1874; *Mercy Philbrick's Choice.* 1876.

Selected Criticism: Banning, Evelyn. *Helen Hunt Jackson.* New York: Vanguard, 1973; Coultrap-McQuin; Dobson; Higginson, T. W. *Contemporaries.* 1899; Sewall, Richard B. *The Life of Emily Dickinson.* Vol. 2. New York: Farrar, 1974; Whitaker, Rosemary. *Helen Hunt Jackson.* Boise: Boise State UP, 1987.

IN TIME OF FAMINE

"She has no heart," they said, and turned away,
Then, stung so that I wished my words might be
Two-edged swords, I answered low:—
        "Have ye
Not read how once when famine held fierce sway

In Lydia, and men died day by day
Of hunger, there were found brave souls whose glee
Scarce hid their pangs, who said, 'Now we
Can eat but once in two days; we will play
Such games on those days when we eat no food
That we forget our pain.'
                "Thus they withstood
Long years of famine; and to them we owe
The trumpets, pipes, and balls which mirth finds good
To-day, and little dreams that of such woe
They first were born.
            "That woman's life I know
Has been all famine. Mock now if ye dare,
To hear her brave sad laughter in the air."

THE PRINCE IS DEAD

A room in the palace is shut. The king
And the queen are sitting in black.
All day weeping servants will run and bring,
But the heart of the queen will lack
All things; and the eyes of the king will swim
With tears which must not be shed,
But will make all the air float dark and dim,
As he looks at each gold and silver toy,
And thinks how it gladdened the royal boy,
And dumbly writhes while the courtiers read
How all the nations his sorrow heed.
      The Prince is dead.

The hut has a door, but the hinge is weak,
And to-day the wind blows it back;

There are two sitting here who do not speak;
They have begged a few rags of black.
They are hard at work, though their eyes are wet
With tears which must not be shed;
They dare not look where the cradle is set;
They hate the sunbeam which plays on the floor,
But will make the baby laugh out no more;
They feel as if they were turning to stone,
They wish the neighbors would leave them alone.
   The Prince is dead.

POPPIES ON THE WHEAT

Along Ancona's hills the shimmering heat,
A tropic tide of air with ebb and flow
Bathes all the fields of wheat until they glow
Like flashing seas of green, which toss and beat
Around the vines. The poppies lithe and fleet
Seem running, fiery torchmen, to and fro
To mark the shore.
     The farmer does not know
That they are there. He walks with heavy feet,
Counting the bread and wine by autumn's gain,
But I,—I smile to think that days remain
Perhaps to me in which, though bread be sweet
No more, and red wine warm my blood in vain,
I shall be glad remembering how the fleet,
Lithe poppies ran like torchmen with the wheat.

Helen Hunt Jackson

MEMOIR OF A QUEEN

Her name, before she was a queen, boots not.
When she was crowned, her kingdom said, "The Queen!"
And, after that, all other names too mean
By far had seemed. Perhaps all were forgot,
Save "Queen, sweet queen."
                    Such pitiable lot
As till her birth her kingdom had, was seen
Never in all fair lands, so torn between
False grasping powers, that toiled and fought, but got
No peace.
           All curious search is wholly vain
For written page or stone whereon occurs
A mention of the kingdom which obeyed
This sweet queen's rule. But centuries have laid
No dead queen down in royal sepulchres
Whose reign was greater or more blest than hers.

COVERT

One day, when sunny fields lay warm and still,
    And from their tufted hillocks, thick and sweet
    With moss and pine and ferns, such spicy heat
Rose up, it seemed the air to overfill,
And quicken every sense with subtle thrill,
    I rambled on with careless, aimless feet,
    And lingered idly, finding all so sweet.

Sudden, almost beneath my footsteps' weight,
    Almost before the sunny silence heard
    Their sound, from a low bush, which scarcely stirred

A twig at lightening of its hidden freight,
Flew, frightened from her nest, the small brown mate
  Of some melodious, joyous, soaring bird,
  Whose song that instant high in air I heard.

   . . . .

"Ah! Heart," I said, "when days are warm and sweet,
  And sunny hours for very joy are still,
  And every sense feels subtle, languid thrill
Of voiceless memory's renewing heat,
Fly not at sound of strangers' aimless feet!
  Of thy love's distant song drink all thy fill!
  Thy hiding-place is safe. Glad heart, keep still!"

RENUNCIATION

  O wherefore thus, apart with drooping wings
    Thou stillest, saddest angel,
  With hidden face, as if but bitter things
    Thou hadst, and no evangel
  Of good tidings?
  Thou know'st that through our tears
    Of hasty, selfish weeping,
  Comes surer sun; and for our petty fears
    Of loss, thou hast in keeping
  A greater gain than all of which we dreamed.
    Thou knowest that in grasping
  The bright possessions which so precious seemed,
    We lose them; but, if clasping
  Thy faithful hand, we tread with steadfast feet
    The path of thy appointing,
  There waits for us a treasury of sweet
    Delight; royal anointing

With oil of gladness and of strength!
                              O, things
    Of Heaven, Christ's evangel
Bearing, call us with shining face and poised wings,
    Thou sweetest, dearest angel!

CORONATION

At the king's gate the subtle noon
    Wove filmy yellow nets of sun;
Into the drowsy snare too soon
    The guards fell one by one.

Through the king's gate, unquestioned then,
    A beggar went, and laughed, "This brings
Me chance, at last, to see if men
    Fare better, being kings."

The king sat bowed beneath his crown,
    Propping his face with listless hand;
Watching the hour-glass sifting down
    Too slow its shining sand.

"Poor man, what wouldst thou have of me?"
    The beggar turned, and, pitying,
Replied, like one in dream, "Of thee,
    Nothing. I want the king."

Uprose the king, and from his head
    Shook off the crown and threw it by.
"O man, thou must have known," he said,
    "A greater king than I."

Through all the gates, unquestioned then,
 Went king and beggar hand in hand.
Whispered the king, "Shall I know when
 Before *his* throne I stand?"

The beggar laughed. Free winds in haste
 Were wiping from the king's hot brow
The crimson lines the crown had traced.
 "This is his presence now."

At the king's gate, the crafty noon
 Unwove its yellow nets of sun;
Out of their sleep in terror soon
 The guards waked one by one.

"Ho here! Ho there! Has no man seen
 The king?" The cry ran to and fro;
Beggar and king, they laughed, I ween,
 The laugh that free men know.

On the king's gate the moss grew gray;
 The king came not. They called him dead:
And made his eldest son one day
 Slave in his father's stead.

MY NEW FRIEND

A shallow voice said, bitterly, "New friend!"
As if the old alone were true, and, born
Of sudden freak, the new deserved but scorn
And deep distrust.
     If love could condescend,
What scorn in turn! Do men old garments mend

With new? And put the new wine, red at morn,
Into the last year's bottles, thin and worn?
But love and loving need not to defend
Themselves. The new is older than the old;
And newest friend is oldest friend in this,
That, waiting him, we longest grieved to miss
One thing we sought.
                I think when we behold
Full Heaven, we say not, "Why was this not told?"
But, "Ah! For years we've waited for this bliss!"

HER EYES

That they are brown, no man will dare to say
He knows. And yet I think that no man's look
Ever those depths of light and shade forsook,
Until their gentle pain warned him away.
Of all sweet things I know but one which may
Be likened to her eyes.
                When, in deep nook
Of some green field, the water of a brook
Makes lingering, whirling eddy in its way,
Round soft drowned leaves; and in a flash of sun
They turn to gold, until the ripples run
Now brown, now yellow, changing as by some
Swift spell.
              I know not with what body come
The saints. But this I know, my Paradise
Will mean the resurrection of her eyes.

Helen Hunt Jackson

FOUND FROZEN

She died, as many travellers have died,
O'ertaken on an Alpine road by night;
Numbed and bewildered by the falling snow,
Striving, in spite of falling pulse, and limbs
Which faltered and grew feeble at each step,
To toil up the icy steep, and bear
Patient and faithful to the last, the load
Which, in the sunny morn seemed light!
                                    And yet
'T was in the place she called her home, she died;
And they who loved her with the all of love
Their wintry natures had to give, stood by
And wept some tears, and wrote above her grave
Some common record which they thought was true;
But I, who loved her first, and last, and best,—*I* knew.

DANGER

With what a childish and short-sighted sense
Fear seeks for safety; reckons up the days
Of danger and escape, the hours and ways
Of death; it breathless flies the pestilence;
It walls itself in towers of defence;
By land, by sea, against the storm it lays
Down barriers; then, comforted, it says:
"This spot, this hour is safe." Oh, vain pretence!
Man born of man knows nothing when he goes;
The winds blow where they list, and will disclose
To no man which brings safety, which brings risk.

The mighty are brought low by many a thing
Too small to name. Beneath the daisy's disk
Lies hid the pebble for the fatal sling.

ESTHER

A face more vivid than he dreamed who drew
Thy portrait in that thrilling tale of old!
Dead queen, we see thee still, thy beauty cold
As beautiful; thy dauntless heart which knew
No fear,—not even of a king who slew
At pleasure; maiden heart which was not sold,
Though all the maiden flesh the king's red gold
Did buy! The loyal daughter of the Jew,
No hour saw thee forget his misery;
Thou wert not queen until thy race went free;
Yet thoughtful hearts, that ponder slow and deep,
Find doubtful reverence at last for thee;
Thou heldest thy race too dear, thyself too cheap;
Honor no second place for truth can keep.

After divorcing Vashti (see Frances Harper's poem and the note) King
Ahasuerus married a Jewish woman, Esther. She kept her race a secret until her
people were threatened, but eventually revealed herself and pleaded their cause.
Though Esther was not killed, Jackson seems to imply she took too great a risk for
her people.

Helen Hunt Jackson

VASHTI

In all great Shushan's palaces was there
Not one, O Vashti, knowing thee so well.
Poor uncrowned queen, that he the world could tell
How thou wert pure and loyal-souled as fair?
How it was love which made thee bold to dare
Refuse the shame which madmen would compel?
Not one, who saw the bitter tears that fell
And heard thy cry heart-rending on the air:
"Ah me! My Lord could not this thing have meant!
He well might loathe me ever, if I go
Before these drunken princes as a show.
I am his queen; I come of king's descent.
I will not let him bring our crown so low;
He will but bless me when he doth repent!"

A WOMAN'S DEATH-WOUND

It left upon her tender flesh no trace.
The murderer is safe. As swift as light
The weapon fell, and, in the summer night,
Did scarce the silent, dewy air displace;
'T was but a word. A blow had been less base.
Like dumb beast branded by an iron white
With heat, she turned in blind and helpless flight,
But then remembered, and with piteous face
Came back.
             Since then, the world has nothing missed
In her, in voice or smile. But she—each day
She counts until her dying be complete.

One moan she makes, and ever doth repeat:
"O lips that I have loved and kissed and kissed,
Did I deserve to die this bitterest way?"

ACQUAINTED WITH GRIEF

Dost know Grief well? Hast known her long?
    So long, that not with gift or smile,
Or gliding footstep in the throng,
    She can deceive thee by her guile?

So long, that with unflinching eyes
    Thou smilest to thyself apart,
To watch each flimsy, fresh disguise
    She plans to stab anew thy heart?

So long, thou barrest up no door
    To stay the coming of her feet?
So long, thou answerest no more,
    Lest in her ear thy cry be sweet?

Dost know the voice in which she says,
    "No more henceforth our paths divide;
In loneliest nights, in crowded days,
    I am forever by thy side"?

Then dost thou know, perchance, the spell
    The gods laid on her at her birth,—
The viewless gods who mingle well
    Strange love and hate of us on earth.

Weapon and time, the hour, the place,
    All these are hers to take, to choose,

Helen Hunt Jackson

To give us neither rest nor grace,
    Not one heart-throb to miss or lose.

All these are hers; yet stands she, slave,
    Helpless before our one behest:
The gods, that we be shamed not, gave,
    And locked the secret in our breast.

She to the gazing world must bear
    Our crowns of triumph, if we bid;
Loyal and mute, our colors wear,
    Sign of her own forever hid.

Smile to our smile, song to our song,
    With songs and smiles our roses fling,
Till men turn round in every throng,
    To note such joyous pleasuring.

And ask, next morn, with eyes that lend
    A fervor to the words they say,
"What is her name, that radiant friend
    Who walked beside you yesterday?"

CELIA THAXTER

(1835–1894)

꙰꙰꙰꙰꙰

THE DAUGHTER of a lighthouse keeper on one of New England's Isles of Shoals, Celia Laighton grew up in a very isolated environment without school, church, or friends. Early she developed an interest in literature and a passionate love for the stark landscape of her native island world.

When she was thirteen, the family moved to Appledore Island where her father built a large resort hotel, managed at first by Levi Thaxter, who also tutored Celia. Though Levi was fifteen years older than Celia, they married in 1851. The marriage faltered, however, due to Celia's nostalgia for the isles and what seems to have been Levi's financial extravagance and overbearing attitude toward his wife. To supplement the family income and give herself some economic independence, Thaxter began to publish poetry. Her first poem "Land-Locked" appeared in the *Atlantic Monthly* in 1861 and earned her $10.

From that time on, Celia Thaxter continued to publish both poetry and prose despite her husband's resentment at her growing popularity. Though they never divorced, they began to live separate lives, Celia returning to Appledore Island to spend long periods with her mother. Barbara White has recently maintained that Levi's chummy behavior with his cronies suggests homosexuality. For her part, Celia was deeply devoted to women, writing several love poems, such as "Alone" and "S. E.," which represent females as the beloved. Since women poets often adopted male personae, however, one cannot be sure that such poems indicate homoeroticism. Love poems written by women to women were common.

Thaxter's poetry earned her the support of writers and publishers such as Whittier and Annie and James Fields. Though Celia was always ashamed of her lack of education, she was a popular hostess, entertaining many prominent visitors at her salon on Appledore Island, including Harriet Beecher Stowe, Lucy Larcom, and Sarah Orne Jewett, who named Thaxter "the sandpiper."

Throughout her life Celia Thaxter was plagued by financial worries. In addition to publishing poetry, she made money (as did many women poets) by producing children's literature. After her mother's death in 1877—which left Celia devastated—she turned to religion for the first time and dabbled in spiritualism and theosophy, but like Melville she remained unable to maintain a firm belief in religious consolation. Her principal contributions are not her religious writings but her poems of classic nineteenth-century female frustration and her realistic memoir of offshore New England life, *Among the Isles of Shoals* (1873).

Selected Works: Poems for Children. 1884; *The Letters of Celia Thaxter.* Ed. Annie Fields and Rose Lamb. 1895; *The Poems of Celia Thaxter.* Preface by Sarah Orne Jewett. 1896; *The Heavenly Guest.* Ed. O. Laighton—privately printed 1935.

Selected Criticism: Colby Library Quarterly 6 (1964), Celia Thaxter Issue; Fields, Annie. *Authors and Friends.* 1896; Thaxter, Rosamond. *Sandpiper: The Life and Letters of Celia Thaxter*—rev. ed. Francestown, NH: Marshall Jones, 1963; Vallier, Jane. *Poet on Demand: The Life, Letters, and Works of Celia Thaxter.* Camden, ME: Down East, 1982; Westbrook, Perry. *Acres of Flint.* Washington: Scarecrow, 1951; White, Barbara. "Profile of Celia Thaxter." *Legacy* 7:1 (1990); Woodward, Pauline. "Celia Thaxter's Love Poems." *Colby Library Quarterly* 23 (1987): 144–53.

Celia Thaxter

LAND-LOCKED

Black lie the hills; swiftly doth daylight flee;
   And, catching gleams of sunset's dying smile,
   Through the dusk land for many a changing mile
The river runneth softly to the sea.

O happy river, could I follow thee!
   O yearning heart, that never can be still!
   O wistful eyes, that watch the steadfast hill,
Longing for level line of solemn sea!

Have patience; here are flowers and songs of birds,
   Beauty and fragrance, wealth of sound and sight,
   All summer's glory thine from morn till night,
And life too full of joy for uttered words.

Neither am I ungrateful; but I dream
   Deliciously how twilight falls to-night
   Over the glimmering water, how the light
Dies blissfully away, until I seem

To feel the wind, sea-scented, on my cheek,
   To catch the sound of dusty flapping sail
   And dip of oars, and voices on the gale
Afar off, calling low,—my name they speak!

O Earth! thy summer song of joy may soar
   Ringing to heaven in triumph. I but crave
   The sad, caressing murmur of the wave
That breaks in tender music on the shore.

Celia Thaxter

THE MINUTE-GUNS

I stood within the little cove,
   Full of the morning's life and hope,
While heavily the eager waves
   Charged thundering up the rocky slope.

The splendid breakers! How they rushed,
   All emerald green and flashing white,
Tumultuous in the morning sun,
   With cheer and sparkle and delight!

And freshly blew the fragrant wind,
   The wild sea wind, across their tops,
And caught the spray and flung it far
   In sweeping showers of glittering drops.

Within the cove all flashed and foamed
   With many a fleeting rainbow hue;
Without, gleamed bright against the sky
   A tender wavering line of blue,

Where tossed the distant waves, and far
   Shone silver-white a quiet sail;
And overhead the soaring gulls
   With graceful pinions stemmed the gale.

And all my pulses thrilled with joy,
   Watching the winds' and waters' strife,
With sudden rapture,—and I cried,
   "Oh, sweet is life! Thank God for life!"

Sailed any cloud across the sky,
   Marring this glory of the sun's?

Celia Thaxter

Over the seas, from distant forts,
    There came the boom of minute-guns!

War-tidings! Many a brave soul fled,
    And many a heart the message stuns!
I saw no more the joyous waves,
    I only heard the minute-guns.

IMPRISONED

Lightly she lifts the large, pure, luminous shell,
    Poises it in her strong and shapely hand.
"Listen," she says, "it has a tale to tell,
    Spoken in language you may understand."

Smiling, she holds it at my dreaming ear:
    The old, delicious murmur of the sea
Steals like enchantment through me, and I hear
    Voices like echoes of eternity.

She stirs it softly. Lo, another speech!
    In one of its dim chambers, shut from sight,
Is sealed the water that has kissed the beach
    Where the far Indian Ocean leaps in light.

Those laughing ripples, hidden evermore
    In utter darkness, plaintively repeat
Their lapsing on the glowing tropic shore,
    In melancholy whispers low and sweet.

O prisoned wave that may not see the sun!
    O voice that never may be comforted!

You cannot break the web that Fate has spun;
    Out of your world are light and gladness fled.

The red dawn nevermore shall tremble far
    Across the leagues of radiant brine to you;
You shall not sing to greet the evening star,
    Nor dance exulting under heaven's clear blue.

Inexorably woven is the weft
    That shrouds from you all joy but memory;
Only this tender, low lament is left
    Of all the sumptuous splendor of the sea.

MODJESKA

Deft hands called Chopin's music from the keys.
    Silent she sat, her slender figure's poise
Flower-like and fine and full of lofty ease;
    She heard her Poland's most consummate voice
From power to pathos falter, sink and change;
    The music of her land, the wondrous high,
Utmost expression of its genius strange,—
    Incarnate sadness breathed in melody.
Silent and thrilled she sat, her lovely face
    Flushing and paling like a delicate rose
    Shaken by summer winds from its repose
Softly this way and that with tender grace,
    Now touched by sun, now into shadow turned,—
    While bright with kindred fire her deep eyes burned!

Helena Modjeska (1840–1909) was a Polish-born actress who emigrated to America.

Celia Thaxter

ALONE

The lilies clustered fair and tall;
I stood outside the garden wall;
I saw her light robe glimmering through
The fragrant evening's dusk and dew.

She stooped above the lilies pale;
Up the clear east the moon did sail;
I saw her bend her lovely head
O'er her rich roses blushing red.

Her slender hand the flowers caressed,
Her touch the unconscious blossoms blessed;
The rose against her perfumed palm
Leaned its soft cheek in blissful calm.

I would have given my soul to be
That rose she touched so tenderly!
I stood alone, outside the gate,
And knew that life was desolate.

SUBMISSION

The sparrow sits and sings, and sings;
    Softly the sunset's lingering light
        Lies rosy over rock and turf,
            And reddens where the restless surf
    Tosses on high its plumes of white.

Celia Thaxter

Gently and clear the sparrow sings,
   While twilight steals across the sea,
      And still and bright the evening-star
      Twinkles above the golden bar
   That in the west lies quietly.

Oh, steadfastly the sparrow sings,
   And sweet the sound; and sweet the touch
      Of wooing winds; and sweet the sight
      Of happy Nature's deep delight
   In her fair spring, desired so much!

But while so clear the sparrow sings
   A cry of death is in my ear:
      The crashing of the riven wreck,
      Breakers that sweep the shuddering deck,
   And sounds of agony and fear.

How is it that the birds can sing?
   Life is so full of bitter pain;
      Hearts so wrung with hopeless grief;
      Woe is so long and joy so brief;
   Nor shall the lost return again.

Though rapturously the sparrow sings,
   No bliss of Nature can restore
      The friends whose hands I clasped so warm,
      Sweet souls that through the night and storm
   Fled from the earth for evermore.

Yet still the sparrow sits and sings,
   Till longing, mourning, sorrowing love,
      Groping to find what hope may be
      Within death's awful mystery,
   Reaches its empty arms above;

And listening, while the sparrow sings,
    And soft the evening shadows fall,
        Sees, through the crowding tears that blind,
        A little light, and seems to find
    And clasp God's hand, who wrought it all.

S. E.

She passes up and down life's various ways
    With noiseless footfall and with serious air:
Within the circle of her quiet days
    She takes of sorrow and joy her share.
In her bright home, like some rare jewel set,
    The lustre of her beauty lives and glows,
With all the fragrance of the violet,
    And all the radiant splendor of the rose.
As simple and unconscious as a flower,
    And crowned with womanhood's most subtle charm,
She blesses her sweet realm with gentle power,
    And keeps her hearth-fires burning clear and warm.
To know her is to love her. Every year
Makes her more precious and more wise and dear.

MARY TUCKER LAMBERT

(1838–?)

❦❦❦❦❦❦

ACCORDING TO JOAN R. SHERMAN, Mary Tucker Lambert was a nine-
teenth-century black woman poet, the editor of *St. Matthew's Lyceum
Journal* and two volumes of poetry, as well as a work entitled *Life of
Mark M. Pomeroy* (1868). Almost nothing is known of her, not even the
date of her death. One biographical source simply lists her as a woman
of Philadelphia, but her publications suggest that she lived in New York
City in the 1860s. Her first book of verse, *Poems* (1867), is dedicated to
the Honorable Charles J. Jenkins, governor of Georgia, and to Mrs.
Governor Jenkins "my honoured and trusted friends." Many of her
poems are about the South, whose torment after the Civil War Lambert
seems to feel keenly.

One guesses that Lambert was a mulatto and may even have
passed for a Creole gentlewoman. In *Invisible Poets* Sherman lists the
sources for Lambert's racial identification as the AME *Church Review* and
Gertrude Mossell's *The Work of the Afro-American Woman.* As Mary E.
Tucker she published *Poems* in 1867; the same year *Loew's Bridge: A
Broadway Idyl* was printed anonymously. None of her lyrics address
issues of race directly, though slavery is one of the social issues men-
tioned in her panoramic poem about New York street life. Lambert's
work is mostly conventional. In the selections reprinted here, two nine-
teenth-century *topoi*—drug use ("The Opium-Eater") and cries of the
city ("Loew's Bridge")—are represented.

Of special interest, however, are Tucker's poems about food and
food preparation, which are not typical of the period. Her poem "Upon

Receipt of a Pound of Coffee" is refreshingly explicit about the process of making a pot of warm Java, while "Apple Dumplings" is a playful commentary on the old theme of appearance and reality. It is tantalizing to speculate about whether Lambert intended these poems to imply some judgments about racial matters, such as the disconnection between process and products that makes the speaker in the coffee poem able to pass over the oppressive circumstances of the coffee plantation in a neutralizing fantasy of pleasing a Turkish pacha. Similarly, "Apple Dumplings" may be intended to suggest a commentary upon racial distinctions in its deconstruction of the opposition between inside and outside. Without more information about Lambert, however, one can only guess about such authorial intentions.

In *A Broadway Idyl* the poet does toy with the subject of slavery. Her surprising shift from the slaves who pick cotton to "slaves / Of Fashion, whose vile hands / Pollute [the cotton's] purity" certainly suggests some race-related sleight-of-hand. Her comment in another section that "White, glaring white, is all the earth below" adds further ammunition to the argument that the text is carrying on a metatextual discourse about color, a discourse one does not need to know authorial intentions to analyze.

Selected Criticism: Mossell, Gertrude E. H. Bustill. *The Work of the Afro-American Woman.* 1894. Intro. by Joanne Braxton. Schomburg Library of Nineteenth-Century Black Women Writers. New York: Oxford UP, 1988; Sherman, Joan R. Intro. to *Collected Black Women's Poetry.* Vol. 1; Sherman, *Invisible Poets.*

LOEW'S BRIDGE: A BROADWAY IDYL (selection)

Our City rulers pass in grand array,
Some whose each step pollutes this snowy way,

"Loew's, or as it is commonly called, Fulton Street Bridge, was completed March 1866, the building being supervised by the Hon. Charles E. Loew, whose name has been bestowed upon it" (author's note).

Whose nervous glances tell that they have sold
Their honor for position and for gold.
Others, whose pure lives can command
Respect, aye love, of all e'en in this land,
　　　Where merit's granted but to favored few.
Our present Mayor, with abstracted air,
Comes with kind greeting, for high, low and fair.
　In each heart holds he a much envied placed,
And his position fills with nameless grace.
And yet he bears upon his brow the badge
Of hope deferred, Ambition's goal half won—
The race for station only just begun.[1]

His rival follows, and determination
Within his eye shows will to do, or dare—
Not only will, but power,
Dame Nature's priceless dower.
From very foot the mount of fame he trod:
Sprung from the people, he's the people's god.[2]

And Authors, too, the devils of the quill,
Who daily, hourly their poor brains distil:
Exalted, trampled by the public will;
And yet they cater, and will cater still,
Undaunted by the missiles hurled
　　　Each day by a censorious world.
Some with their faces beaming bright
See in their eyes success' light;
Some who on yesterday were naught,
To-day they find themselves the sought

---

1. "Hon. John T. Hoffman is Mayor of New York at this writing, November 11, 1867" (author's note).

2. "The Hon. Fernando Wood, the rival candidate for the Mayoralty" (author's note).

And courted, for their genius bright,
    A reputation
      Made by the "Nation,"
Growing like Jonah's gourd all in a night.
And some poor sinner who awoke
From dream of fame, alas to find
His fancy's child, child of his mind,
Damned by the critics,
    Or unnoticed passed.
Ah, well, when he is dead, perchance his name
May live forever, immortalized by fame.
Such is the world's great largess to the dead,
The genius who when living wanted bread.

'Tis marvellous how mortals can invent
The ways and means to increase worldly stores.
Scorn not beginnings, and each small thing prize,
From e'en a cord, sometimes large fortunes rise.[3]
Yon apple-woman, vender of small wares,
Stale lozenges, fruit, candy, and vile cakes,
Who sells to urchins pennies' worth of aches,
Has now the gold safe hoarded in the bank,
With which to buy high place in fashion's rank.
Merit is nothing, money rules the day
Right royally, with rare despotic sway.

Something familiar comes before me now,
A picture of the Southern cotton-plant.
Broadway to-day, with its white glittering shield,
Is not as pure as Southern cotton field;
    With flakes of snow bursting from bolls of green,
Like some imprisoned genius scorning to be
Confined by laws, which bind society,

---

3. A reference to toys made to dance by an elastic string; they proved very profitable.

And breaking bonds is wafted on the breeze
Of public favor, or gathered by the slaves
    Of Fashion, whose vile hands
        Pollute its purity.
True, fragments now and then
Are gently taken to the hearts of men—
White flowers of fancy oftimes sink to rest
Deep in the wells of some fair maiden's breast:
Pure in themselves, they yet become more fair
By contact with the holy thoughts in there.

Cotton and slaves, 'twas thus we counted gold,
The slaves are free, the free in bondage sold;
And now some man with rare prolific brains,
Genius inventive, by the name of Gaines,[4]
Has made a bitters of the cotton plant;
Polluting thus the hitherto white name
By clothing it in the vile badge of shame.

White, glaring white, is all the earth below,
And Broadway seems a "universe of snow."
Or like the Ocean's silver-crested waves,
Upon whose breasts thousands of barks are tossed;
Some brave the storm,—by cautious pilots mann'd,
Some strike on breakers, ere they reach the land,
    And are forever lost.

---

4. This is probably George Strother Gaines (c. 1784–1873) Alabama pioneer, Indian agent, merchant, and planter who was elected to the Mississippi legislature in 1861.

Mary Tucker Lambert

REVENGE

Ah! I could curse them in my woe,
    E'en as the viper stings,
And to the heel that strikes it clings,
So I could plant my blow.

Yes, I could pray that fell disease
Should torture them with pain—
That plague should fall in every rain,
Miasma taint each breeze.

That wealth should vanish, and the curse
Of poverty should reign;
That cries for bread should be in vain!
An always empty purse.

That friends should die, and every pride
Should vanish in a day;
'Till even hope withdraws her ray,
And naught of joys abide.

Yes, I could whisper in the ear
Of one who loves to tell
Some fabrication, dark as hell,
As scandal loves to hear.

Revenge is sweet; I could invent
Full many a thousand way,
That would my heartfelt wrongs repay,
Could they my soul content.

But could I go to sleep in peace,
And could I dream of heaven—

Could I e'er hope to be forgiven
When death came to release?

Revenge is sweet to those who live;
But when we think of death—
The ebbing of this life-tide breath—
'Tis sweeter to forgive.

LIFT ME HIGHER

Lift me higher! Lift me higher!
    From this sphere of earthly dross;
Upward still! far yonder gleaming,
    Shines my Saviour's glorious cross.

Oh, very beautiful is life,
    And earthly flowers are passing fair:
But lift, oh lift me up to heaven,
    And let me rest forever there.

There, no care shall plough its furrows;
    There, no sin shall blur my heart;
There, in blessed choirs of angels,
    I shall sing a humble part.

Lift me higher! Lift me higher!
    Friends of earth, no tears for me!
From temptation, sin, and sorrow,
    Let me be forever free!

Ah! I hear my Saviour call me!
    Clad in heavenly robes of white;

He will lift me higher, higher,
    From this world of storm and night.

Lift me higher! Lift me higher!
    Farewell earthly friends I love.
Lift me higher! Lift me higher!
    To that better world above!

"Lift me higher!" And our darling
    Gently closed her wearied eyes;
And her spirit, lifted higher,
    Reached its home beyond the skies.

She is sleeping, and white marble
    This inscription only bears:
"Our lost flower—thirteen summers—
    Lifted higher"—than life's cares.

WAIL OF THE DIVORCED

How can I give thee up, my child, my dearest, earliest born,
While fond hopes are 'round thee clustered, like bright clouds o'er
    morning's dawn?
No, I will not leave thee, darling; thou at least shall never say
That no tender hand did guide thee through the cares of childhood's day.

My child! when first thy mother heard thy feeble, first-born wail,
Love's tide came rushing through the heart, I thought encased in mail.
For the few years of my young life had been scenes of mirth and woe,
For I grasped the pleasures, darling, grasped them, ere I let them go!

Mary Tucker Lambert

E'en the brightest days of summer have their sunshine and their showers;
And the piercing thorn will wound us, as we pluck the fairest flowers;
But the perfume of the flowers makes us glory in the pain,
And exulting in the sunshine, we forget the chilling rain.

I know 'twould break my aching heart to leave thee, precious one!
How can they brand me with a curse—what have I ever done?
I know that I have never sent a sister down to shame,
By casting blots of foulest sin upon a snow-white name.

Have charity, have charity, my child, for every sin—
For the sore temptation, darling, may all-powerful have been;
And always lend a helping hand to those who chance to fall;
Forgive, forget, be ready to obey your Saviour's call.

Learn, learn, my child, and ne'er forget, learn while thou art still young,
That he will have the truest friends, who bridleth his tongue.
Speak well of all, if aught you know of evil, or of ill;
Deep in thy bosom let it rest, and keep the scandal still.

My baby, should you ever choose a partner for this life,
Oh, darling, ever strive to be a fond, devoted wife;
And never let thy husband's name be spoken but in praise;
For some will, if you let them, sadly misconstrue his ways.

Seek not happiness in pleasure, for the dregs of every cup
Are so bitter, darling, bitter, as we quaff the latest sup!
And never seek, my child, to win the laurel wreath of fame,
Unless thou hast a heart to bear the world's taunts, even shame.

Kind, noble, generous, they will give thy sister to me, dear:
But I must leave thee, child, and seek a home away from here.
Ah! I defy them to the last; they shall not part us, child
And thy mother's hand shall rear thee—rear thee, pure and undefiled!

May the fond prayers of thy mother prove a love-protecting shield
From each sorrow, and each harrowing care, that life doth ever yield.
And may the hand of love, my child, pluck thorns from thy bright
    flowers;
And may'st thou find a home at last in heaven's celestial bowers.

THE OPIUM-EATER

[*Before taking a dose.*]

Life's pathway to me is dreary;
I am ill, and cold, and weary;
Would my lonely walk were done,
And my heavenly race begun!

Once all things to me were bright,
Things that now seem dark as night:
Is the darkness all within?
Dark without from inward sin?

The present dark; eyes dim with age
Can see no joy, save memory's page.
The present, future, ne'er can be
Bright as the past they once did see.

My hair is turning quite grey now;
I see some wrinkles on my brow;
My teeth—they must be failing too,—
And corns are growing in my shoe.

I muffle up my aching face,
And pray from pangs a moment's grace.

Mary Tucker Lambert

Ah! now the misery seeks my head—
Would I were with the pangless dead!
There is a cure for pain and grief—
Come, Opium, come to my relief!
Soothed by thy influence, I shall find
A moment's rest, and peace of mind.

[*After taking a dose.*]

Ah! now I sit in bowers of bliss,
Soothed by an angel's balmy kiss!
Delicious languor o'er me stealing
Is now my only sense of feeling.

The breath of flowers perfumes the air;
The forms around are—oh, so fair!
The once cold air seems warm and bright,
And I, too, seem a being of light.

My hair is not so very grey—
Some dye will take that hue away;
A little powder shall, I vow,
Hide the small wrinkles on my brow.

My teeth are sound—I feel no pain—
Their slight ache was but sign of rain;
And then the twinging of my feet
Was nothing but a dream, a cheat.

To me, the night, though dark, seems day,
Colored by Hope's most beauteous ray:
No sorrow hence shall give me pain—
I know I'll never weep again!

Mary Tucker Lambert

APPLE DUMPLINGS

By Request

Gaze not upon my outside, friend,
　　With scorn or with disgust—
Judge not, until you condescend
　　To look beneath the crust.

Rough and unsightly is my shell,
　　But you just dues will render;
And to the world the truth will tell,
　　And say my heart is tender.

The young may scorn my olden ways,
　　With their new-fashioned notions;
The old the insult soon repays
　　By claiming double portions.

'Tis true, like modern Misses, gay,
　　The truth is sad, distressing!
But I must now say out my say—
　　I need a little *dressing!*

My sauce, my rich apparel, hides
　　My ugly form from sight;
The goodness of my heart, besides,
　　Will always come to light.

Then judge not by the surface, dear;
　　Look deeper at the heart:
Above the faults of earth appear
　　Beneath the better part.

Mary Tucker Lambert

UPON RECEIPT OF A POUND OF COFFEE IN 1863

The sight of the coffee was good for sore eyes,
For I have not learned yet its worth to despise;
I welcomed each grain as I culled with care o'er,
And in fancy increased it to ten thousand more.

I put it on fire, and stirred round and round,
Then took it off gently when it was quite browned;
When cool I proceeded to fill up my mill,
And ground up a boiling with very good will.

I measured three spoons full, you see, for us three—
The old Lady Lane, my Grand-mother and me;
I added some water, then put it to boil,
And stood close by, watching, for fear it might spoil.

I put cream and sugar in three of our cups,
Then poured out our coffee, and took some good sups.
I thought of the Turk, sitting on his curled knees,
And was sure that our coffee, his Lordship would please.

It spoiled me, and now I'm beginning to think,
When that coffee gives out, what the mischief I'll drink;
I must get some coffee—beg, borrow, or steal—
For after that Java, I can't drink parched meal!

Thus down to the bottom we drank your good health!
May God shower o'er you of blessings a wealth;
May you never want for good coffee and tea—
And, friend, in your buying, remember poor me!

The date here may be important in calling attention to the difficulty of getting
coffee (as opposed to "parched meal") during the Civil War.

ADAH ISAACS MENKEN

(1839?–1868)

爻爻爻爻爻

OF ALL THE WOMEN POETS in this collection, the one whose tombstone was inscribed Adah Isaacs Menken surely led the most unconventional and romantic life. She used many names during her lifetime, claimed to have been married six times (though she died at the age of twenty-nine), posed as Euro-American, Jewish, and Negro, electrified audiences in America and Europe with her scantily clad performances of Byron's *Mazeppa,* and fraternized with Walt Whitman, Bret Harte, Charles Dickens, Mark Twain, George Sand, Alexander Dumas (père), and Algernon Swinburne. With the last two men on the list, she apparently had scandalous love affairs.

Recent biographical studies of her life claim that she was probably born in New Orleans to a "free man of color" and his wife, her given name being Philomène Croi Théodore. Her career began when at fifteen she gave public readings of Shakespeare, published some poetry, and married her first husband Alexander Isaac Menken, a rich Jewish businessman. After her marriage she converted to Judaism and learned Hebrew. Claiming that she was of Jewish descent, Adah published poems fervently endorsing Hebrew culture and is still revered as an important Jewish artist by some scholars. Though her marriage to Menken did not last, she retained her first husband's name in death and asked for Jewish burial rites.

There is evidence of three more marriages in 1859, 1862, and 1866, but these had even less stability than her first one. Menken's most prominent and continuous career was as an actress, and she is said to

have earned as much as $5,000 a week during the height of her popu-
larity. She lived lavishly, suffered terribly, was sometimes penniless, and
not infrequently suicidal. In her more gregarious moods, she charmed
and delighted Bohemians on both sides of the Atlantic, but she was
forever searching for a stability she found impossible to achieve. She
died in Paris on 10 August 1868, probably of pneumonia. In her poem
"Infelix" she conveys her sense that her life has been a failure.

After her death, a volume of her collected poems appeared, en-
titled *Infelicia*, and, probably because of her notoriety, it went through
twelve editions between 1868 and 1902. Joan R. Sherman, in her intro-
duction to the poems, comments: "The poet of *Infelicia* speaks with two
voices: hysterical and extremely hysterical." Nevertheless, some of her
poems are fascinating in their defiance of nineteenth-century conven-
tions. "Judith" is a fearless assault upon feminine standards of pro-
priety, an early version of what would later become a female genre: the
woman warrior's revenge poem. In contrast, a work like "Aspiration"
would not seem out of place in Rufus Griswold's anthology.

Adah Isaacs Menken was undoubtedly a talented woman. She cer-
tainly had a facility for learning languages and she rightly assessed the
value of poets such as Whitman and Poe, both of whom (along with
Swinburne) strongly influenced her work. On the other hand, she never
put much time into developing her talents as a poet, and today her life
seems more interesting than her art.

Selected Criticism: Mankowitz, Wolf. *Mazeppa: The Lives, Loves, and Legends
of Adah Isaacs Menken.* London: Blond & Briggs, 1982; Miller, Joaquin.
Adah Isaacs Menken. Austin: U of Texas P, 1934; Sherman, Intro. to *Col-
lected Black Women's Poetry.* Vol. I; Stoddard, Charles Warren. "La Belle
Menken." *National Magazine* (Feb. 1905): 477–88.

JUDITH

*"Repent, or I will come unto thee quickly, and will fight thee with the sword of my
mouth."*—Revelation *ii. 16.*

In the Apocrypha, Judith is the heroine who saves her native Bethulia by
creeping into the enemy camp and slaying Nebuchadnezzar's general, Holofernes.

Adah Isaacs Menken

I

Ashkelon is not cut off with the remnant of a valley.
  Baldness dwells not upon Gaza.
The field of the valley is mine, and it is clothed in verdure.
The steepness of Baal-perazim is mine;
And the Philistines spread themselves in the valley of Rephaim.
They shall yet be delivered into my hands.
For the God of Battles has gone before me!
The sword of the mouth shall smite them to dust.
I have slept in the darkness—
But the seventh angel woke me, and giving me a sword of flame, points
    to the blood-ribbed cloud, that lifts his reeking head above the
    mountain.
Thus am I the prophet.
I see the dawn that heralds to my waiting soul the advent of power.
    Power that will unseal the thunders!
    Power that will give voice to graves!

    Graves of the living;
    Graves of the dying;
    Graves of the sinning;
    Graves of the loving;
    Graves of despairing;
And oh! graves of the deserted!
These shall speak, each as their voices shall be loosed.
And the day is dawning.

Place names given here refer to the Ashkelon area in southwest Palestine. The
Plain of Rephaim is west of Jerusalem. In Friedrich Hebbell's play (1841) Holo-
fernes is Judith's lover. Menken seems to be drawing on this variant.

Adah Isaacs Menken

II

Stand back, ye Philistines!

Practice what ye preach to me;

I heed ye not, for I know ye all.

Ye are living burning lies, and profanation to the garments which with
stately steps ye sweep your marble palaces.

Your palaces of Sin, around which the damning evidence of guilt hangs
like a reeking vapor.

Stand back!

I would pass up the golden road of the world.

A place in the ranks awaits me.

I know that ye are hedged on the borders of my path.

Lie and tremble, for ye well know that I hold with iron grasp the battle
axe.

Creep back to your dark tents in the valley.

Slouch back to your haunts of crime.

Ye do not know me, neither do ye see me.

But the sword of the mouth is unsealed, and ye coil yourselves in slime
and bitterness at my feet.

I mix your jeweled heads, and your gleaming eyes, and your hissing
tongues with the dust.

My garments shall bear no mark of ye.

When I shall return this sword to the angel, your foul blood will not
stain its edge.

It will glimmer with the light of truth, and the strong arm shall rest.

III

Stand back!

I am no Magdalene waiting to kiss the hem of your garment.

It is mid-day.

See ye not what is written on my forehead?

Adah Isaacs Menken

I am Judith!

I wait for the head of my Holofernes!

Ere the last tremble of the conscious death-agony shall have shuddered, I
will show it to ye with the long black hair clinging to the glazed
eyes, and the great mouth opened in search of voice, and the strong
throat all hot and reeking with blood, that will thrill me with wild
unspeakable joy as it courses down my bare body and dabbles my
cold feet!

My sensuous soul will quake with the burden of so much bliss.

Oh, what wild passionate kisses will I draw up from that bleeding mouth!

I will strangle this pallid throat of mine on the sweet blood!

I will revel in my passion.

At midnight I will feast on it in the darkness.

For it was that which thrilled its crimson tides of reckless passion
through the blue veins of my life, and made them leap up in the
wild sweetness of Love and agony of Revenge!

I am starving for this feast.

Oh forget not that I am Judith!

And I know where sleeps Holofernes.

ASPIRATION

Poor, impious Soul! that fixes its high hopes
 In the dim distance, on a throne of clouds,
And from the morning's mist would make the ropes
 To draw it up amid acclaim of crowds—
Beware! That soaring path is lined with shrouds;
 And he who braves it, though of sturdy breath,
May meet, half way, the avalanche and death!

O poor young Soul!—whose year-devouring glance
 Fixes in ecstasy upon a star,

Whose feverish brilliance looks a part of earth,
   Yet quivers where the feet of angels are,
And seems the future crown in realms afar—
   Beware! A spark *thou* art, and dost but see
Thine own reflection in Eternity!

INFELIX

Where is the promise of my years;
   Once written on my brow?
Ere errors, agonies and fears
Brought with them all that speaks in tears,
Ere I had sunk beneath my peers;
   Where sleeps that promise now?

Naught lingers to redeem those hours,
   Still, still to memory sweet!
The flowers that bloomed in sunny bowers
Are withered all; and Evil towers
Supreme above her sister powers
   Of Sorrow and Deceit.

I look along the columned years,
   And see Life's riven fane,
Just where it fell, amid the jeers
Of scornful lips, whose mocking sneers,
For ever hiss within mine ears
   To break the sleep of pain.

The title of the poem is Latin, meaning, the unfortunate one.

Adah Isaacs Menken

I can but own my life is vain
    A desert void of peace;
I missed the goal I sought to gain,
I missed the measure of the strain
That lulls Fame's fever in the brain,
    And bids Earth's tumult cease.

Myself! alas for theme so poor
    A theme but rich in Fear;
I stand a wreck on Error's shore,
A spectre not within the door,
A houseless shadow evermore,
    An exile lingering here.

INA COOLBRITH

(1841–1928)

&ZdZdZdZd&

BORN JOSEPHINE SMITH (named after her famous uncle, the founder of the Mormon Church), Ina moved from Illinois to St. Louis and then to California, making a difficult crossing on the Overland Trail with her mother and gold-seeking stepfather. The family eventually settled in Los Angeles, which at that time was a little town of Mexican pueblos. Ina went to a tiny local school but, like the Cary sisters and Celia Thaxter, she was mostly self-educated. She published her first poem at fifteen and in 1858 married Robert Carsley, part owner of a local iron works.

A handsome and romantic figure, Carsley was also jealous and unstable. His wild accusations of infidelity against Ina led to a gunfight with her stepfather resulting in the amputation of Carsley's hand. Though it seems the accusations were unfounded, and Ina filed for divorce, she was deeply humiliated and decided to leave the area. Apparently she also had a child who died.

Settling in San Francisco, Ina decided to take her mother's maiden name of Coolbrith. She began to publish her poetry in local journals, eventually developing a national reputation that brought her to the attention of Whittier, Stedman, and others. Coolbrith soon fell in with local writers and became part of what was called the "Golden Gate Trinity": herself, Bret Harte, and Charles Warren Stoddard. For many years she held a weekly salon that entertained Joaquin Miller, Ambrose Bierce, John Muir, Jack London, Isadora Duncan, and many other traveling artists and writers.

However, Coolbrith was often depressed and troubled by financial pressures. She took care of Joaquin Miller's half-Indian daughter (who became an alcoholic) and ultimately took in a niece and nephew as well as her mother. In 1874 she accepted a position as the first librarian of the Oakland Free Library. The hours were long (eleven hours a day, six days a week) and the salary small, but the early years at the library were happy. Ina had many friends and, it was rumored, several suitors.

During the 1880s Coolbrith was tormented by the library's directors. In 1892 they fired her, replacing her with the nephew whom Coolbrith had supported at some sacrifice. The rest of her life was difficult despite other librarianships, friendships with Mary Austin and Gertrude Atherton, and the publication of several books of poetry. In 1906 Coolbrith was caught in the San Francisco earthquake. Her home destroyed, her manuscripts lost, her job gone, the severely rheumatic poet had to sleep outside for two days. Eventually, her friends collected money for her support, and a new home was built for her. In 1915 she was made the first poet laureate of California. Today a library, a park, a poppy, a mountain, and a poetry prize all bear her name.

Coolbrith's poetry is often melancholy, but "The Captive of the White City" demonstrates her ability to criticize her own culture. Her even-handed pity for both Custer and his killer was ahead of its time, and her poems of the West remain striking. Her narrated poem "Concha"—though too long to include here—is probably her best work.

Selected Works: A Perfect Day. 1881; *Songs of the Golden Gate.* 1896; *Wings of Sunset.* 1928.

Selected Criticism: Graham, Ina Agnes. "My Aunt, Ina Coolbrith." *Pacific Historian* 17 (Fall 1973): 12–19; Hubbard, George U. "Ina Coolbrith's Friendship with John Greenleaf Whittier." *New England Quarterly* 45 (March 1972): 109–18; Rhodehamel, J., and R. F. Wood. *Ina Coolbrith, Librarian and Laureate of California.* Provo: Brigham Young UP, 1973; Walker, Cheryl. "Ina Coolbrith and the Nightingale Tradition." *Legacy* 6: 1 (Spring 1989): 27–33.

Ina Coolbrith

WHEN THE GRASS SHALL COVER ME

When the grass shall cover me,
Head to foot where I am lying,—
    When not any wind that blows,
    Summer-blooms nor winter-snows,
Shall awake me to your sighing:
    Close above me as you pass,
    You will say, "How kind she was,"
    You will say, "How true she was,"
When the grass grows over me.

When the grass shall cover me,
Holden close to earth's warm bosom,—
    While I laugh, or weep, or sing,
    Nevermore, for anything,
You will find in blade and blossom,
    Sweet small voices, odorous,
    Tender pleaders in my cause,
    That shall speak me as I was—
When the grass grows over me.

When the grass shall cover me!
Ah, belovëd, in my sorrow
    Very patient, I can wait,
    Knowing that, or soon or late,
There will dawn a clearer morrow:
    When your heart will moan: "Alas!
    Now I know how true she was;
    Now I know how dear she was"—
When the grass grows over me!

Ina Coolbrith

THE MARIPOSA LILY

Insect or blossom? Fragile, fairy thing,
Poised upon slender tip, and quivering
　　To flight! a flower of the fields of air;
　　A jeweled moth; a butterfly, with rare
And tender tints upon his downy wing
　　A moment resting in our happy sight;
　　A flower held captive by a thread so slight
Its petal-wings of broidered gossamer
Are, light as the wind, with every wind astir,—
　　Wafting sweet odor, faint and exquisite.
O dainty nursling of the field and sky,
　　What fairer thing looks up to heaven's blue
　　And drinks the noontide sun, the dawning's dew?
Thou wingëd bloom! thou blossom-butterfly!

WITHHELD

Therein is sunlight, and sweet sound:
　　Cool flow of waters, musical,
　　Soft stir of insect-wings, and fall
Of blossom-snow upon the ground.

The birds flit in and out the trees,
　　Their bright, sweet throats strained full with song.
　　The flower-beds, the summer long,
Are black and murmurous with bees.

Th' unrippled leaves hang faint with dew
　　In hushes of the breezeless morn.
　　At eventide the stars, new born,
And the white moonlight, glimmer through.

Therein are all glad things whereof
   Life holdeth need through changing years;
   Therein sweet rest, sweet end of tears,
Therein sweet labors, born of love.

This is my heritage, mine own,
   That alien hands from me withhold.
   From barrëd windows, dark and cold,
I view, with heart that maketh moan.

They fetter feet and hands; they give
   Me bitter, thankless tasks to do;
   And, cruel wise, still feed anew
My one small hope, that I may live.

And, that no single pang I miss,
   Lo! this one little window-space
   Is left, where through my eyes may trace
How sweeter than all sweet it is.

I CANNOT COUNT MY LIFE A LOSS

I cannot count my life a loss,
   With all its length of evil days.
I hold them only as the dross
   About its gold, whose worth outweighs:
   For each and all I give Him praise.

For, drawing nearer to the brink
   That leadeth down to final rest,
I see with clearer eyes, I think,
   And much that vexed me and oppressed,
   Have learned was right, and just, and best.

So though I may but dimly guess
　　Its far intent, this gift of His
I honor; nor would know the less
　　One sorrow, or in pain or bliss
　　Have other than it was and is.

THE CAPTIVE OF THE WHITE CITY

Flower of the foam of the waves
　　Of the beautiful inland sea,—
White as the foam that laves
　　The ships of the Sea-Kings past,—
　　Marvel of human hands,
Wonderful, mystical, vast,
　　The great White City stands;
And the banners of all the lands
Are free on the western breeze,
　　Free as the West is free.
And the throngs go up and down
In the streets of the wonderful town
　　In brotherly love and grace,—
Children of every zone
The light of the sun has known:
　　And there in the Midway Place,
　　In the House of the Unhewn Trees,
There in the surging crowd,
Silent, and stern, and proud,
　　Sits Rain-in-the-Face![1]

"The White City" was the name given to the Columbian Exposition in Chicago, 1893.

1. The man who was supposed to have killed Custer was displayed at the fair, his wigwam having been brought all the way from Montana for the purpose.

Why is the captive here?
Is the hour of the Lord so near
When slayer and slain shall meet
In the place of the Judgment seat
   For the word of the last decree?
   Ah, what is that word to be?
For the beautiful City stands
On the Red Man's wrested lands,[2]
    The home of a fated race;
And a ghostly shadow falls
Over the trophied walls[3]
   Of the House of the Unhewn Tree,
    In the pleasant Midway Place.
There is blood on the broken door,
There is blood on the broken floor,
Blood on your bronzed hands,
    O Rain-in-the-Face!

    Shut from the sunlit air,
Like a sun-god overthrown,
   The soldier, Custer, lies.
Dust is the sun-kissed hair,
   Dust are the dauntless eyes,
Dust and a name alone;—
   While the wife holds watch with grief
   For the never-returning chief.
What if she walked to-day
In the City's pleasant way,
   The beautiful Midway Place,
   And there to her sudden gaze,
Dimmed with her widow's tears,

---

2. "The Indians claim that the land upon which Chicago is built was never fully paid for" (Coolbrith's note).

3. "The walls were hung with relics of the fight" (Coolbrith's note).

Ina Coolbrith

After the terrible years,
Stood Rain-in-the-Face!

Quench with a drop of dew
From the morning's cloudless blue
    The prairies' burning plains—
    The seas of seething flame;
Turn from its awful path
The tempest, in its wrath;
    Lure from his jungle-lair
    The tiger, crouching there
For the leap on his sighted prey:
    Then seek as well to tame
The hate in the Red Man's veins,
    His tiger-thirst to cool,
In the hour of the evil day
When his foe before him stands!
    From the wrongs of the White Man's rule
    Blood only may wash the trace.
    Alas, for the death-heaped plain!
    Alas, for slayer and slain!
    Alas for your blood-stained hands,
        O Rain-in-the-Face!

And the throngs go up, go down,
In the streets of the wonderful town;
And jests of the merry tongue,
And the dance, and the glad songs sung,
    Ring through the sunlit space.
And there, in the wild, free breeze,
In the House of the Unhewn Trees,
    In the beautiful Midway Place,
        The captive sits apart,
        Silent, and makes no sign.
        But what is the word in your heart,

Ina Coolbrith

O man of a dying race?
What tale on your lips for mine,
O Rain-in-the-Face?

HELEN HUNT JACKSON

("H. H.")

What songs found voice upon those lips,
    What magic dwelt within the pen,
Whose music into silence slips,
    Whose spell lives not again!

For her the clamorous to-day
    The dreamful yesterday became;
The brands upon dead hearths that lay
    Leaped into living flame.

Clear ring the silvery Mission bells[1]
    Their calls to vesper and to mass;
O'er vineyard slopes, thro' fruited dells,
    The long processions pass;

The pale Franciscan lifts in air
    The Cross above the kneeling throng;
Their simple world how sweet with prayer,
    With chant and matin-song!

"H. H." stands for Helen Hunt and is the acronym Jackson used to sign many of her poems.

1. The references to the Mission, the Franciscan, Alessandro, and Ramona all allude to Jackson's well-known novel *Ramona* (1884).

Ina Coolbrith

There, with her dimpled, lifted hands,
    Parting the mustard's golden plumes,
The dusky maid, Ramona, stands
    Amid the sea of blooms.

And Alessandro, type of all
    His broken tribe, for evermore
An exile, hears the stranger call
    Within his father's door.

The visions vanish and are not,
    Still are the sounds of peace and strife,
Passed with the earnest heart and thought
    Which lured them back to life.

O, sunset land! O, land of vine,
    And rose, and bay! in silence here
Let fall one little leaf of thine,
    With love, upon her bier.

SAN FRANCISCO

April 18, 1906

In olden days, a child, I trod thy sands,
    Thy sands unbuilded, rank with brush and briar
And blossom—chased the sea-foam on thy strands,
    Young City of my love and my desire.

The date here refers to the great earthquake.

Ina Coolbrith

I saw thy barren hills against the skies,
   I saw them topped with minaret and spire;
Wall upon wall thy myriad mansions rise,
   Fair City of my love and my desire.

With thee the Orient touched heart and hands,
   The world-wide argosies lay at thy feet;
Queen of the queenliest land of all the lands—
   Our sunset glory, regal, glad and sweet!

I saw thee in thine anguish tortured! prone!
   Rent with the earth-throes, garmented in fire!
Each wound upon thy breast upon my own,
   Sad City of my grief and my desire.

Gray wind-blown ashes, broken, toppling wall
   And ruined hearth—are these thy funeral pyre?
Black desolation covering as a pall—
   Is this the end—my love and my desire?

Nay! strong, undaunted, thoughtless of despair,
   The Will that builded thee shall build again,
And all thy broken promise spring more fair,
   Thou mighty mother of as mighty men.

Thou wilt arise, invincible! supreme!
   The world to voice thy glory never tire;
And song, unborn, shall chant no nobler theme—
   Great City of my faith and my desire.

But I will see thee ever as of old!
   Thy wraith of pearl, wall, minaret and spire,
Framed in the mists that veil thy Gate of Gold—
   Lost City of my love and my desire.

EMMA LAZARUS

(1849–1887)

EMMA LAZARUS was born into a Sephardic Jewish family whose American roots on both sides went back to the seventeenth century. The beloved and privileged fourth daughter of a very wealthy New York businessman, Emma was educated by private tutors who taught her French, German, and Italian. Intelligent and precocious, Lazarus published her first book, *Poems and Translations,* at the age of eighteen. A second came out four years later, dedicated to Emerson whom she deeply admired.

As a young woman, Emma was indulged but also sheltered from contact with the outside world. T. W. Higginson met her in 1872 and, according to Morris Schappes, wrote his sisters: "She is rather an interesting person. . . . She has never seen an author till lately, though she has corresponded with Emerson. It is curious to see how mentally famished a person may be in the very best literary society" (9). In 1876 she stayed for a week with the Emersons. She later traveled to Europe and met with literary figures there, such as Henry James, Robert Browning, William Morris, and Thomas Huxley. When her novel *Alide* (based on the life of Goethe) came out in 1874, she sent it to Turgenev who responded with enthusiasm.

Her early work was rather romantic and conventional, but in the 1880s she became fired with a desire to write of Jewish culture and the woes experienced by European Jews. Her entire orientation to life and art changed, and she became an ardent supporter of Jewish causes, whereas earlier she had seen herself as only tenuously connected to that heritage. In addition to writing, she became actively engaged in charity work, supported socialist economic changes, and the creation of a Jewish state in

Palestine. "Until we are all free," she wrote, "we are none of us free. Today, wherever we are free, we are at home."

Lazarus saw herself as representing a wider world than Jews alone, however, and in 1883 she composed "The New Colossus" to help raise funds for the Statue of Liberty. After her death it was engraved on the pedestal. Lazarus was sympathetic to the laboring poor, women, immigrants, and those who were denied access to the privileges of a free and prosperous society. With its new politics her poetry gained the passion it lacked earlier. Such works as "The New Ezekiel" are both ardent and memorable.

Emma Lazarus died at the age of thirty-eight of cancer. She received memorial tributes from Browning, Whittier, Stedman, Stowe, Higginson, and Walt Whitman, who commented: "She must have had a great, sweet, unusual nature." In fact, she was lifted into greatness by her deep-felt connection to the issues of her time. In 1956 Eve Merriam wrote: "One of the finest women poets our country has produced, she enriched the treasure-house of American democratic writing. She should be reclaimed and honored" (154).

Selected Works: Poems and Translations. 1867; *Admetus, and Other Poems.* 1871; *Songs of a Semite.* 1882; *By the Waters of Babylon.* 1887; *The Poems of Emma Lazarus.* 2 vols. 1889; *The Letters of Emma Lazarus.* Ed. Morris Schappes. 1949.

Selected Criticism: Jacob, Heinrich E. *The World of Emma Lazarus.* New York: Schocken, 1949; Kessner, Carole. "The Emma Lazarus–Henry James Connection: Eight Letters." *American Literary History* 3 (Spring 1991): 46–62; Lyons, Joseph. "In Two Divided Streams." *Midstream* 7 (Aug. 1961): 78–85; Merriam, Eve. *Emma Lazarus: Woman with a Torch.* New York: Citadel, 1956; Schappes, Morris, ed. *Emma Lazarus: Selections.* New York: Book League, 1944.

ECHOES

Late-born and woman-souled I dare not hope,
The freshness of the elder lays, the might
Of manly, modern passion shall alight

Upon my Muse's lips, nor may I cope
(Who veiled and screened by womanhood must grope)
With the world's strong-armed warriors and recite
The dangers, wounds, and triumphs of the fight;
Twanging the full-stringed lyre through all its scope.
But if thou ever in some lake-floored cave
O'erbrowed by rocks, a wild voice wooed and heard,
Answering at once from heaven and earth and wave,
Lending elf-music to thy harshest word,
Misprize thou not these echoes that belong
To one in love with solitude and song.

CRITIC AND POET

No man had ever heard a nightingale,
When once a keen-eyed naturalist was stirred
To study and define —what is a bird,
To classify by rote and book, nor fail
To mark its structure and to note the scale
Whereon its song might possibly be heard.
Thus far, no farther;—so he spake the word.
When of a sudden,—hark, the nightingale!

Oh deeper, higher than he could divine
That all-unearthly, untaught strain! He saw
The plain, brown warbler, unabashed. "Not mine"
(He cried) "the error of this fatal flaw.
No bird is this, it soars beyond my line,
Were it a bird, 'twould answer to my law.

Emma Lazarus

VENUS OF THE LOUVRE

Down the long hall she glistens like a star,
The foam-born mother of Love, transfixed to stone,
Yet none the less immortal, breathing on.
Time's brutal hand hath maimed but could not mar.
When first the enthralled enchantress from afar
Dazzled mine eyes, I saw not her alone,
Serenely poised on her world-worshipped throne,
As when she guided once her dove-drawn car,—
But at her feet a pale, death-stricken Jew,
Her life adorer, sobbed farewell to love.
Here *Heine*[1] wept! Here still he weeps anew,
Nor ever shall his shadow lift or move,
While mourns one ardent heart, one poet-brain,
For vanished Hellas and Hebraic pain.

IN THE JEWISH SYNAGOGUE AT NEWPORT

Here, where the noises of the busy town,
  The ocean's plunge and roar can enter not,
We stand and gaze around with tearful awe,
  And muse upon the consecrated spot.—

No signs of life are here: the very prayers
  Inscribed around are in a language dead;
The light of the "perpetual lamp" is spent
  That an undying radiance was to shed.

---

1. Heinrich Heine, German Jewish poet (1797–1856), who lived almost his entire adult life in Paris.

What prayers were in this temple offered up,
    Wrung from sad hearts that knew no joy on earth,
By these lone exiles of a thousand years,
    From the fair sunrise land that gave them birth!

Now as we gaze, in this new world of light,
    Upon this relic of the days of old,
The present vanishes, and tropic bloom
    And Eastern towns and temples we behold.

Again we see the patriarch with his flocks,
    The purple seas, the hot blue sky o'erhead,
The slaves of Egypt,—omens, mysteries,—
    Dark fleeing hosts by flaming angels led.

A wondrous light upon a sky-kissed mount,
    A man who reads Jehovah's written law,
'Midst blinding glory and effulgence rare,
    Unto a people prone with reverent awe.

The pride of luxury's barbaric pomp,
    In the rich court of royal Solomon—
Alas! we wake: one scene alone remains,—
    The exiles by the streams of Babylon.

Our softened voices send us back again
    But mournful echoes through the empty hall;
Our footsteps have a strange, unnatural sound,
    And with unwonted gentleness they fall.

The weary ones, the sad, the suffering,
    All found their comfort in the holy place,
And children's gladness and men's gratitude
    Took voice and mingled in the chant of praise.

The funeral and the marriage, now, alas!
   We know not which is sadder to recall;
For youth and happiness have followed age,
   And green grass lieth gently over all.

Nathless the sacred shrine is holy yet,
   With its lone floors where reverent feet once trod.
Take off your shoes as by the burning bush,
   Before the mystery of death and God.[1]

THE BANNER OF THE JEW

Wake, Israel, wake! Recall to-day
   The glorious Maccabean rage,
The sire heroic, hoary-gray,
   His five-fold lion-lineage:
The Wise, the Elect, the Help-of-God,
The Burst-of-Spring, the Avenging Rod.[2]

From Mizpeh's mountain-ridge they saw
   Jerusalem's empty streets, her shrine
Laid waste where Greeks profaned the Law
   With idol and with pagan sign.
Mourners in tattered black were there,
With ashes sprinkled on their hair.

Then from the stony peak there rang
   A blast to ope the graves: down poured

---

1. See also Longfellow's poem "The Jewish Cemetery at Newport."
2. "The sons of Matthias—Jonathan, John, Eleazar, Simon, (also called the Jewel), and Judas, the Prince" (author's note).

The Maccabean clan, who sang
   Their battle-anthem to the Lord.
Five heroes lead, and, following, see
Ten thousand rush to victory!

Oh for Jerusalem's trumpet now,
   To blow a blast of shattering power,
To wake the sleepers high and low,
   And rouse them to the urgent hour!
No hand for vengeance—but to save,
A million naked swords should wave.

Oh deem not dead that martial fire,
   Say not the mystic flame is spent!
With Moses' law and David's lyre,
   Your ancient strength remains unbent.
Let but an Ezra[2] rise anew,
To lift the *Banner of the Jew!*

A rag, a mock at first—erelong,
   When men have bled and women wept,
To guard its precious folds from wrong,
   Even they who shrunk, even they who slept,
Shall leap to bless it, and to save.
Strike! for the brave revere the brave!

---

2. In the Old Testament, the priest Ezra led a band of 1,500 Jews back to Jerusalem after their captivity in Babylon (Ezra 2.1–70).

Emma Lazarus

THE CROWING OF THE RED COCK

Across the Eastern sky has glowed
    The flicker of a blood-red dawn;
Once more the clarion cock has crowed,
    Once more the sword of Christ is drawn.
A million burning roof-trees light
The world-wide path of Israel's flight.

Where is the Hebrew's fatherland?
    The folk of Christ is sore bestead;
The Son of Man is braised and banned,
    Nor finds whereon to lay his head.
His cup is gall, his meat is tears,
His passion lasts a thousand years.

Each crime that wakes in man the beast,
    Is visited upon his kind.
The lust of mobs, the greed of priest,
    The tyranny of kings, combined
To root his seed from earth again,
His record is one cry of pain.

When the long roll of Christian guilt
    Against his sires and kin is known,
The flood of tears, the life-blood spilt,
    The agony of ages shown,
What oceans can the stain remove
From Christian law and Christian love?

Nay, close the book; not now, not here,
    The hideous tale of sin narrate;
Reëchoing in the martyr's ear,
    Even he might nurse revengeful hate,

Even he might turn in wrath sublime,
With blood for blood and crime for crime.

Coward? Not he, who faces death,
   Who singly against worlds has fought,
For what? A name he may not breathe,
   For liberty of prayer and thought.
The angry sword he will not whet,
His nobler task is—to forget.

THE NEW EZEKIEL

What, can these dead bones live, whose sap is dried
   By twenty scorching centuries of wrong?
Is this the House of Israel, whose pride
Is as a tale that's told, an ancient song?
Are these ignoble relics all that live
   Of psalmist, priest, and prophet? Can the breath
Of very heaven bid these bones revive,
   Open the graves and clothe the ribs of death?

Yea, Prophesy, the Lord hath said. Again
   Say to the wind, Come forth and breathe afresh,
Even that they may live upon these slain,
   And bone to bone shall leap, and flesh to flesh.
The Spirit is not dead, proclaim the word,
   Where lay dead bones, a host of armed men stand!
I ope your graves, my people, saith the Lord,
   And I shall place you living in your land.

Ezekiel was a Hebrew prophet during the Babylonian exile.

Emma Lazarus

THE NEW COLOSSUS

Not like the brazen giant of Greek fame,
With conquering limbs astride from land to land;
Here at our sea-washed, sunset gates shall stand
A mighty woman with a torch, whose flame
Is the imprisoned lightning, and her name
Mother of Exiles. From her beacon-hand
Glows world-wide welcome; her mild eyes command
The air-bridged harbor that win cities frame.
"Keep, ancient lands, your storied pomp!" cries she
With silent lips. "Give me your tired, your poor,
Your huddled masses yearning to breathe free,
The wretched refuse of your teeming shore.
Send these, the homeless, tempest-tost to me,
I lift my lamp beside the golden door!"

ELLA WHEELER WILCOX

(1850–1919)

ＥＬＬＡ ＷＨＥＥＬＥＲ was born on an isolated Wisconsin farm where cultural opportunities were few. Her mother was fond of literature, however, and encouraged Ella to develop a love for both reading and writing. Though she enrolled at the University of Wisconsin, Ella soon returned home and by 1880 was actively involved with a group of writers in Milwaukee.

Her work got sudden attention when she published *Poems of Passion* in 1883. Though many of these poems had been printed in periodicals already, the book as a whole became notorious, especially because one publisher had rejected it as obscene. The Chicago publisher who was willing to bring it out soon sold 60,000 copies of these poems which he said "out-Swinburned Swinburne and out-Whitmaned Whitman."

Nevertheless, Ella Wheeler was no Adah Isaacs Menken. Though she became part of what was called "the erotic school"—a group of artists who refused to sublimate their sensuality in conformity with Victorian standards—Ella married Robert Wilcox in 1884 and lived a highly respectable life. She was active in the temperance movement and believed that women should glorify rather than denigrate the role of wife. Shortly before her death in 1919, she attacked Amy Lowell for writing what she thought were obscene poems, demonstrating that, for all her rebelliousness, she was more a Victorian than a modernist.

Wilcox was enormously productive, publishing forty-six books and many articles. She was championed (appropriately) by William Randolph Hearst, but her reputation went into decline quickly as more modern women such as Edna St. Vincent Millay and Dorothy Parker overshadowed her. In the heydey of New Criticism, she was the subject of attacks by I. A. Richards and W. K. Wimsatt, who claimed that works such as "Friendship after Love" were full of clichés and facile resolutions. Her name took on the negative connotations associated with popular "fireside" poets.

Nevertheless, Ella Wheeler Wilcox remains an important figure among late nineteenth-century women poets. She was enormously influential in liberalizing attitudes about women's passions. Her work was still widely known and read in the 1920s. At a time when prevailing wisdom claimed that morality depended upon women's instinctive resistance to sexual desire, Wilcox wrote in *Men, Women, and Emotions:* "It is impossible for an absolutely passionless woman to be either just or generous in her judgments of humanity at large. It is a strange fact that she needs an admixture of the baser physical element, to broaden her spiritual vision, and quicken her sympathies" (298).

Selected Works: Drops of Water. 1872; *Maurine.* 1876; *Perdita and Other Stories.* 1886; *Poems of Pleasure.* 1888; *Custer and Other Poems.* 1896; *Men, Women, and Emotions.* 1896; *New Thought Common Sense and What Life Means to Me.* 1908; *Collected Poems.* 1924.

Selected Criticism: Ballou, Jenny. *Period Piece: Ella Wheeler and Her Times.* Boston: Houghton, 1940; Haeffner, Paul. "Auden and Ella Wheeler Wilcox." *Notes and Queries* 9 (Mar. 1962): 110–11; Lewis, Naomi. "Wilcox Revisited." *New Statesman.* 24 Dec. 1971. 901; Pittock, Malcolm. "In Defense of Ella Wheeler Wilcox." *Durham University Journal* 65 (Dec. 1972): 86–89; Walker.

INDIVIDUALITY

O yes, I love you, and with all my heart;
Just as a weaker woman loves her own,
Better than I love my beloved art,
Which, till you came, reigned royally, alone,
My king, my master. Since I saw your face
I have dethroned it, and you hold that place.

Ella Wheeler Wilcox

I am as weak as other women are—
Your frown can make the whole world like a tomb.
Your smile shines brighter than the sun, by far,
Sometimes I think there is not space or room
In all the earth for such a love as mine,
And it soars up to breathe in realms divine.

I know that your desertion or neglect
Could break my heart, as women's hearts do break,
If my wan days had nothing to expect
From your love's splendor all joy would forsake
The chambers of my soul. Yes, this is true.
And yet, and yet—one thing I keep from you.

There is a subtle part of me which went
Into my long pursued and worshiped art;
Though your great love fills me with such content
No other love finds room now, in my heart.
Yet that rare essence was my art's alone.
Thank God, you cannot grasp it; 'tis mine own.

Thank God, I say, for while I love you so,
With that vast love, as passionate as tender,
I feel an exultation as I know
I have not made you a complete surrender.
Here is my body: bruise it, if you will.
And break my heart; I have that something still.

You cannot grasp it. Seize the breath of morn,
Or bind the perfume of the rose as well.
God put it in my soul when I was born;
It is not mine to give away, or sell,
Or offer up on any altar shrine.
IT was my art's; and when not art's, 'tis mine.

For love's sake, I can put the art away,
Or anything which stands 'twixt me and you.
But that strange essence God bestowed, I say,
To permeate the work He gave to do:
And it cannot be drained, dissolved, or sent
Through any channel, save the one He meant.

FRIENDSHIP AFTER LOVE

After the fierce midsummer all ablaze
    Has burned itself to ashes, and expires
    In the intensity of its own fires,
There come the mellow, mild, St. Martin days
Crowned with the calm of peace, but sad with haze.
    So after Love has led us, till he tires
    Of his own throes, and torments, and desires,
Comes large-eyed friendship: with a restful gaze,
He beckons us to follow, and across
    Cool verdant vales we wander free from care.
    Is it a touch of frost lies in the air?
Why are we haunted with a sense of loss?
We do not wish the pain back, or the heat;
And yet, and yet, these days are incomplete.

AS BY FIRE

Sometimes I feel so passionate a yearning
    For spiritual perfection here below,
This vigorous frame with healthful fervor burning,
    Seems my determined foe.

So actively it makes a stern resistance,
So cruelly sometimes it wages war
Against a wholly spiritual existence
    Which I am striving for.

It interrupts my soul's intense devotions,
Some hope it strangles of divinest birth,
With a swift rush of violent emotions
    Which link me to the earth.

It is as if two mortal foes contended
Within my bosom in a deadly strife,
One for the loftier aims for souls intended,
    One for the earthly life.

And yet I know this very war within me,
Which brings out all my will-power and control;
This very conflict at the last shall win me
    The loved and longed-for goal.

The very fire which seems sometimes so cruel.
Is the white light, that shows me my own strength.
A furnace, fed by the divinest fuel
    It may become at length.

Ah! When in the immortal ranks enlisted,
I sometimes wonder if we shall not find
That not by deeds, but by what we've resisted,
    Our places are assigned.

MISALLIANCE

I am troubled to-night with a curious pain;
    It is not of the flesh, it is not of the brain,

Nor yet of a heart that is breaking:
But down still deeper, and out of sight—
In the place where the soul and the body unite—
    There lies the seat of the aching.

They have been lovers, in days gone by;
But the soul is fickle, and longs to fly
    From the fettering misalliance:
And she tears at the bonds which are binding her so,
And pleads with the body to let her go,
    But he will not yield compliance.

For the body loves, as he loved in the past
When he wedded the soul; and he holds her fast,
    And swears that he will not loose her;
That he will keep her and hide her away
For ever and ever and for a day
    From the arms of Death, the seducer.

Ah! this is the strife that is wearying me—
The strife 'twixt a soul that would be free
    And a body that will not let her.
And I say to my soul, "Be calm, and wait;
For I tell ye truly that soon or late
    Ye surely shall drop each letter.

And I say to the body, "Be kind, I pray;
For the soul is not of the mortal clay,
    But is formed in spirit fashion."
And still through the hours of the solemn night
I can hear my sad soul's plea for flight,
    And my body's reply of passion.

Ella Wheeler Wilcox

THE YEAR OUTGROWS THE SPRING

The year outgrows the spring it thought so sweet
    And clasps the summer with a new delight,
Yet wearied, leaves her languors and her heat
    When cool-browed autumn dawns upon his sight.

The tree outgrows the bud's suggestive grace
    And feels new pride in blossoms fully blown.
But even this to deeper joy gives place
    When bending boughs 'neath blushing burdens groan.

Life's rarest moments are derived from change,
    The heart outgrows old happiness, old grief,
And suns itself in feelings new and strange.
    The most enduring pleasure is but brief.

Our tastes, our needs, are never twice the same.
    Nothing contents us long, however dear.
The spirit in us, like the grosser frame,
    Outgrows the garments which it wore last year.

Change is the watchword of Progression. When
    We tire of well-worn ways, we seek for new.
This restless craving in the souls of men
    Spurs them to climb, and seek the mountain view.

So let who will erect an altar shrine
    To meek-browed Constancy, and sing her praise
Unto enlivening Change I shall build mine.
    Who lends new zest, and interest to my days.

Ella Wheeler Wilcox

THE TIGER

In the still jungle of the senses lay
A tiger soundly sleeping, till one day
A bold young hunter chanced to come that way.

"How calm," he said, "that splendid creature lies,
I long to rouse him into swift surprise!"
The well aimed arrow-shot from amorous eyes,

And lo! the tiger rouses up and turns,
A coal of fire his glowing eyeball burns,
His mighty frame with savage hunger yearns.

He crouches for a spring; his eyes dilate—
Alas! bold hunter, what shall be thy fate?
Thou canst not fly, it is too late, too late.

Once having tasted human flesh, ah! then,
Woe, woe unto the whole rash world of men,
The wakened tiger will not sleep again.

TWIN-BORN

He who possesses virtue at its best,
    Or greatness in the true sense of the word,
    Has one day started even with that herd
Whose swift feet now speed, but at sin's behest.
It is the same force in the human breast
    Which makes men gods or demons. If we gird
    Those strong emotions by which we are stirred

With might of will and purpose, heights unguessed
   Shall dawn for us; or if we give them sway
We can sink down and consort with the lost.
All virtue is worth just the price it cost.
    Black sin is oft white truth, that missed its way
And wandered off in paths not understood.
Twin-born I hold great evil and great good.

A FABLE

Some cawing Crows, a hooting Owl,
   A Hawk, a Canary, an old Marsh-Fowl,
    One day all met together,
To hold a caucus and settle the fate
Of a certain bird (without a mate),
    A bird of another feather.

   "My friends," said the Owl, with a look most wise,
"The Eagle is soaring too near the skies,
   In a way that is quite improper;
Yet the world is praising her, so I'm told,
And I think her actions have grown so bold
   That some of us ought to stop her."

"I have heard it said," quoth Hawk, with a sigh,
"That young lambs died at the glance of her eye.
   And I wholly scorn and despise her.
This, and more, I am told they say—
And I think that the only proper way
   Is never to recognize her."

Ella Wheeler Wilcox

"I am quite convinced," said Crow, with a caw,
"That the Eagle minds no moral law,
She's a most unruly creature."
"She's an ugly thing," piped Canary Bird;
"Some call her handsome—it's so absurd—
She hasn't a decent feature."

Then the old Marsh Hen went hopping about,
She said she was sure—she hadn't a doubt—
   Of the truth of each bird's story:
And she thought it a duty to stop her flight,
To pull her down from her lofty height,
   And take the gilt from her glory.

But, lo! from a peak on the mountain grand
That looks out over the smiling land
   And over the mighty ocean,
The Eagle is spreading her splendid wings—
She rises, rises, and upward swings,
   With a slow, majestic motion

Up in the blue of God's own skies,
With a cry of rapture, away she flies,
   Close to the Great Eternal:
She sweeps the world with her piercing sight—
Her soul is filled with the infinite
   And the joy of things supernal.

Thus rise forever the chosen of God,
The genius-crowned or the power-shod.
   Over the dust-world sailing;
And back, like splinters blown by the winds,
Must fall the missiles of silly minds,
   Useless and unavailing.

HENRIETTA CORDELIA RAY

(1850?–1916)

☙☙☙☙☙☙

CORDELIA RAY was one of three sisters, all of whom had distinguished careers. Their father, the Reverend Charles B. Ray, was a Congregational minister in New York City when Cordelia (as she preferred to be called) was born. A black man of considerable distinction, Reverend Ray was an outspoken abolitionist and an editor of the *Colored American*. He had a deep influence on his daughters, who received an excellent education. Cordelia probably attended the Sauveneur School of Languages, learning Greek, Latin, French, and German; she also received a graduate degree in pedagogy from the University of the City of New York. Her sister Charlotte graduated from Howard University Law School in 1872, becoming the District of Columbia's first black woman lawyer.

Cordelia remained in New York where she and her older sister Florence taught school. Neither of the women married; their devotion to one another throughout their lives, much like Alice and Phoebe Cary's, was deeply satisfying. Cordelia published poems in periodicals from 1880 to 1900, and a volume entitled *Sonnets* was published in 1893. She was naturally modest and scholarly, inspiring the following tribute in Hallie Brown's *Homespun Heroines:* "Her curious air of detachment from things ordinary, her entire absence from affectation, her genuine self-forgetfulness, made her charming. A classmate once said of her that she appeared as one unspotted by the world" (172).

Cordelia did have one moment of worldliness when her long commemoration ode, "Lincoln," was read at President Grant's unveiling of the Freedman's Monument in 1876, at which Frederick Douglass also spoke.

Henrietta Cordelia Ray

Ray's poetry is not highly regarded by critics today, however, because its range of references (to Beethoven, Milton, Shakespeare, Dante, Long-fellow, Thoreau) seems to acknowledge only hegemonic cultural debts. Ray's originality lies in her many experiments with stanzaic patterns. Though her subject matter allies her with an earlier era, her endings in such poems as "At the Cascade" and "Incompleteness" suggest modern experiments with unresolving or imagistic final lines.

H. Cordelia Ray spent her last years in retirement, living on Long Island with Florence. In her sonnet "Life" she describes her sense of human existence as "one restless strife from fetters to be free." Though most of her poems are reminiscent of those written by nineteenth-century white women poets, and like theirs show the influence of Goethe and Felicia Hemans, perhaps her ability to assume the voice of the dominant Other was for her a triumph in the struggle "from fetters to be free." Her tributes to Lincoln and to Paul Laurence Dunbar prove that she was not insensitive to issues of race or to the voice of a fellow-poet who had chosen a different path, who "woke to utterance"—as she puts it—with a different dream of art.

Selected Works: Sketch of the Life of Rev. Charles B. Ray. With Florence T. Ray. 1887; *Poems.* 1910.

Selected Criticism: Brown, Hallie Q. *Homespun Heroines and Other Women of Distinction.* 1926—rpt. Oxford UP, 1988; Sherman. Intro to *Collected Black Women's Poetry.* Vol. 3; Sherman. *Invisible Poets.*

THE SCULPTOR'S VISION

A sculptor musing sat one eve,
When crimson clouds began to weave
Their sunset drapery in the sky;
Cold was his studio and bare,
But golden sunbeams lingered there,
And robins caroling flew by.

Henrietta Cordelia Ray

A vision on his dreaming broke;
With parted lips and eyes that spoke,
A statue stood of beauty rare,
And chiseled with such exquisite care,
It seemed no mortal hand had share
In what was like embodied prayer.

The sculptor woke to find his dream
Of loveliness was but a gleam
Of what the future might unfold;
And then resolved to labor late,
Until his work his dream could mate,
And daily carved with joy untold.

But sometimes sorrow mingled there,
For naught he fashioned could compare
With that chaste form which ev'ry night,
Would come to give him impulse new,
To bid him seek the pure, the true,
And lead him to a clearer light.

Nor wrought the sculptor all in vain;
The statue grew despite his pain,
In curves of beauty, strength and grace;
And so he loved his magic art,
His very soul seemed to impart
A something human to the face.

Yet was the vision fairer still;
Its subtle presence seemed to fill
The space before his troubled gaze.
It beckoned him to heights unknown,
And charmed him like the undertone
That floats through many olden lays.

Henrietta Cordelia Ray

LIFE

Life! Ay, what is it? E'en a moment spun
From cycles of eternity. And yet,
What wrestling 'mid the fever and the fret
Of tangled purposes and hopes undone!
What affluence of love! What vict'ries won
In agonies of silence, ere trust met
A manifold fulfillment, and the wet,
Beseeching eyes saw splendors past the sun!
What struggle in the web of circumstance,
And yearning in the wingèd music! All,
One restless strife from fetters to be free;
Till, gathered to eternity's expanse,
Is that brief moment at the Father's call;
Life! Ay, at best, 'tis but a mystery!

ASPIRATION

We climb the slopes of life with throbbing heart,
And eager pulse, like children toward a star.
Sweet siren music cometh from afar,
To lure us on meanwhile. Responsive start
The nightingales to richer song than Art
Can ever teach. No passing shadows mar
Awhile the dewy skies; no inner jar
Of conflict bids us with our quest to part.
We see adown the distance, rainbow-arched,
What melting aisles of liquid light and bloom!
We hasten, tremulous, with lips all parched,
And eyes wide-stretched, nor dream of coming gloom.
Enough that something held almost divine
Within us ever stirs. Can we repine?

Henrietta Cordelia Ray

INCOMPLETENESS

What soul hath struck its need of melody,
From life's strange instrument whereon it plays?
Are the aspiring strains of weary days
E'er gathered in their full intensity,
Swelling a psalm incomparable, free
To utter all their yearning? Nay! the lays
Moan on inadequately, for the ways
Of God in shaping souls we may not see.
'Mid baffled hopes we cry out in our need,
And wrestle in the shadows, wond'ring when
Such dissonance can e'er be sweet, and how.

SELF-MASTERY

To catch the spirit in its wayward flight
Through mazes manifold, what task supreme!
For when to floods has grown the quiet stream,
Much human skill must aid its rage to fight;
And when wild winds invade the solemn night,
Seems not man's vaunted power but a dream?
And still more futile, ay, we e'en must deem
This quest to tame the soul, and guide aright
Its restless wanderings,—to lure it back
To shoals of calm. Full many a moan and a sigh
Attend the strife; till, effort merged in prayer,
Oft uttered, clung to—when of strength the lack
Seems direst—brings the answer to our cry:
A gift from Him who lifts our ev'ry care.

Henrietta Cordelia Ray

THE QUEST OF THE IDEAL

Fair Hope with lucent light in her glad eyes,
Fleet as Diana, through the meadow speeds;
Nor dewy rose nor asphodel she heeds,
For lo! unwonted radiance in the skies
Bids her not pause. The silv'ry shimmer lies
'Mid blooming vistas, whence the pathway leads
To heights aerial. The glow recedes
As panting Hope toils on, while awed surprise
Fills her sweet glances; will the vision fade
Ere she can reach it? Nay, 'tis lovelier far,
Rarer perspectives open to her gaze;
Then hasten on, expectantly, glad maid!
The splendor still will tremble there afar;
Yet count this quest the holiest of thy days.

MIGNON

What art thou, Mignon, child of mystery?
A woodbird e'en in galling fetters caught?
Dwelling apart in charmèd reverie,
Crushed by the weight of undeveloped thought,
Though seem'st some weird, sad spirit of the Past,
Guarding a secret life cannot unfold;
Yet was thy soul's calm rapture lily-pure,
Thy heart's fond treasures bright as rarest gold.

In Goethe's *Wilhelm Meister's Apprenticeship* (1795–96) Mignon is the strange young girl whom Wilhelm saves from a brutal life as a sideshow performer. Her love is pure and mystical.

Dim pictures of soft skies and orange groves,
Of marble statues with their pitying gaze,[1]
Lured thee to musing; while the cloudlets built
An airy path for thee amid the haze.
Sweet are thy songs of longing; thou didst dream
Of sunny isles where no rude questioner
Shall need to ask of man or woman more,
And no unrest thy weary soul shall stir.

What depths of sorrow in thy dreamy life,
Around which Mem'ry wove a subtle chain;
Thy ev'ry gesture, ev'ry glance expressed
Intensity of yearning deep with pain,
Yet lit by Hope's illuminating smile;
Faith hov'ring over thee, thou phantom bright,
Shed gleams along thy tragic path, until
Thy spirit's wings unfolded in the Light.

LIFE'S BOUNDARY

Life is a glass wherein we dimly see
    Foreshadowings of our devious plans and ways;
Life is a glass. Lo! 'tis Eternity
    That bounds the dim perspective of our days.

CHARITY

I saw a maiden, fairest of the fair,
    With every grace bedight beyond compare.

---

1. These lines refer to the poem that opens Book 3: "Kennst du das Land, wo die Zitronen blühen?"

Said I, "What doest thou, pray, tell to me!"
"I see the good in others," answered she.

LOST OPPORTUNITIES

When it is past—the golden moment—gone!
How we do rend ourselves, undone, forlorn!
The jewel left a moment in our hands,
We search, yet find it not o'er widest lands.

AMBITION

What is ambition? 'tis unrest, defeat!
A goad, a spur, a quick'ning the heart's beat;
A fevered pulse, a grasp at shadows fleet,
A beck'ning vision, fair, illusive, sweet!

FULL VISION

But look a trial down from some far height,
And 'twill diminish to a speck in air.
Half-vision irks and frets. Let on the light!
The demon vanishes before a prayer.

Henrietta Cordelia Ray

AFTER THE STORM

Sol took his nightcap off and gazed
Through cloudy curtains. At the sight
The mists fled scared to windy haunts;
    And lo! the earth was filled with light.

AT THE CASCADE

The waters rippled, gleamed and fell;
Sweet Jessie tripped adown the dell.
She heard his voice, their fond lips met;
The rocks with silver spray were wet.

IN MEMORIAM

Paul Laurence Dunbar

The Muse of Poetry came down one day,
And brought with willing hands a rare, sweet gift;
She lingered near the cradle of a child,
Who first unto the sun his eyes did lift.
She touched his lips with true Olympian fire,
And at her bidding Fancies hastened there,
To flutter lovingly around the one
So favored by the Muse's gentle care.

Who was this child? The offspring of a race
That erst had toiled 'neath slavery's galling chains.

Paul Laurence Dunbar (1872–1906) was an African-American poet. His best-known work is *Lyrics of a Lowly Life* (1896), written for the most part in Negro dialect. The son of former slaves, he died of tuberculosis at the age of thirty-four.

And soon he woke to utterance and sang
In sweetly cadenced and in stirring strains,
Of simple joys, and yearnings, and regrets;
Anon to loftier themes he turned his pen;
For so in tender, sympathetic mood
He caught the follies and the griefs of men.

His tones were various: we list, and lo!
"Malindy Sings,"[1] and as the echoes die,
The keynote changes and another strain
Of solemn majesty goes floating by;
And sometimes in the beauty and the grace
Of an impassioned, melancholy lay,
We seem to hear the surge, and swell, and moan
Of soft orchestral music far away.

Paul Dunbar dead! His genius cannot die!
It lives in songs that thrill, and glow, and soar;
Their pathos and their joy will fill our hearts,
And charm and satisfy e'en as of yore.
So when we would lament our poet gone,
With sorrow that his lyre is resting now,
Let us remember, with the fondest pride,
That Fame's immortal wreath has crowned his brow.

LINCOLN

We lift the curtain of the past to-day,
And chase the mists and stains of years away,
Once more, O martyred chief, to gaze on thee,
The worth and purpose of thy life to see.
'Twas thine, not worlds to conquer, but men's hearts,

---

1. "Malindy Sings" is a poem by Dunbar.

To change to balm the sting of slavery's darts,
In lowly charity thy joy to find,
And open "gates of mercy on mankind."
Long will they come, the freed, with grateful gift,
From whose sad path the shadows thou didst lift.

The years have rolled their changeful seasons round,
Since its most tragic close thy life-work found.
Yet through the vistas of the vanished days
We see thee still, responsive to our gaze,
As ever to thy country's solemn needs.
Not regal coronets, but princely deeds
Were thy chaste diadem; of truer worth
Thy modest virtues than the gems of earth.
Stanch, honest, fervent in the purest cause,
Truth was thy guide; her mandates were thy laws.

Rare heroism, spirit-purity,
The storied Spartan's stern simplicity,
Such moral strength as gleams like burnished gold
Amid the doubt of men of weaker mould,
Were thine. Called in thy country's sorest hour
When brother knew not brother—mad for power—
To guide the helm through bloody deeps of war,
While distant nations gazed in anxious awe,
Unflinching in the task, thou didst fulfill
Thy mighty mission with a deathless will.

Born to a destiny the most sublime,
Thou wert, O Lincoln! in the march of time,
God bade thee pause and bid the oppressed go free—
Most glorious boon giv'n to humanity.
While slavery ruled the land, what deeds were done!
What tragedies enacted 'neath the sun!
Her page is blurred with records of defeat,
Of lives heroic lived in silence, meet

For the world's praise; of woe, despair and tears,
The speechless agony of weary years.

Thou utteredst the word, and Freedom fair
Rang her sweet bells on the clear winter air;
She waved her magic wand, and lo! from far
A long procession came. With many a scar
Their brows were wrinkled, in the bitter strife,
Full many had said their sad farewell to life.
But on they hastened, free, their shackles gone;
The aged, young,—e'en infancy was borne
To offer unto thee loud pæans of praise,—
Their happy tribute after saddest days.

A race set free! The deed brought joy and light!
It bade calm Justice from her sacred height,
When faith and hope and courage slowly waned,
Unfurl the stars and stripes, at last unstained!
The nations rolled acclaim from sea to sea,
And Heaven's vault range with Freedom's harmony.
The angels 'mid the amaranths must have hushed
Their chanted cadences, as upward rushed
The hymn sublime: and as the echoes pealed,
God's ceaseless benison the action sealed.

Exalted patriot! illustrious chief!
Thy life's immortal work compels belief.
To-day in radiance thy virtues shine,
And how can we a fitting garland twine?
Thy crown most glorious is a ransomed race!
High on our country's scroll we fondly trace,
In lines of fadeless light that softly blend,
Emancipator, hero, martyr, friend!
While Freedom may her holy sceptre claim,
The world shall echo with Our Lincoln's name.

EDITH M. THOMAS

(1854–1925)

𝕏𝕏𝕏𝕏𝕏

EDITH THOMAS precisely captures the transition between nineteenth- and twentieth-century women's verse. Her thematics of hunger, secret sorrow, and limitation connect her to the past and Emily Dickinson. Her adoption of a Greek persona, musicality, and love for New York City make her the forerunner of such poets as H. D., Elinor Wylie, Sara Teasdale, and Louise Bogan. Though archaic in certain ways, her verse is also modern. Like Amy Lowell and Edna St. Vincent Millay, she sought to unite an admiration for Keats with a modernist resistance to religious consolation.

Thomas was born in Ohio where her Welch father was a farmer and taught school. Precocious and literary, Edith found her talents nurtured by both her parents and a favorite uncle. She graduated in 1872 from the Geneva Normal School, where she had followed a special course in Greek, and enrolled for only one semester at Oberlin College before dropping out to earn a living. The most significant event of her literary life was her entry, one evening in 1881, into the New York salon of Anne Lynch Botta. Botta introduced her to Helen Hunt Jackson, who agreed to read her poems and responded to them with enthusiasm. To Thomas, the city seemed exciting and friendly, and she decided in 1887 to move there permanently. Her poem "Anima Urbis" celebrates her love for the city, a love that remained constant over the years.

Thomas never married, though her beauty might have won her many suitors. Instead, the poet became an editor for the *Century Dictionary* and *Harper's*. Her early years in New York were very exciting, especially when she frequented the home of the cultured physician Samuel Elliott, which was a meeting place for writers and intellectuals such as Charles Dana and Parke Godwin. Edith, however, was aware of having missed out on many of the joys of life. In her last years she became much like Louise Bogan would later become: a hardworking journalist, increasingly withdrawn, who lived alone and whose best poetry had been written decades earlier. In 1925 Edith Thomas died of a cerebral hemorrhage at the age of seventy-one. The following year Jessie Rittenhouse published a volume of *Selected Poems* with a long retrospective in which she spoke of Thomas's "burning spirit."

Edith Thomas's diction often seems archaic to a modern ear. Yet one cannot help thinking of Bogan's work when one reads "The Good Furies." "Frost To-Night," Thomas's most popular poem, has a definitely modern resonance, and "Fabrique of Things Spent" could take its place among many of the poems published by much younger women in the twenties. "Losses" even hints at Elizabeth Bishop's "One Art." Edith Thomas was represented by three poems in Sara Teasdale's anthology of female love poets, *The Answering Voice* (1917). Indeed, her work captured the longings of many like her, women who felt love had passed them by.

Selected Works: Lyrics and Sonnets. 1887; *The Inverted Torch.* 1890; *Fair Shadow Land.* 1893; *A Winter Swallow.* 1896; *The Flower from the Ashes.* 1915.

Selected Criticism: Pattee, Fred Lewis. *A History of American Literature since 1870.* New York: Century, 1915; Rittenhouse, Jessie. Memoir in *Selected Poems of Edith Thomas.* New York: Harper, 1926; Rittenhouse. *The Younger American Poets.* 1914—rpt. Freeport, NY: Books for Libraries, 1968; Stedman; Watts.

EVOE!

"Many are the wand-bearers, few are the true bacchanals."

Many are the wand-bearers;
　　Their windy shouts I hear,

Evoe is the cry of the followers of Bacchus (here Iacchus). The epigraph comes from Plato's *Phaedo* 69c.

Along the hillside vineyard,
　　And where the wine runs clear;
They show the vine-leaf chaplet,
　　The ivy-wreathen spear;
But the god, the true Iacchus,
　　He does not hold them dear.

Many are the wand-bearers,
　　And bravely are they clad;
Yes, they have all the tokens
　　His early lovers had.
They sing the master passions,
　　Themselves unsad, unglad;
And the god, the true Iacchus—
　　He knows they are not mad!

Many are the wand-bearers;
　　The fawn-skin bright they wear;
There are among them mænads [1]
　　That rave with unbound hair.
They toss the harmless firebrand—
　　It spends itself in air;
And the god, the true Iacchus,
　　He smiles—and does not care.

Many are the wand-bearers;
　　And who (ye ask) am I?
One who was born in madness,
　　"Evoe!" my first cry—
Who dares, before your spear-points,
　　To challenge and defy;
And the god, the true Iacchus,
　　So keep me till I die!

---

1. Maenads are the Bacchants or mad, frenzied women who follow Bacchus
(also known as Dionysus).

Edith M. Thomas

Many are the wand-bearers.
    I bear with me no sign;
Yet, I was mad, was drunken,
    Ere yet I tasted wine;
Nor bleeding grape can slacken
    The thirst wherewith I pine;
And the god, the true Iacchus,
    Hears now this song of mine.

FROST TO-NIGHT

Apple-green west and an orange bar,
And the crystal eye of a lone, one star . . .
And, "Child, take the shears and cut what you will.
Frost to-night—so clear and dead-still."

Then, I sally forth, half sad, half proud,
And I come to the velvet, imperial crowd,
The wine-red, the gold, the crimson, the pied,—
The dahlias that reign by the garden-side.

The dahlias I might not touch till to-night!
A gleam of the shears in the fading light,
And I gathered them all,—the splendid throng,
And in one great sheaf I bore them along.

In my garden of Life with its all-late flowers,
I heed a Voice in the shrinking hours:
"Frost to-night—so clear and dead-still . . ."
Half sad, half proud, my arms I fill.

POPPIES IN OUR WHEAT

Let no blame upon us fall,
Thrifty ones of cot and hall,
That, while ye take care to hoard
Corn and wine for winter's board,
We beside the hedgerow lie,
Heedless how bright hours go by.
Wonder not we dread no want,
When the year is bare and gaunt:
Idle bread we have to eat,—
Poppies grew amidst our wheat.

Blame not us, ye revelers blithe,
Who have lodged the rake and scythe,
And with fan and flail no more
Tread the granary's breezy floor:
Though, with humming wire and flute,
The boon Season well ye suit,
Call us not by word or glance;
We will neither feast nor dance.
Blame not us that sleep is sweet,—
Poppies grew amidst our wheat.

CURE-ALL

Tell me, is there sovereign cure
    For heart-ache, heart-ache,—
Cordial quick and potion sure
    For heart-ache, heart-ache?

Fret thou not. If all else fail
    For heart-ache, heart-ache,

One thing surely will avail,—
    That's heart-break, heart-break!

LOSSES

Speed had not served, strength had not flowed amain,
Heart had not braced me, for this journey's strain,
Had I foreseen what losses must be met;
But drooping losel[1] was I never yet!

So rich in losses through long years I've grown,
So rich in losses (and so proud, I own)
Myself I pity not, but only such
As have not had, nor therefore lost, so much.

Behind me ever grew a hungry Vast
Which travelers fear to face, but call the Past;
So much it won from me I can but choose
To exult that I've so little left to lose.

When that shall go, as fain it is to go,
Like some full sail when winds of voyage blow,
At this late nick of time to murmur sore
Were idle, since so much I've lost before!

So much I've lost, lost out of hand—ah, yes!
But were that all, my fortune I could bless;
For whensoever aught has slipped away,
Some dearer thing has gone to find the stray;

---

1. A losel is a worthless person.

And then, to find the finder loth or slow,
Yet dearer thing my wistful heart let go,
With hope like his whose glancing arrow gave
The clue to Pari-banou's palace-cave.[2]

Perchance one loss the more, regains the whole,
Lost loves and faith and young delight of soul:
I'm losing—what? Ah, Life, join thou the quest;
It may be, to be lost, is not unblest!

THE SOUL OF THINGS

Day by day the soul of things
Up its countless ladders springs,
Fleeting back to whence it came,—
Inviolate, etherial flame!
I have pierced its changing shapes,
Coils and turnings, deft escapes!
Up yon swaying shaft it stole,
Of the scarlet gladiole.
First, the lowest bud it caught,
And with fire its chalice fraught;
Then, with aspiration new,
To the bloom above withdrew.
Every flower, thus bereft,
Like a quenchèd brand was left,—
Quickly into ashes fell
When the Genius fled its cell!
On the morrow it will rest

---

2. Pari-banou is a fairy in the *Arabian Nights* who gives Prince Ahmed a tent with magical powers to expand from a tiny toy to a palace big enough to cover an army.

In the topmost blossom-crest;
Waving thence its light adieus,
Some unseen way it pursues.
Airy pyramid of grass
At its motion yields a pass.
Through the wind-loved wheat it flows,
Up the tufted sedge-flower goes,
Scales the foxglove's leaning spire,
Fans the wild lobelia's fire,
Where beside the pool it flashes;
And the slender vervain's lashes,
By the climbing spirit swayed,
All their purple length unbraid.
Thus the soul of blooming things
Up its countless ladders springs.

THE QUIET PILGRIM

When on my soul in nakedness
His swift, avertless hand did press,
Then I stood still, nor cried aloud,
Nor murmured low in ashes bowed;
And, since my woe is utterless,
To supreme quiet I am vowed;
Afar from me be moan and tears,—
I shall go softly all my years.

Whenso my quick, light-sandaled feet
Bring me where Joys and Pleasures meet,
I mingle with their throng at will;
They know me not an alien still,
Since neither words nor ways unsweet
Of storèd bitterness I spill;

Edith M. Thomas

Youth shuns me not, nor gladness fears,—
For I go softly all my years.

Whenso I come where Griefs convene,
And in my ear their voice is keen,
They know me not, as on I glide,
That with Arch Sorrow I abide.
They haggard are, and drooped of mien,
And round their brows have cypress tied:
Such shows I leave to light Grief's peers,—
I shall go softly all my years.

Yea, softly! heart of hearts unknown.
Silence hath speech that passeth moan,
More piercing-keen than breathèd cries
To such as heed, make sorrow-wise.
But save this voice without a tone,
That runs before me to the skies,
And rings above thy ringing spheres,
Lord, I go softly all my years!

THE DEEP-SEA PEARL

The love of my life came not
    As love unto others is cast;
For mine was a secret wound—
    But the wound grew a pearl, at last.

The divers may come and go,
    The tides, they arise and fall;
The pearl in its shell lies sealed,
    And the Deep Sea covers all.

Edith M. Thomas

INSOMNIA

A house of sleepers—I, alone unblest,
   Am yet awake and empty vigil keep.
When these, who spend life's day with me, find rest
   Oh, let me not be last to fall asleep!

LONE FREEDOM

How lonely is vast Freedom! I may go,
   Or come, or sit in the still house of thought,
   All idleness, unseeking and unsought,
From the gray morn to noon, to evening's glow;
None shall reprove, if vacant hands I show,
   Or question why the task remains unwrought;
   Or done, or never done, 'twill be as naught,
To every creature on the earth below.

How lonely is vast Freedom! I were fain
   To follow any who would be my liege;
     To say, "Do this," or, "To the world's end ride!"
I am as he who once sought all in vain
   To enter his loved city, in her siege;
     "How lone is Freedom!" at her gate he cried.

THE REFLECTION

It was the eve my mother died.
   The bowl with water had been set;

The candle shone, the bier beside—
   The room, I see it yet!

Above the bowl I chanced to lean;
   The water like a mirror lay—
My mother's face therein was seen!
   Half-wild I turned away.

And long my tears flowed unassuaged . . .
   But now I know, since years are gone,
It was my face I saw—but aged,
   With lines of sorrow drawn!

THE ETHERIAL HUNGER

I have been hungry all my days—
   (Oh, when shall I be fed?)
They saw my pinched and wistful gaze,
   And some there were gave wine and bread,
And some gave love and praise.

I was as hungry as before—
   (Oh, when shall I be fed?)
Good souls! they shared their choicest store,
   Another had been surfeited—
I did but hunger more.

I am an ingrate in all eyes—
   (Oh, when shall I be fed?)
From their best feasts I famished rise,
   I dream of tables ampler spread—
O tables of the skies!

Edith M. Thomas

FABRIQUE OF THINGS SPENT

All must have Beauty, else they pine and die.
  Some to possess her the far quest must lead,
Ascend Olympus and invade the sky!
  I will create the Beauty that I need
Out of spent things that disregarded lie,
  From every mundane use dismissed and freed.

Give me your dust, O delicate gone things
  That were so worshipped in the ascendent year,
That now the harpy guest befouling flings
  Under their feet who have nor love nor fear.
Give me the moultings from yon wonder wings
  And I to Heliopolis[1] will steer
And find the phoenix at those crimson springs
  Where he renews him on his cradle-bier!

I will take shard and wave-shot laminae
  Of shells that lie along the slope-brown sand,
Housings of life, scarce more than foam of sea
  That shaped them, whirling—whirling would disband.
Bring the long ribbons of the dulse[2] to me,
  These will I braid together, strand by strand.

Bring me but from the cottage hearth a toll
  Of filmy ash that gives soft death to fire,
Like a gray moss o'ergrowing the live coal
  Until its substance it has wormed entire,
Within such driftage there abides a soul
  Will recreate itself at my desire.

---

1. Heliopolis is the city of the sun.
2. dulse—edible seaweed found in the Northern hemisphere.

Edith M. Thomas

So now I warp my loom and sit to weave,
    Shuttle in hand, the woof I seek alone.
But I will take whatso the rest would leave—
    Treasurable once but now unvalued grown.
I, that come after, riches will I sheave
    In the waste fields where careless ones have sown.
All must have Beauty—but I can retrieve
    The lovely semblance when ye say 'tis flown!

THE GOOD FURIES

From time to time I meet with those who cry
    Peccavi,[1] and the bitter cup still drink
For errors of a season long gone by;
    Though once I held with them, this now I think—

At last is outlawed one's account for sins,
    The thorn of conscience—let it cease to turn!
'Tis then a time of thankfulness begins;
    We find some gifts our virtues could not earn!

Read how Orestes, years of torment done,
    Felt suddenly withdrawn the Furies' goad:
'Twas when Athene and Latona's son[2]
    Checked those pursuers, and compassion showed.

On Ares' Hill the Furies' temple stood:
    Orestes, now his spirit filled with ease,

---

1. I have sinned (Lat.).
2. Latona (or Leto) was the mother of Apollo.

Their altar wreathed with flowers and called them Good—
    The favoring, the kind, Eumenides![3]

Can I do less than he—young Greek of old?
    How well I know what felt that fugitive
Who could not with his torturing memories hold,
    Nor yet without them had he learned to live!

Oh, let them be my friends, who were my dread,
    With several lash for every ill thing done—
Whose brazen feet pursued where'er I fled,
    Whose torch lit up whatever shade I won!

Drop, scourge, at last—and heavy hand, uplift! . . .
    Now, since they send me such abounding ease,
Should I not bring to them some little gift—
    The favoring, the kind, Eumenides?

What I have done amiss must so remain,
    Not mine to longer grieve therefor, or brood;
Both sins and lashes have not been in vain;
    I call my own departing Furies *"Good"!*

This have I written for those souls who still
    Peccavi cry—because their sins were sore,
When better they might climb the templed hill,
    And carry there their flowers—and grieve no more!

---

3. After Orestes murdered his mother, he was pursued by the Furies. They eventually gave up their torment of him, due to the intervention of Athena and Apollo, and became known as "The Kindly Ones," the Eumenides.

Edith M. Thomas

ANIMA URBIS

You, City, by two rivers made an isle,
　　To whom the sea a tidal tribute pays,
What is it in you that could so beguile
　　My heart to leave its love of earlier days
Till now its passion seems a fable far,
Dissolved and faded with life's morning star?

For I am lost and strange unease is mine,
　　If ever I turn back to that old love:
Great Nature is no more to me benign,
　　I fear her vacant heavens spread above;
The lonely wind-tides drawing through her trees
Are sad to me as Sophoclean seas.

Your casual glimpses of the stars suffice,
　　Your chary sunsets are of precious sard;
Your yearning towers bloom agate as they rise,
　　Where men enskied do work—and Heaven keep guard!
And oftentimes I let my thought take flight
Around those shafts half-veiled in misty light.

City, I do not know what charm you wield
　　That to my spirit has been subtle balm;
From stabbing memories it oft has healed.
　　Your very tumults can my tumults calm.
Who speaks of guile, of harm your spells can do?
Enchantress City—I am safe with you!

Yes, I have been your lover many years.
　　Like any lover I your praise could sing,

The Latin title of the poem means the soul of the city.

For this—for that—which so my heart endears.
 And yet, and yet, beyond each several thing,
Like any lover I despair, and say,
 "It is your *soul* I've loved so many a day!"

Your soul of many souls well mingled up!
 I sometimes drink it with a giddy joy.
And I here pledge you in a loving-cup
 Service and faith that nothing can destroy.
A conscious soul? O City, can it be—
Since I have so loved you—do you love me?

FAITHFUL OVER A FEW THINGS

All that was mine—I have loved it, and loved it both true and well.
Quick to its call I uprose, as the heart to the sacring-bell.[1]
Never so long ago, nor aught that I loved as a child,
And lost, but I love it still and would seek it unreconciled.
Never so far past by, that broken its image appears,
Blent with dissolving visions or dim in the rush of the years!
Never so cast away, flung out on the world's rough wake,
But only the more would I love it—at need would go down for its sake.

All that was mine—I have loved it. Had greater than this been mine,
I know not how greater my love—how mounting nearer divine.
All that was mine in the world—its Maker my witness be!
I loved it, and love it still, as I leave it and pass unto Thee.
If more and greater than this be my share, in some Heaven above,
The soul that was mine will live on, and measure its life by its love.

---

1. This small bell is rung to call parishioners to Communion.

LIZETTE WOODWORTH REESE

(1856–1935)

✠✠✠✠✠✠

OF THE SAME GENERATION as Edith Thomas, Lizette Reese also had Welch forebears, worked hard into old age, and never married. Both writers grew up in rural areas (Reese in Maryland), and both developed a great love for nature that often manifested itself in their poetry. There the similarities end, for whereas Edith Thomas made a significant move to New York City and went to work in publishing, Lizette Reese spent her entire life in the greater Baltimore area teaching school. For four years (1877–81), she taught at the black high school, years she remembered as some of her happiest. Though Reese was often critical of the "System," as she called it, she insisted that "the pupils were in school to do their duty, and I was there to do mine" (*NB* 123).

Her sensibility was not as stern as this quotation implies, however. A contemporary Mae Dietrich, wrote of her: "Shy, modest, possessing a keen whimsical sense of humor, she nevertheless created the impression of fearless courage and staunch loyalty to her ideals, founded upon her boundless faith in God" (120). This description would fit many women in this collection equally well.

Lizette Reese published her first poem, "The Deserted House," in 1874. Though she continued to write into the 1930s, and published some especially fine poetry in the twenties, she developed her voice and her style before 1900 and never changed it significantly. Louis Untermeyer, who published fifteen of her poems in his *Modern American Poetry,* describes Reese's style as "an artistry which, for all its seemingly old-fashioned elegance, is as spontaneous as it is skillful" (116). A typical common diction, traditional rhymes and metrics. In this mode she made a profound impression upon younger women poets, such as Sara Teasdale, Edna St. Vincent Millay, and Louise Bogan. Bogan's poem "Women" pays homage to Reese's earlier poem with the same title.

Yet, even more than Edith Thomas, Lizette Reese remains a Victorian lady: upright, unself-pitying, a believer in universal human truths, sustained by a sense of certainty that her life, if not ecstatic, was at least useful. She was one of the founders of the Women's Literary Club in Baltimore. Her most popular poem was "Tears" and this lyric, with its insistence that "each hath back what once he stayed to weep," measures the distance between herself and the far less confident Thomas.

Though childless, Reese wrote with deep feeling about the deaths of children. In addition to "Rachel," included here, she produced a long narrative poem on this subject, *Little Henrietta* (1927). Her own death, however, she regarded with equanimity. Reese wrote her own epitaph which appears on her headstone: "The long day sped, / A roof, a bed; / No years, / No tears."

Selected Works: A Branch of May. 1887; *A Handful of Lavender.* 1891; *A Quiet Road.* 1896; *Wild Cherry.* 1925; *Selected Poems.* 1926; *A Victorian Village.* 1929; *White April.* 1930.

Selected Criticism: Dietrich, Mae. "Lizette Woodworth Reese." *Emily Dickinson Bulletin* 15 (1970): 114–22; Harriss, R. P. "April Weather: The Poetry of Lizette Woodworth Reese." *South Atlantic Quarterly* (Apr. 1934): 200–07; Jones, Robert J., ed. *In Praise of Common Things: Lizette Woodworth Reese Revisited.* Westport, CT: Greenwood Press, 1992. Rittenhouse, Jessie. *The Younger American Poets.* 1914—rpt. Freeport, NY: Books for Libraries, 1968; Untermeyer, Louis. *Modern American Poetry.* New York: Harcourt, 1930; Walker.

THE DESERTED HOUSE

The old house stands deserted, gray,
    With sharpened gables high in air,
And deep-set lattices, all gay
    With massive arch and framework rare;

And o'er it is a silence laid,
That feeling, one grows sore afraid.

The eaves are dark with heavy vines;
   The steep roof wears a coat of moss;
The walls are touched with dim designs
   Of shadows moving slow across;
The balconies are damp with weeds,
Lifting as close as streamside reeds.

The garden is a loved retreat
   Of melancholy flowers, of lone
And wild-mouthed herbs, in companies sweet,
   'Mid desolate green grasses thrown;
And in its gaps the hoar stone wall
Lets sprays of tangled ivy fall.

The pebbled paths drag, here and there,
   Old lichened faces, overspun
With silver spider-threads—they wear
   A silence sad to look upon:
It is so long since happy feet
Made them to thrill with pressure sweet.

'Mid drear but fragrant shrubs there stands
   A saint of old made mute in stone,
With tender eyes and yearning hands,
   And mouth formed in a sorrow lone;
'Tis thick with dust, as long ago
'Twas thick with fairest blooms that grow.

Swallows are whirring here and there;
   And oft a little soft wind blows
A hundred odors down the air;
   The bees hum 'round the red, last rose;

And ceaselessly the crickets shrill
Their tunes, and yet, it seems so still.

Or else, from out the distance steals,
    Half heard, the tramp of horses, or
The bleak and harsh stir of slow wheels
    Bound cityward; but more and more,
As these are hushed, or yet increase,
About the old house clings its peace.

DOUBT

Creeds grow so thick along the way,
Their boughs hide God; I cannot pray.

TRUTH

The old faiths light their candles all about.
But burly Truth comes by and blows them out.

A RHYME OF DEATH'S INN

A rhyme of good Death's inn!
    My love came to that door;
And she had need of many things,
    The way had been so sore.

My love she lifted up her head,
  "And is there room?" said she;
"There was no room in Bethlehem's inn
  For Christ who died for me."

But said the keeper of the inn,
  "His name is on the door."
My love then straightway entered there:
  She hath come back no more.

TELLING THE BEES

(A Colonial Custom)

Bathsheba came out to the sun,
Out to our wallèd cherry-trees;
The tears adown her cheek did run,
Bathsheba standing in the sun,
Telling the bees.[1]

My mother had that moment died;
Unknowing, sped I to the trees,
And plucked Bathsheba's hand aside;
Then caught the name that there she cried
Telling the bees.

Her look I never can forget,
I that held sobbing to her knees;
The cherry-boughs above us met;
I think I see Bathsheba yet
Telling the bees.

---

1. In rural New England beehives were dressed in mourning when a family member died and the bees informed of the death in order to forestall their leaving in search of a new home. See Whittier's poem "Telling the Bees."

Lizette Woodworth Reese

SUNSET

In the clear dusk upon the fields below,
The blossoming thorn-bush, white, and spare, and tall,
Seems carved of ivory 'gainst the dark wall:
Shut from the sunset sharp the farm-roofs show.
But here upon this height, the straggling hedge
Burns in the wind, and is astir with bees;
The little pool beneath the willow trees,
Yellow as topaz flames from edge to edge;
A line of light the deserted highway glows.
Odors like sounds down the rich air do pass,
Spice from each bough, musk from the brier rose
Dropping its five sweet petals on the grass.
Swallows are whirring black against the blaze;
I hear the creek laugh out from pebbly ways.

RACHEL

No days that dawn can match for her
    The days before her house was bare;
Sweet was the whole year with the stir
    Of young feet on the stair.

Once was she wealthy with small cares,
    And small hands clinging to her knees;
Now is she poor, and, weeping, bears
    Her strange, new hours of ease.

Lizette Woodworth Reese

HEROISM

Whether we climb, whether we plod,
    Space for one task the scant years lend—
To choose some path that leads to God,
    And keep it to the end.

RENUNCIATION

Loose hands and part: I am not she you sought,
    The fair one whom in all our dreams you see,
    But something more of earth and less than she,
That crowded her an instant from your thought.
Blameless we face the fate this hour has brought.
    Unwitting I took hers; I set you free
    From all that you unwitting gave to me;
Seek her and find her; I do grudge her naught.
Love, after daylight, dark; so there is left
    This season stripped of you; but yet I know,
    Remembering the old, I cannot make
These new days bitter or myself bereft.
    I know, O love, that I do love you so,
        While peace is yours my true heart cannot break!

IN TIME OF GRIEF

Dark, thinned, beside the wall of stone,
The box[1] dripped in the air;

---

1. This evergreen tree or shrub is used for borders.

Its odor through my house was blown
Into the chamber there.

Remote and yet distinct the scent,
The sole thing of the kind,
As though one spoke a word half meant
That left a sting behind.

I knew not Grief would go from me,
And naught of it be plain,
Except how keen the box can be
After a fall of rain.

KEATS

An English lad, who, reading in a book,
A ponderous, leathern thing set on his knee,
Saw the broad violet of the Egean Sea
Lap at his feet as it were village brook.
Wide was the east; the guests of morning shook;
Immortal laughter beat along that shore;
Pan crouching in the reeds, piped as of yore;
The gods came down and thundered from that book.
He lifted his sad eyes; his London street
Swarmed in the sun and strove to make him heed;
Boys spun their tops, shouting and fair of cheek:
But still, that violet lapping at his feet,—
An English lad had he sat down to read;
But he rose up and knew himself a Greek.

Lizette Woodworth Reese

TEARS

When I consider Life and its few years—
A wisp of fog betwixt us and the sun;
A call to battle, and the battle done
Ere the last echo dies within our ears;
A rose choked in the grass; an hour of fears;
The gusts that past a darkening shore do beat;
The burst of music down an unlistening street,—
I wonder at the idleness of tears.

Ye old, old dead, and ye of yesternight
Chieftains, and bards, and keepers of the sheep,
By every cup of sorrow that you had,
Loose me from tears, and make me see aright
How each hath back what once he stayed to weep:
Homer his sight, David his little lad!

TO LIFE

Unpetal the flower of me,
And cast it to the gust;
Betray me if you will;
Trample me to dust.

But that I should go bare,
But that I should go free
Of any hurt at all—
Do not this thing to me.

Lizette Woodworth Reese

BARGAIN

A rose will cost you more
Than its gathering;
A song be such a price
You dare not sing.

What must you pay for each,
Else loveliness fare amiss?
Yourself nailed to a Tree—
This.

WOMEN

Some women herd such little things—a box
Oval and glossy, in its gilt and red,
Or squares of satin, or a high, dark bed—
But when love comes, they drive to it all their flocks;
Yield up their crooks; take little; gain for fold
And pasture each a small, forgotten grave.
When they are gone, then lesser women crave
And squander their sad hoards; their shepherds' gold.
Some gather life like faggots in a wood,
And crouch its blaze, without a thought at all
Past warming their pinched selves to the last spark.
And women as a whole are swift and good,
In humor scarce, their measure being small;
They plunge and leap, yet somehow miss the dark.

Lizette Woodworth Reese

CROWS

Earth is raw with this one note,
  This tattered making of a song,
Narrowed down to a crow's throat,
  Above the willow-trees that throng

The crooking field from end to end.
  Fixed as the sun, the grave, this sound;
Of what the weather has to spend
  As much a part as sky or ground.

The primal yellow of that flower,
  The tansy making August plain;
And the stored wildness of this hour
  It sucks up like a bitter rain.

Miss it we would, were it not here,
  Simple as water, rough as spring,
It hurls us at the point of spear,
  Back to some naked, early thing.

Listen now. As with a hoof
  It stamps an image on the gust;
Chimney by chimney a lost roof
  Starts for a moment from its dust.

LOUISE IMOGEN GUINEY

(1861–1920)

LOUISE IMOGEN GUINEY was a dedicated, scholarly Irish Catholic whose preoccupation with the past eventually led her to settle in England in 1901. Born in Roxbury, Massachusetts, she was educated at a convent school in Providence, but her education was cut short when her father—a dashing soldier, lawyer, and politician—died suddenly when she was sixteen. All her life she would treasure his memory, and many of her poems use military imagery that reflects her idealization of his martial spirit.

In addition to leaving her with a legacy of longing, the death of Patrick Robert Guiney plunged Louise and her mother into financial difficulties similar to those she would endure for the rest of her life. Like Reese and Thomas, Guiney never married. Her methods of self-support included a stint as postmistress of the Auburndale Post Office (where she was cruelly ostracized because of her sex, politics, and religion), years spent as a cataloguer in the Boston Public Library, and a lifetime of journeywoman writing for both popular and scholarly publications.

Guiney had a wonderful sense of humor, a tough spirit, and a finely-developed sensibility that somehow survived despite adverse conditions. She was an ardent Keatsian, but she also devoted much time and research to seventeenth-century poets such as Donne, Herbert, and especially Vaughan. For many years she worked on a Catholic anthology, entitled *Recusant Poets,* which was published after her death. In addition, she welcomed the Aesthetes, championing Aubrey Beardsley and Lionel Johnson. Though not a feminist, Guiney supported women's suffrage and was enthusiastic about other women poets, writing a long study of Katherine Philips, "the Matchless Orinda," and praising both Reese and Thomas.

She had many friends and supporters, including Oliver Wendell Holmes, Thomas Bailey Aldrich, T. W. Higginson, and especially two women, Annie Adams Fields (also important to Celia Thaxter) and Alice Brown. But the years of trial took their toll on her. She suffered two nervous breakdowns. Her health was poor throughout her final years—she often felt a complete failure—and she died of a stroke in England at the age of fifty-nine.

Guiney's readership was always small, and therefore it is misleading to call her a "popular" poet. She was greatly admired by her peers, however. Her poems influenced Louise Bogan and Amy Lowell, among others. Many have justly praised her letters; her criticism, published in *Patrins,* is also thoughtful and witty. Guiney's poems are still effective, although one senses unresolved anger in the strain of masochism that colors "The Kings" for example. Guiney's life was blighted by the restrictions placed upon women of her day, though in "Talisman" she tries to claim a "sweet" renunciation. About Pascal she wrote: "Spirit so abstinent, in thy deeps lay / What passion of possession?" This question might be applied to her own character as well.

Selected Works: Songs at the Start. 1884; *A Roadside Harp.* 1893; *Patrins.* 1898; *The Martyr's Idyl.* 1900; *Katherine Philips.* 1904; *Letters.* 2 vols. Ed. Grace Guiney. 1926; *Recusant Poets.* 1938.

Selected Criticism: Fairbanks, H. G. *Louise Imogen Guiney: Laureate of the Lost.* Albany: Magi, 1972; Lears, T. J. Jackson. *No Place of Grace.* New York: Pantheon, 1981; Lucey, William L. "Louise I. Guiney on American Women Poets." *Boston Public Library Quarterly* 12 (Apr. 1960): 110–15; Tenison, E. M. *Louise Imogen Guiney: Her Life and Works.* London: Macmillan, 1923; Walker.

Louise Imogen Guiney

THE KINGS

A man said unto his Angel:
"My spirits are fallen low,
    And I cannot carry this battle:
    O brother! where might I go?

"The terrible Kings are on me
    With spears that are deadly bright;
    Against me so from the cradle
    Do fate and my fathers fight."

Then said to the man his Angel:
"Thou wavering witless soul,
    Back to the ranks! What matter
    To win or to lose the whole,

"As judged by the little judges
    Who hearken not well, nor see?
    Not thus, by the outer issue,
    The Wise shall interpret thee.

"Thy will is the sovereign measure
    And only event of things:
    The puniest heart, defying,
    Were stronger than all these Kings.

"Though out of the past they gather,
    Mind's Doubt, and Bodily Pain,
    And pallid Thirst of the Spirit
    That is kin to the other twain,

"And Grief, in a cloud of banners,
    And ringletted Vain Desires,

And Vice, with the spoils upon him
Of thee and thy beaten sires,—

"While Kings of eternal evil
  Yet darken the hills about,
  Thy part is with broken sabre
  To rise on the last redoubt;

"To fear not sensible failure,
  Nor covet the game at all,
  But fighting, fighting, fighting,
  Die, driven against the wall."

OPEN, TIME

Open, Time, and let him pass
Shortly where his feet would be!
Like a leaf at Michaelmas
Swooning from the tree,

Ere its hour the manly mind
Trembles in a sure decrease,
Nor the body now can find
Any hold on peace.

Take him, weak and overworn;
Fold about his dying dream
Boyhood, and the April morn,
And the rolling stream:

Weather on a sunny ridge,
Showery weather, far from here;

Louise Imogen Guiney

Under some deep-ivied bridge,
Water rushing clear:

Water quick to cross and part
(Golden light on silver sound),
Weather that was next his heart
All the world around!

Soon upon his vision break
These, in their remembered blue;
He shall toil no more, but wake
Young, in air he knew.

He hath done with roofs and men.
Open, Time, and let him pass,
Vague and innocent again,
Into country grass.

THE KNIGHT ERRANT

(Donatello's Saint George)

Spirits of old that bore me,
And set me, meek of mind,
Between great dreams before me,
And deeds as great behind,
Knowing humanity my star
As first abroad I ride,
Shall help me wear with every scar
Honour at eventide.
Let claws of lightning clutch me

Donatello was an Italian sculptor (1386–1466). One of his major works is *St. George* (1415–16), which he did for the exterior of Or San Michele in Florence.

From summer's groaning cloud,
Or ever malice touch me,
And glory make me proud.
Oh, give my youth, my faith, my sword,
Choice of the heart's desire:
A short life in the saddle, Lord!
Not long life by the fire.

Forethought and recollection
Rivet mine armour gay!
The passion for perfection
Redeem my failing way!
The arrows of the upper slope
From sudden ambush cast,
Rain quick and true, with one to ope
My Paradise at last!

I fear no breathing bowman,
But only, east and west,
The awful other foeman
Impowered in my breast.
The outer fray in the sun shall be,
The inner beneath the moon;
And may Our Lady lend to me
Sight of the Dragon soon!

ROMANS IN DORSET

A.D. MDCCCXCV[1]

A stupor on the heath,
And wrath along the sky;
Space everywhere; beneath
A flat and treeless wold for us, and darkest noon on high.

---

1. Date given here (1895) is the date of the poem.

Sullen quiet below,
But storm in upper air!
A wind from long ago,
In mouldy chambers of the cloud had ripped an arras there,

And singed the triple gloom,
And let through, in a flame,
Crowned faces of old Rome:
Regnant o'er Rome's abandoned ground, processional they came.

Uprisen as any sun
Through vistas hollow grey,
Aloft, and one by one,
In brazen casques the Emperors loomed large, and sank away.

In ovals of wan light
Each warrior eye and mouth:
A pageant brutal bright
As if once over loudly passed Jove's laughter in the south;

And dimmer, these among,
Some cameo'd head aloof,
With ringlets heavy-hung,
Like yellow stonecrop comely grown around a castle roof.

An instant: guests again,
Then heaven's impacted wall,
The hot insistent rain,
The thunder-shock; and of the Past mirage no more at all,

No more the alien dream
Pursuing, as we went,
With glory's cursed gleam:
Nor sin of Caesar's ruined line engulfed us, innocent.

Louise Imogen Guiney

The vision great and dread
Corroded; sole in view
Was empty Egdon[2] spread,
Her crimson summer weeds ashake in tempest: but we knew

What Tacitus[3] had borne
In that wrecked world we saw;
And what, thine heart uptorn,
My Juvenal![4] distraught with love of violated Law.

ASTRÆA

Since I avail no more, O men! with you,
I will go back unto the gods content;
For they recall me, long with earth inblent,
Lest lack of faith divinity undo.
I served you truly while I dreamed you true,
And golden pains with sovereign pleasure spent:
But now, farewell! I take my sad ascent,
With failure over all I nursed and knew.

---

2. Egdon is the mythical heath in Thomas Hardy's novel *The Return of the Native* (1878).

3. Tacitus (c. AD 55–117) was a Roman historian who scrupulously recounted the history of his own time, which after the fall of Caesar was known for its corruption.

4. Juvenal (c. AD 60–140) was a contemporary of Tacitus. He was a satirist, but he placed himself among the foolish and corrupt he often satirized.

Daughter of Zeus and Themis, Astræa was the goddess of justice, the last of the immortals to withdraw from the earth after the Golden Age.

Are ye unwise, who would not let me love you?
Or must too bold desires be quieted?
Only to ease you, never to reprove you,
I will go back to heaven with heart unfed:
Yet sisterly I turn, I bend above you,
To kiss (ah, with what sorrow!) all my dead.

W. H.

A.D. MDCCLXXVIII–MDCCCXXX

Between the wet trees and the sorry steeple,
Keep, Time, in dark Soho,[1] what once was Hazlitt,
Seeker of Truth, and finder oft of Beauty;

Beauty's a sinking light, ah, none too faithful;
But Truth, who leaves so here her spent pursuer,
Forgets not her great pawn: herself shall claim it.

Therefore sleep safe, thou dear and battling spirit,
Safe also on our earth, begetting ever
Some one love worth the ages and the nations!

Falleth no thing that was to thee eternal.
Sleep safe in dark Soho: the stars are shining,
Titian and Wordsworth live; the People marches.

William Hazlitt (1778–1830), English essayist and critic, was politically liberal, a friend of Wordsworth and Coleridge (though he broke with them when they became conservative), and a supporter of both Renaissance and Romantic theories of art.

1. Soho is a district in central London.

SANCTUARY

High above hate I dwell:
O storms! farewell.
Though at my sill your daggered thunders play
Lawless and loud to-morrow as to-day, . . .
To me they sound more small
Than a young fay's footfall:
Soft and far-sunken, forty fathoms low
In Long Ago,
And winnowed into silence on that wind
Which takes wars like a dust, and leaves but love behind.

Hither Felicity
Doth climb to me,
And bank me in with turf and marjoram
Such as bees lip, or the new-weaned lamb;
With golden barberry-wreath,
And bluets thick beneath;
One grosbeak, too, mid apple-buds a guest
With bud-red breast,
Is singing, singing! All the hells that rage
Float less than April fog below our hermitage.

EMILY BRONTË

What sacramental hurt that brings
The terror of the truth of things
Had changed thee? Secret be it yet.
'T was thine, upon a headland set,
To view no isles of man's delight,
With lyric foam in rainbow flight,

But all a-swing, a-gleam, mid slow uproar,
Black sea, and curved uncouth sea-bitten shore.

THE WILD RIDE

I hear in my heart, I hear in its ominous pulses
All day, on the road, the hoofs of invisible horses,
All night, from their stalls, the importunate pawing and neighing.

Let cowards and laggards fall back! but alert to the saddle
Weather-worn and abreast, go men of our galloping legion,
With a stirrup-cup each to the lily of women that loves him.

The trail is through dolour and dread, over crags and morasses;
There are shapes by the way, there are things that appal or entice us:
What odds? We are Knights of the Grail, we are vowed to the riding.

Thought's self is a vanishing wing, and joy is a cobweb,
And friendship a flower in the dust, and glory a sunbeam:
Not here is our prize, nor, alas! after these our pursuing.

A dipping of plumes, a tear, a shake of the bridle,
A passing salute to this world and her pitiful beauty:
We hurry with never a word in the track of our fathers.

(I hear in my heart, I hear in its ominous pulses
All day, on the road, the hoofs of invisible horses,
All night, from their stalls, the importunate pawing and neighing.)

We spur to a land of no name, out-racing the storm-wind;
We leap to the infinite dark like sparks from the anvil.
Thou leadest, O God! All's well with Thy troopers that follow.

Louise Imogen Guiney

A TALISMAN

Take Temperance to thy breast,
While yet is the hour of choosing,
As arbitress exquisite
Of all that shall thee betide;
For better than fortune's best
Is mastery in the using,
And sweeter than any thing sweet
The art to lay it aside!

MONOCHROME

Shut fast again in Beauty's sheath
Where ancient forms renew,
The round world seems above, beneath,
One wash of faintest blue,

And air and tide so stilly sweet
In nameless union lie,
The little far-off fishing fleet
Goes drifting up the sky.

Secure of neither misted coast
Nor ocean undefined,
Our flagging sail is like the ghost
Of one that served mankind,

Who in the void, as we upon
This melancholy sea,
Finds labour and allegiance done,
And Self begin to be.

Louise Imogen Guiney

WHEN ON THE MARGE OF EVENING

When on the marge of evening the last blue light is broken,
And winds of dreamy odour are loosened from afar,
Or when my lattice opens, before the lark hath spoken,
On dim laburnum-blossoms, and morning's dying star,

I think of thee (O mine the more if other eyes be sleeping!),
Whose greater noonday splendours the many share and see,
While sacred and for ever, some perfect law is keeping
The late, the early twilight, alone and sweet for me.

PLANTING THE POPLAR

Because thou'rt not an oak
To breast the thunder-stroke,
Or flamy-fruited yew
Darker than Time, how few
Of birds or men or kine
Will love this throne of thine,
Scant Poplar, without shade
Inhospitably made!
Yet, branches never parted
From their straight secret bole,
Yet, sap too single-hearted!
Prosper as my soul.

In loneliness, in quaint
Perpetual constraint,
In gallant poverty,
A girt and hooded tree,
See if against the gale

Our leafage can avail:
Lithe, equal, naked, true,
Rise up as spirits do,
And be a spirit crying
Before the folk that dream!
My slender early-dying
Poplar, by the stream.

PASCAL

Thou lovedst life, but not to brand it thine (O rich in all forborne
        felicities!),
Nor use it with marauding power, to seize
And stain the sweet earth's blue horizon-line.
Virgin the grape might in the trellis twine
Where thou hadst long ago an hour of ease,
And foot of thine across the unpressed leas
Went light as some Idæan[1] foot divine.

Spirit so abstinent, in thy deeps lay
What passion of possession? Day by day
Was there no thirst upon thee, sharp and pure,
In forward sea-like surges unforgot?
Yes: and in life and death those joys endure
More blessedly, that men can name them not.

---

1. This reference is to Mt. Ida, a sacred mountain in Greece.

Louise Imogen Guiney

BORDERLANDS

Through all the evening,
Al the virginal long evening,
Down the blossomed aisle of April it is dread to walk alone;
For there the intangible is nigh, the lost is ever-during;
And who would suffer again beneath a too divine alluring,
Keen as the ancient drift of sleep on dying faces blown?

Yet in the valley,
At a turn of the orchard alley,
When a wild aroma touched me in the moist and moveless air,
Like breath indeed from out Thee, or as airy vesture round Thee,
Then was it I went faintly, for fear I had nearly found Thee,
O Hidden, O Perfect, O Desired! O first and final Fair!

TARPEIA

Woe: lightly to part with one's soul as the sea with its foam!
Woe to Tarpeia, Tarpeia, daughter of Rome!

Lo, now it was night, with the moon looking chill as she went:
It was morn when the innocent stranger strayed into the tent.

The hostile Sabini were pleased, as one meshing a bird;
She sang for them there in the ambush: they smiled as they heard.

Her sombre hair purpled in gleams, as she leaned to the light;
All day she had idled and feasted, and now it was night.

See note for "Tarpeia" by Anne Lynch Botta.

The chief sat apart, heavy-browed, brooding elbow on knee;
The armlets he wore were thrice royal, and wondrous to see:

Exquisite artifice, whorls of barbaric design,
Frost's fixed mimicry; orbic imaginings fine

In sevenfold coils: and in orient glimmer from them,
The variform voluble swinging of gem upon gem.

And the glory thereof sent fever and fire to her eye.
'I had never such trinkets!' she sighed,—like a lute was her sigh.

'Were they mine at the plea, were they mine for the token, all told,
Now the citadel sleeps, now my father the keeper is old,

'If I go by the way that I know, and thou followest hard,
If yet at the touch of Tarpeia the gates be unbarred?'

The chief trembled sharply for joy, then drew rein on his soul:
'Of all this arm beareth I swear I will cede thee the whole,'

And up from the nooks of the camp, with hoarse plaudit outdealt,
The bearded Sabini glanced hotly, and vowed as they knelt,

Bare-stretching the wrists that bore also the glowing great boon:
'Yea! surely as over us shineth the lurid low moon,

'Not alone of our lord, but of each of us take what he hath!
Too poor is the guerdon, if thou wilt but show us the path.'

Her nostril upraised, like a fawn's on the arrowy air,
She sped; in a serpentine gleam to the precipice stair,

They climbed in her traces, they closed on their evil swift star:
She bent to the latches, and swung the huge portal ajar.

Repulsed where they passed her, half-tearful for wounded belief,
'The bracelets!' she pleaded. Then faced her the leonine chief,

And answered her: 'Even as I promised, maid-merchant, I do.'
Down from his dark shoulder the baubles he sullenly drew.

'This left arm shall nothing begrudge thee. Accept. Find it sweet.
Give, too, O my brothers!' The jewels he flung at her feet,

The jewels hard, heavy; she stooped to them, flushing with dread,
But the shield he flung after: it clanged on her beautiful head.

Like the Apennine bells when the villagers' warnings begin,
Athwart the first lull broke the ominous din upon din;

With a 'Hail, benefactress!' upon her they heaped in their zeal
Death: agate and iron; death: chrysoprase, beryl and steel.

'Neath the outcry of scorn, 'neath the sinewy tension and hurl,
The moaning died slowly, and still they massed over the girl

A mountain of shields! and the gemmy bright tangle in links,
A torrent-like gush, pouring out on the grass from the chinks,

Pyramidical gold! the sumptuous monument won
By the deed they had loved her for, doing, and loathed her for, done.

Such was the wage that they paid her, such the acclaim:
All Rome was aroused with the thunder that buried her shame.

On surged the Sabini to battle. O you that aspire!
Tarpeia the traitor had fill of her woman's desire.

Woe: lightly to part with one's soul as the sea with its foam!
Woe to Tarpeia, Tarpeia, daughter of Rome!

MARY WESTON FORDHAM

(1862?–?)

𝕏𝕏𝕏𝕏𝕏

ALMOST NOTHING is known of this black woman who published *Magnolia Leaves* in 1897, a book of poems introduced by Booker T. Washington, who wrote: "I give my cordial endorsement to this little 'Book of Poems,' because I believe it will do its part to awaken the Muse of Poetry which I am sure slumbers in very many of the Sons and Daughters of the Race of which the Author of this work is a representative." It is perhaps fitting that selections from *Magnolia Leaves* should conclude this anthology. As Joan Sherman points out in her introduction to the Oxford reprint, Fordham's poetry is consistent with that published by Griswold at mid-century: "Turn to any page of Rufus W. Griswold's *Female Poetry of America* (all white) and you find poems identical to the sixty-six in *Magnolia Leaves*" (xxx). Thus, Fordham is a "representative" poet. Yet she also embodies the new criterion of representation provided in this, the first interracial anthology of nineteenth-century women poets.

It is true, as Sherman says, that Fordham avoids openly racial topics. But some poems may very well make coded references to race. "The Saxon Legend of Language," for instance, invites a racial interpretation, first by its title and then by its mocking rewriting of the Fall. These fish who missed the Angel's (Lucifer's?) visit, might they not be those traditionally silenced by [Anglo-]Saxon culture and thus protected from the Fall, destined to speak a different language, as yet unheard?

If so, "To the Mock-Bird," which concludes the longest section of her volume, may present the poet's adaptive strategies as those of a "little trickster," building a nest for her children by insinuating herself into the midst of the dominant discourse, from which the poet can "Say to sombre winter—up and away." A hundred years earlier, Phillis Wheatley, another black woman, used the old, "austere," white man Winter as a metonomy for all that "forbids me to aspire."

The last section of Fordham's book, "In Memoriam," chronicles the deaths of many loved ones, including several children—Alphonse, Charlie, Queenie—who died in infancy. Fordham's careful attention to her grandparents, her father (Rev. Samuel Weston), her mother, and other relatives including Mrs. Mary Furman Weston Byrd (born in the eighteenth-century, the product of a mixed marriage) suggests that her family had deep roots in America and remained intact despite adversity.

Though rough and unrefined, Fordham's poetry displays flashes of imaginative force, and even humor in "The Coming Woman." "Alaska" and "To the Mock-Bird," for example, suggest that Fordham longed to develop the native force of homegrown materials, celebrating diversity instead of hegemony. In her work we encounter the aspirations of many nineteenth-century women poets who insisted that "the pen" might become a woman's instrument, prophesying the triumph of "myriads then unborn."

Selected Criticism: Sherman. Intro. to *Collected Black Women's Poetry.* Vol. 2; Walker, Cheryl. "Nineteenth-Century American Women Poets and Realism." *American Literary Realism* 23: 3 (Spring 1991): 25–41.

THE WASHERWOMAN

With hands all reddened and sore,
    With back and shoulders low bent,
She stands all day, and part of the night
    Till her strength is well-nigh spent.
With her rub—rub—rub,
    And her wash, rinse, shake,
Till the muscles start and the spirit sinks,
    And the bones begin to ache.

Mary Weston Fordham

At morn when the sunbeams scatter
   In rays so golden and bright,
She yearns for the hour of even,
   She longs for the restful night.
Still she rubs—rubs—rubs,
   With the energy born of want,
For the larder's empty and must be filled,—
   The fuel's growing scant.

As long as the heart is blithesome,
   Will her spirit bear her up,
And kindness and love imparteth a zest
   To sweeten hard life's bitter cup.
But to toil—toil—toil,
   From the grey of the morn till eve,
Is an ordeal so drear for a human to bear,
   Which the rich can hardly conceive.

What part in the world of pleasure?
   What holidays are her own?
For the rich reck not of privations and tears,
   Saying, "she is to the manor born."
So dry those scalding tears
   That furrow so deeply thy cheek,
For rest—rest—rest
   Will come at the end of the week.

Yes, even on earth there's a day
   When labor and toil must cease,
The world at its birth received the mandate
   Of the seventh day of rest.
When the sweet-toned Sabbath bells
   Break o'er the balmy air,
Then sing—sing—sing
   That the morning stars may hear.

For the frugal table spread,
    For the crust and the humble bed,
When He to whom all earth belongs
    Had not where to lay His head,
Then toil for thy daily bread,
    Let thy heart like thy hands be clean,
And rub—rub—rub
    T'ill thy bones all ache, I ween.

With hands all reddened and sore,
    With back and shoulders bent low,
Thou hast for thy comfort that rest, sweet rest,
    Will be found on the other shore.
Then they who've washed their souls
    Will dip in the crystal tide
Of the fountain clear that was oped to man
    From the Saviour's wounded side.

THE SNOWDROP

How comest thou, O flower so fair,
To bud and bloom while wintry air
    Still hovers o'er the land?

How comest from the cold, dark earth?
That fostered thee and gave thee birth,
    Studding thy brow with snow

Say, didst thou yearn for sunny bowers?
To gladden with thy pure, pale flowers,
    The valley and the hill?

Down in the darkness whence thou came,
Hear'st aught of passion, fashion, fame,
   Or even greed for gold?

And when the old earth's bosom heaves,
And scatters man like autumn's leaves,
   With its low thundered voice.

Thou sleep'st serene with eyelids closed,
No earthquake shock breaks thy repose,
   Till comes the breath of Spring.

THE SAXON LEGEND OF LANGUAGE

The earth was young, the world was fair,
And balmy breezes filled the air,
Nature reposed in solitude,
When God pronounced it "very good."

The snow-capped mountain reared its head,
The deep, dark forests widely spread,
O'er pebbly shores the stream did play
On glad creation's natal day.

But silence reigned, nor beast nor bird
Had from its mate a whisper heard,
E'en man, God's image from above,
Could not, to Eve, tell of his love.

Where the four rivers met there strayed
The man and wife, no whit afraid,
For the arch-fiend expelled from heaven
Had not yet found his way to Eden.

But lo! a light from 'mid the trees,
But hark! a rustling 'mongst the leaves,
Then a fair Angel from above,
Descending, sang his song of love.

Forth sprang the fierce beasts from their lair,
Bright feathered songsters fill the air,
All nature stirred to centre rang
When the celestial song began.

The Lion, monarch of the plain,
First tried to imitate the strain,
And shaking high his mane he roared,
Till beast and bird around him cowered.

The little Linnet tuned her lay,
The Lark, in turn, did welcome day,
And cooing soft, the timid Dove
Did to his mate tell of his love.

Then Eve, the synonym of grace,
Drew nearer to the solemn place,
And heard the words to music set
In tones so sweet, she ne'er forgot.

The anthems from the earth so rare,
Higher and higher filled the air,
Till Seraphs caught the inspiring strain,
And morning stars together sang.

Then laggard Adam sauntered near,
What Eve had heard he too must hear,
But ah! for aye will woman's voice
Make man to sigh or him rejoice.

Only the fishes in the deep
Did not arouse them from their sleep,
So they alas! did never hear
Of the Angel's visit to this sphere.
Nor have they ever said one word
To mate or man, or beast or bird.

CHICAGO EXPOSITION ODE

Columbia, all hail!
　　May thy banner ne'er be furled
Till Liberty, with her beauteous rays,
　　Enlighten all the world.
Columbia, to thee
　　From every clime we come,
To lay our trophies at thy feet—
　　Our sunbright, glorious home.
　　*　*　*　*　*　*　*　*
'Twas a lovely autumn morn,
　　And the leaves were turning red,
And the sturdy oaks and graceful pines
　　Then branches over-spread;
And the breezes softly swept
　　The hills and valleys o'er;
And the dew-kissed earth with incense sweet,
　　Crowned forest, grove and flower.

On a grassy knoll near by
　　Where the rustling leaves were piled,
Knelt a mighty chief of a mighty tribe,
　　And his band of warriors wild.

Mary Weston Fordham

For the rising sun had shown
    To the trained eyes of that band,
That vessels three, like white-winged birds,
    Were steering straight for land.

Whence comes this stranger fleet?
    Whence hails this Pale Face crew?
And the chieftain's brow was wrapped in pain
    As his tomahawk he drew.
Then, with quivering voice, he said
    Some evil may betide;
From the land of the sky this host has come—
    Let's haste to the river side.

And the warriors started forth
    Like fawns through the forest trees;
When lo! what a wondrous, solemn sight—
    "Pale Faces" on their knees!
Before the Holy Cross,
    Each with uncovered brow,
Prayed the mighty God, that His blessings e'er
    Might this fair land endow.

And the stalwart braves—awe-struck—,
    With heads bowed low on breast
As the veteran sailor proudly cried
    San Salvador, the blest!
And this first, grand solemn act
    Has been chronicled in heaven;
For, from East to West of this broad, fair land,
    Has God's benison been given.

Then hail! bright, sunny land!
    Home of the free, the brave!
From the eastern shores to the western plains,
    Let thy banner proudly wave.

Nations beyond the seas
   Shall worship at thy shrine.
Honor and wealth, and matchless power.
   Columbia! be thine.

ALASKA

With thy rugged, ice-girt shore,
Draped in everlasting snow,
   Thou'rt enthroned a queen.
Crown of moss and lichen grey,
Frosted o'er with ocean spray,
All thy long, long wintry day,
   Dark and stern thy mien.

From the cloudland fresh and fair,
Falls the snow through crispy air,
   Mantling vale and hill.
Then old "Borealis" glows,
With his fiery light that shows,
Frozen nature in repose,
   River, stream and rill.

On thy north the Polar Sea
Thunders forth in wild melée,
   'Mid gorges dark and steep
Full many a ship with noble crew,
Lies low beneath thy waters blue,
Nor left behind a single clew,
   But sleep a dreamless sleep.

Beside the far famed Yukon stands
Hundreds of men from distant lands,
   All with the same desire
Gold, gold's the watchword, yellow ore,
That tempts him from his homestead door,
And Oh! alas he nevermore
    May sit by household fire.

Ah! if men would only toil,
Dig and delve their own rich soil,
   With vigor and with vim;
Forth would spring the golden corn,
Loud would ring the harvest song,
Life and health they would prolong,
    All through nature's prime.

Under his own, his fruitful vine,
Beneath his laden fig tree green,
   He, like a king, would reign.
Bending low with purple yield,
Rivalling fair Eschkol's fields,[1]
He'd a potent influence wield,
    With his corn and wine.

---

1. Eschkol comes from the Hebrew meaning cluster. The reference is to region of Hebron in south central Judea from which spies sent by Moses brought back clusters of grapes, pomegranates, and figs (see Num. 13.23–24).

Mary Weston Fordham

ON PARTING WITH A FRIEND

Can I forget thee? No, while mem'ry lasts,
   Thine image like a talisman entwined,
Around my heart by sacred friendship's ties
   Remains unchanged, in love, pure love, enshrined.

Can I forget thee? Childhood's happy hours
   Would like some flitting phantom mock and jeer;
Life's sunny hours, would quickly lose their charm,
   If Lethe's slumbrous waves but touched me there.

Can I forget thee? 'Tis a sad, sad thought.
   That friend from friend should thus be ruthless riven—
But list, methinks, a sweet voice whispers low,
   Remember, no adieus are spoke in heaven.

Can I forget thee? No, though ocean's waves
   May madly leap and foam 'twixt you and me,
Still o'er my stricken heart this yearning will remain,
   Nor time estrange my love, dear one, from thee.

And though on earth again we never more may meet,
   In that bright Elysian where spirits, holy, dwell,
May we in concert with that transported throng,
   Unite, ne'er more (rapt thought) to say "farewell!"

THE PEN

Mightier than the sword thou art,
Thou can'st pierce like venomed dart,

Time and space count naught with thee,
Leagues of land or leagues of sea.

Thou can'st waves of passion calm,
Griefs assuage like Gilead's balm,
Bring sweet pleasure to the eye,
Give sweet gladness for the sigh.

When thy little point is prest,
Oft it wounds some gentle breast,
Filling chalice to the brim,
Darkening life with sorrows grim.

Learnéd sage in days gone by,
Scanned thee with prophetic eye,
Said to myriads then unborn
Thou would'st rule on many a throne.

Swords may stab with savage ire,
Glistening out like rays of fire,
They can ne'er thy power attain,
O'er the sea or o'er the main.

Mightier than the sword art thou,
Lo! on many a regal brow
Furrows which thy point has wrought,
Troubles which thy work has brought.

Mightier than the sword art thou,
List! a maid records her vow,
That so long as life shall last,
Ne'er a doubt shall love o'ercast

Naught of bliss or naught of woe,
But thou can'st on man bestow,

With thy tiny pointed prow,
Mightier than the sword art thou.

THE CHEROKEE

'Twas a cloudless morn and the sun shone bright,
 And dewdrops sparkled clear;
And the hills and the vales of this Western land
 Were wreathed with garlands rare.
For verdant spring with her emerald robe
 Had decked the forest trees;
Whilst e'er and anon the vine-clad boughs
 Waved in the playful breeze.

All, all was still, not a sound was heard,
 Save the music of each tree,
As gracefully it bent and bowed
 Its branches o'er the lea.
But hark! a sound, 'tis the Red man's tread,
 Breaks on the silent air;
And a sturdy warrior issues forth,
 Robed in his native gear.

And wandering on, he neared the brook;
 Then sat him down to rest;
'Twas a noble sight—that warrior free—
 That Monarch of the West.
He gazed around, O! a wistful gaze
 Saddened his upturned brow,
As he thought of those he'd fondly loved,
 Of those now laid so low.

He mused aloud "Great Spirit!" list
    To the Indian's earnest plea;
And tell me why, from his own loved home,
    Must the Indian driven be,
When the "Pale Face" came to our genial clime,
    We wondered and were glad;
Then hied us to our chieftain's lodge,
    Our noble "Flying Cloud."

We told him all, and he calmly said
    He'd gladly give them place;
And if friends they proved, perchance, extend
    The calumet of peace.
But soon, alas! the dread truth rang
    That the Pale Face was our foe;
For he made our warriors bite the dust—
    Our children lie so low.

So now, my own, dear, sunny land,
    Each woodland and each dell,
Once the Indian's home, now the Indian's grave,
    I bid a last farewell.
To the "Great Spirit's" hunting-ground,
    To meet my long-lost bride,
My "Raven Wing" I gladly hie—
    He said, then calmly died.

THE COMING WOMAN

Just look, 'tis a quarter past six, love—
    And not even the fires are caught;

Mary Weston Fordham

Well, you know I must be at the office—
    But, as usual, the breakfast'll be late.

Now hurry and wake up the children;
    And dress them as fast as you can;
"Poor dearies," I know they'll be tardy,
    Dear me, "what a slow, poky man!"

Have the tenderloin broiled nice and juicy—
    Have the toast browned and buttered all right;
And be sure you settle the coffee:
    Be sure that the silver is bright.

When ready, just run up and call me—
    At eight, to the office I go,
Lest poverty, grim, should o'ertake us—
    "'Tis bread and butter," you know.

The bottom from stocks may fall out,
    My bonds may get below par;
Then surely, I seldom could spare you
    A nickel, to buy a cigar.

All ready? Now, while I am eating,
    Just bring up my wheel to the door;
Then wash up the dishes; and, mind now,
    Have dinner promptly at four;

For to-night is our Woman's Convention,
    And I am to speak first, you know—
The men veto us in private,
    But in public they shout, "That's so."

So "by-by"—In case of a rap, love,
    Before opening the door, you must look;

Mary Weston Fordham

O! how could a civilized woman
Exist, without a man cook.

TO THE MOCK-BIRD

Bird of the woodland, sing me a song,
Fain would I list to thee, all the day long,
Out from thy cosy nest, 'mid leafy bower,
Lift high thy tuneful voice—'tis summer's hour.

Bird of the forest, with voice sublime,
Gladdening with thy music all summer time,
E'en while the Autumn's winds bend low the trees,
Sweetly still thy carols float with the breeze.

Queen of the song-realm, what doest thou?
Up amid the leaflets, rocking on the bough.
Ah! little trickster, building thee a nest.
Cosy, soft and warm, for thy wee ones to rest.

Bird of the south-land, haste thee and bring
Tributes of thy melody, welcoming the spring,
Say to sombre winter—up and away,
This my time of minstrelsy, bright, sunny May.

ORDER FORM
■ ■ ■ ■ ■ ■ *AMERICAN WOMEN WRITERS SERIES* ■ ■ ■ ■ ■ ■

☐ Special Offer on the Complete Set!
**All 18 volumes in the Series (in paperback) for only $200.00,
a 25% discount off the list price of $274.00**

Individual volumes in the American Women Writers Series

☐ **Alternative Alcott**, by Louisa May Alcott.
Elaine Showalter, editor
1987. 462 pp. Paper, $16.00

☐ **"The Amber Gods" and Other Stories**,
by Harriet Prescott Spofford.
Alfred Bendixen, editor
1989. 300 pp. Paper, $15.00

☐ **American Women Poets of the Nineteenth
Century: An Anthology**.
Cheryl Walker, editor
1992. 350 pp. Paper, $15.00

☐ **Clovernook Sketches and Other Stories**,
by Alice Cary. Judith Fetterley, editor
1988. 314 pp. Paper, $15.00

☐ **The Essential Margaret Fuller**, by Margaret
Fuller. Jeffrey Steele, editor
1992. 450 pp. Paper, $17.00

☐ **Gail Hamilton: Selected Writings**, by Gail
Hamilton. Susan Coultrap-McQuin, editor
1992. 280 pp. Paper, $15.00.

☐ *The Hidden Hand*, by E.D.E.N. Southworth.
Joanne Dobson, editor
1988. 450 pp. Paper, $16.00.

☐ *Hobomok* and Other Writings on Indians,
by Lydia Maria Child.
Carolyn L. Karcher, editor
1986. 275 pp. Paper, $15.00

☐ *Hope Leslie*, by Catharine Maria Sedgwick.
Mary Kelly, editor
1987. 373 pp. Paper, $15.00

☐ **"How Celia Changed Her Mind" and
Selected Stories**, by Rose Terry Cooke.
Elizabeth Ammons, editor
1986. 265 pp. Paper, $15.00

☐ *The Lamplighter*, by Maria Susanna
Cummins. Nina Baym, editor
1987. 437 pp. Paper, $17.00

☐ *Moods*, by Louisa May Alcott.
Sarah Elbert, editor
1991. 284 pp. Paper, $15.00

☐ *A New Home—Who'll Follow?*,
by Caroline Kirkland.
Sandra A. Zagarell, editor
1990. 250 pp. Paper, $15.00

☐ *Oldtown Folks*, by Harriet Beecher Stowe.
Dorothy Berkson, editor
1987. 519 pp. Paper, $17.00

☐ *Quicksand* and *Passing*, by Nella Larsen.
Deborah E. McDowell, editor
1986. 246 pp. Paper, $10.00

☐ *Ruth Hall* and Other Writings,
by Fanny Fern. Joyce W. Warren, editor
1986. 380 pp. Paper, $15.00

☐ **Stories from the Country of Lost Borders**,
by Mary Austin. Marjorie Pryse, editor
1987. 310 pp. Paper, $15.00

☐ **Women Artists, Women Exiles: "Miss
Grief" and Other Stories**, by Constance
Fenimore Woolson.
Joan Myers Weimer, editor
1988. 292 pp. Paper, $15.00.

Postage: For the complete set, add $12.00.
For other orders, add $3.00 postage for the
first book, $1.00 for each additional book.
New Jersey residents: please add 6% sales
tax.

Copy or tear out this page and send to:

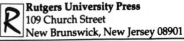
Rutgers University Press
109 Church Street
New Brunswick, New Jersey 08901